Striving
for the
Whole

Striving
for the
Whole

Creating
Theoretical
Syntheses

Rainer
Diriwächter
and
Jaan Valsiner
editors

Transaction Publishers
New Brunswick (U.S.A.) and London (U.K.)

This book is printed on acid-free paper that meets the American National Standard for Permanence of Paper for Printed Library Materials.

Library of Congress Catalog Number: 2008005220
ISBN: 978-1-4128-0738-8
Printed in the United States of America

Library of Congress Cataloging-in-Publication Data

Striving for the whole : creating theoretical syntheses / Rainer Diriwächter
    and Jean Valsiner, editors.
    Includes bibliographical references and index.
    ISBN 978-1-4128-0738-8
        1. Whole and parts (Psychology)   I. Diriwächter, Rainer.
    II. Valsiner, Jaan.

BF202.S77   2008
150.19'31—dc22   2008005220

Contents

Preface:
The Past and Future of the Whole

Rainer Diriwächter
California Lutheran University

Jaan Valsiner
Clark University

Psychology—just like many other disciplines—is still far removed from presenting a unified theory. Instead, we still find a number of schools of thought, each with their own theoretical orientation which is often at striking odds with those of competing schools. Moreover, the institutionalization of theories has traditionally shifted over time, so that we can continuously witness recurring themes emerging (see van der Veer & Valsiner, 2000). In short, it seems that currently the unification of psychology remains predominantly a disciplinary maneuver rather than an epistemological act as one would imagine it should be (see Stam, 2004).

One of the central aims of this current volume is to bring back to psychological discourse the often-neglected ideas of early twentieth century holistically oriented schools of thought. We have found that, all too often, present day mainstream psychology demonstrates little theoretical and philosophical orientation at its core. Instead, we can find a large flux of largely data-driven articles that are published in various journals without serious regard to how their results fit with larger theoretical perspectives.

Data are important—but only if they speak the language of theories and help to modify theories (see Holton, 1998 on Einstein's thinking). Psychology is far from a stance of theoretical clarity—and it is precisely for that reason that an inquiry into the holistic nature of its phenomena is in order. While no single school of thought can claim to have achieved the necessary breakthrough in presenting a unified theory of psychology, the holistic approaches have gone a far way in placing the notion of "unity" beyond any data-driven approach. That is, for truly holistically related approaches, the empirical component needs to be integrated with a general life theory that breaches the boundary of a limiting laboratory setting.

At the heart of most holistic approaches to psychology, we find the intellectual ideas of the Second School of Leipzig: Genetic Ganzheitspsychologie. It is their theoretical credo that openly and clearly aims at a unified theory of psychology. This stands in strong opposition to the data-driven approaches, which usually result in so-called "mini-theories" that merely touch upon certain aspects of human life (cf. attribution or social exchange theories). It is true that the Leipzig Ganzheitspsychologie cannot claim itself to be the originator of holistic ideas, as their approach rests upon the shoulders of early giants of psychology—Franz Brentano, Alexius Meinong, Hans Cornelius, Christian von Ehrenfels, and others. Yet, the Leipzig circle could boast to have mastered the leap between lower and higher psychological processes by uniting both into a whole. That is, to take Wilhelm Wundt's strict distinction between studying simple elementary processes of psychological functioning (such as sensations) and the higher, more complex functions such as language, myths, and customs which originate in social life.

As such, this volume should serve as the basis for professionals and students alike to discuss the necessary foundations for creating theoretical syntheses and, in the end, how to achieve a truly holistic approach that is grounded in solid theory that guides subsequent research and its accompanying methodology. We believe that taking a look into our intellectual past, with a keen eye on our future, will help spur renewed research that breaks free of the data-driven approach that has forgotten to see the larger picture (i.e., the forest behind all the trees).

Hence, the collection of writings[1] the reader will find in this volume largely serve as self-standing pieces that reflect upon a given topic with an eye towards how that topic could relate and be integrated into a holistic approach.

Part I—The Whole and Ganzheitspsychologie

There are many starting points which would be well suited for a discussion surrounding holistic theories of psychology. We have chosen to intercept the time-line of holistic theoretical development at the point where Gottfried Wilhelm von Leibniz (1646-1716) enters the stage. The impact of Leibniz's theories on psychology is often forgotten. While at one time the early intellectual giants paid homage to Leibniz's contributions to psychology (see Wundt, 1917) today, his teachings have largely been contained within philosophy. In our first chapter of this volume, Walter Ehrenstein discusses some of Leibniz's ideas in regards to dynamic holism and its true unity. A key anchor point for discussion surrounds the active units and interactive dynamics of the whole, and naturally Leibniz's famous monadology, which highlights the primacy of the whole.

The central topic of Chapter 2—the contributions by Christian von Ehrenfels (1856-1932)—may be somewhat more easily recognizable as an important contribution to holistically oriented theory by anyone who has spent some time with Ganzheit and Gestalt psychology. Steven Kissinger provides a recount of Ehrenfels' 1890 seminal paper on Gestalt Qualities, which is generally considered a milestone, albeit certainly not the only one, for holistically oriented research programs by both the Berlin (Gestalt) and Leipzig (Ganzheit) psychology circles.

As mentioned earlier, while no unified theory of psychology has emerged to this date, there is no single theory that can claim to be more holistic, yet still grounded in empirical rigor with life's structure intact. That is, a theory that has not removed itself from the reality of life—that being of genetic nature—thereby preserving the structural and developmental complexes that make up our psychological necessities. This approach—Genetic Ganzheitspsychologie—tries to account for everything from the simplest complexes to the most broadly conceived metaphysical explanations, whereby the latter is just one aspect in a long spectrum of provisions. A truly holistic approach—as well as a unified theory of psychology for that matter—will be able to account for, and not shy away from, all issues involving human nature. This reaching from the smallest, moment-by-moment transformative occurrences (speak Aktualgenese or Microgenesis)—as become evident through time-limited studies demonstrated through Wohlfahrt's (1925/1932) studies of emergent percepts or Werner's (1925) studies on micro-melodies—to the broad ranging questions of who we humans really are. Let us not forget that much of psychology one hundred years ago was seen as a branch of (experimental) philosophy, and not natural sciences as (largely for political reasons) institutions today advocate. Yet such institutional blinding of the discipline cannot last for long—the need for generalizable knowledge in psychology will sooner or later overtake the social positioning games of "schools" of psychology. For us, there are no "schools" but different thinkers and researchers who have tried to make sense of complex psychological phenomena.

In order to gain a better appreciation for what the discipline of Genetic Ganzheitspsychologie actually entails, Rainer Diriwächter summarizes its main principles in Chapter 3. The emphasis in that chapter is not only placed on the historical past of Ganzheitspsychologie, but also includes recent developments on both the experimental as well as the theoretical levels, thereby paving the way for further potentials.

The near absence of discourse surrounding Ganzheitspsychologie today could lead some readers to believe that this German approach never made it beyond the borders of German speaking Europe. However, this is not entirely true. As Wellek (1954) recounts, prior to World War II, Ganzheitspsychologie ideas were being exported to countries such as Argentina, Italy, Romania, Sweden, Greece, even the United States and Japan. In all these countries we find translated texts by Krueger and others, with subsequent own developments which, unfortunately, seem to have transpired after the onset of World War II. It would be a worthwhile task for any researcher native to these afore mentioned countries to take a stroll to the library archives and re-examine these texts and their initial impact on the psychology of that country.

For our current volume, we have selected Japan as one example of how intellectual ideas can migrate to far away places—at least temporarily—and how often it necessitates the "right" *Zeitgeist* for something to grab foot. In Chapter 4, Miki Takasuna and Tatsuya Sato provide the reader with a glimpse into Japan's history of psychology and relate it to Felix Krueger's Ganzheitspsychologie. One would imagine that any Eastern country would be particularly receptive to holistic ideas, and so it is particularly interesting to read that it's not just general life philosophies of a majority that dictate what and who becomes embraced, but often also a political elite that may (ab)use certain doctrines to their own advantage.

Yet we must not forget that at the heart of any intellectual approach stand people who are committed and fascinated by what their philosophy promises. Dietmar Görlitz gives us a rare personal account in Chapter 5 of what it was like to study at Heidelberg under Johannes Rudert—an assistant of Felix Krueger in Leipzig. Görlitz's discussion highlights the intellectual discussions, the meaning-making process at Heidelberg, inclusive of philosophers, and, at that time, psychologists work in process.

Part II—The Whole in Other Minds

It would be wrong to claim early twentieth-century efforts towards holistic psychology as exclusively German. For example, the legacy of the South African statesman and philosopher Jan Smuts reaches all the way to Anglo-American holistic psychology. In Chapter 6, Christopher Shelley gives us a good overview of Smuts's life and work, with an emphasis on personality theory. Furthermore, Shelley ties the legacy of Smuts's approach to those of Adler, Meyer, and Perls. It is particularly the latter which may surprise one or the other reader who mistakenly thought the famous Gestalt therapy has direct links with the Berlin approach. In fact, as Shelley points out, it seems the South African and German holistic approaches ran parallel to each other and largely ignorant of their respective advances during those times.

One often and surprisingly neglected aspect of psychological research is the centrality of feelings and emotions that stand at the core of every human experience. While the Leipzig Ganzheitspsychologie had made feelings one of their core areas of interests, they were certainly not the only ones. In Chapter 7, Tania Zittoun discusses the French physician and philosopher Pierre Janet, with particular emphasis placed on the various facets of human emotions and how to channel Janet's ideas into today's psychology. French holism, Janet's whole of human conducts in particular, can boast many good ideas that beg for renewed consideration.

One of the most promising areas of modern day psychology has made its' prime target the examination of how humans' system of organized psychological functions takes place via semiotic mediation (see Valsiner, 2000). Cultural psychology spans many disciplines, from anthropology, ethnology, linguistics, and biology (just to name a few). At the core lie the discoveries of psychological necessities which underlie human psychological functioning. As Krueger (1915: 177) mentions, psychological necessities constitute the core of all we call "culture"—they are the carriers and inner movement which represent the forming forces of every cultural development.

In Chapter 8 of this volume, Lívia Simão introduces us to the cultural psychology of Ernst Boesch and demonstrates its holistic orientation by contrasting it with Ganzheitspsychologie. Of particular importance is Boesch's symbolic action theory, which not only accounts for the importance of semiotic regulation but also captures the non-static nature in human lives. Cultural psychology should be examined from the perspective of developmental sciences—a general orientation that puts the word "Genetic" before Ganzheitspsychologie not only for the Leipzig circle. Simão does a good job in highlighting the subject-object and temporal relationships of a person (actor), through symbolic actions, through the prism of a holistic cultural psychology. The comparisons with Pierre Janet and Jean Piaget help to situate Boesch's approach and in the end help pave the way for a truly Sociogenetic Ganzheitspsychologie.

Part III—The Whole in Biology: Making Sense of Others' Ideas.

Some readers may be surprised to find in a volume devoted to the history and development of holistic approaches not one, but two chapters dedicated to the ideas of Conwy Lloyd Morgan. This especially since what became known as Morgan's canon—that one should not interpret an action as the outcome of the exercise of a higher psychical faculty if it can be interpreted as the outcome of the exercise of one which stands lower in the psychological scale (Morgan, 1894/1977: 53)—has quite conveniently become a rallying point for behaviorists. Yet, the inclusion of Morgan need not necessarily be so surprising after all: As Valsiner discusses in Chapter 9, Morgan's comparative approach—indeed resting upon Ockham's Razor (or the principle of parsimony)—did in no way claim one should oversimplify the subject matter. As Viney and King (2003) point out, some people might argue that by following Morgan's canon, the extreme speculative nature and anthropomorphism of some early comparative psychology could give way to another extreme—that of "preferring precise explanations that may meet the test of simplicity, but fail to do justice to the richness and complexity of the living organism" (p. 181).

As is often the case, the reality of original ideas differs from their later reconstructions. We have reprinted the chapter from Morgan's *Introduction to Comparative Psychology* (Chapter 10 here) to demonstrate that Morgan emphasized the simplicity of explanation on the background of systemic—holistic—organization of the biological phenomena. His ideas gain new light today—when our modern protein genetics discovers complex causal systems of interaction of functional units in the genome that give rise to relatively simple biological structures (e.g., such as 19000 genes of *C. elegans* granting the life of that 1000-cell nematode). The question is no longer how to find simplest explanations but how to reconstruct the simplest of the variety of complex causal systems that explain the outcomes.

Morgan was a philosopher first and naturalist second—his contributions to the ways in which knowledge emerges are very contemporary. By emphasizing the meaning-making scientist whose intuition is as important as careful observation he set the stage for a century of debates on the objectivity of the scientific enterprise. Accepting the subjectivity of the scientist in the construction of objective accounts of reality was a bold step—and worth careful consideration in our time.

Any theory of psychology, a holistic one in particular, needs to also account for the organism's biological make-up and eventually how biological changes may have come to form. In Chapter 11, Camilo Khatchikian reviews the history of holism in biology. Early holistic approaches in biology are often underemphasized. Human interest in biology predates any written record. Our stories begin with the Greeks, whose ideas have been passed down through the ages, recurring in the so-called scientific revolution, the vitalism-mechanism debates, and still guide our present-day discourses. When it comes to holistic approaches, Hans Driesch's study on sea urchin eggs has done much to suggest that developing organisms do not proceed in a mechanical, but rather in an integrative holistic manner. The idea that biological systems are due to their organization, that is, their hierarchies and properties as advocated in Ritter's philosophy of organicism has also found its way into the theories of Werner and Wapner.

Perhaps none other than Darwin's theory of evolution has done more to solidify present-day views on how we, as humans, have come to be. His writings have helped capture the imagination of biologists and psychologists alike. Yet it is interesting to note that current evolutionary theory in psychology surprisingly lacks adequate and explicit discussion on the developmental and holistic nature of evolutionary processes. In the final chapter of this volume, Rosemarie Sokol and Philip Rosenbaum take a closer look at evolutionary psychology, and, by contrasting it with Developmental Systems Theory as well as Ganzheitspsychologie, suggest a new theoretical model of evolutionary psychology that is both developmental as well as holistic in nature—Evolutionary Developmental Psychology.

Rediscovering the Whole—and Making it Meaningful

Science is close to art—even if we study elementary phenomena we are after general knowledge—like art is to evoke generalized subjective understanding. Yet it is not clear how to proceed in this focus on the whole. Our whole book centers on one issue—what to do with the whole? The implications from taking Ganzheitspsychologie seriously require that the researcher accounts for *all* the complex qualities of the whole as such qualities—and is careful in any moves to reduce those to individual constituents. Broadly speaking, this implies not only a momentary snapshot of the whole, but also a capturing of the fluidity of the phenomena at hand. Thus, a truly holistic approach needs to be developmental (genetic) in nature, and attempt to describe its components as well as processes all inclusively—from the biological foundation to the metaphysical integration. We hope that the readings in this volume provide triggers for embarking on new theoretical pathways to discovery and keep focus on the qualities of the wholes as those are subjected to various limitations through inquiry.

Note

Chapters 3, 4, 6, 7, 11, and 12 are revised versions of earlier publications appearing in the journal *From Past to Future, Volume 5, No. 1,* 2004. Chapters 9 and 10 appeared in the journal *From Past to Future, Volume 4, No. 1,* 2003.

References

Holton, G. (1998). *The advancement of science, and its burdens.* Cambridge, MA: Harvard University Press.

Krueger, F. (1915). "Über Entwicklungspsychologie: Ihre sachliche und geschichtliche Notwendigkeit." *Arbeiten zur Entwicklungspsychologie, 1. Band - Heft 1.* Leipzig, Germany: Verlag von Wilhelm Engelmann.

Morgan, C. L. (1977). *Comparative psychology.* Washington, DC: University Publications of America. (Original work published in 1894).

Stam, H. J. (2004). "Unifying psychology: Epistemological act or disciplinary maneuver?" *Journal of Clinical Psychology, 60*(12), 1259-1262.

Valsiner, J. (2000). *Culture and Human Development.* London: Sage Publications.

Van Der Veer, R., & Valsiner, J. (2000). *The Social Mind: Construction of the Idea.* Cambridge: Cambridge University Press.

Viney, W., & King, D. B. (2003). *A History of Psychology: Ideas and Context (3rd. Ed.).* Boston: Allyn and Bacon.

Wellek, A. (1954). "Die genetische Ganzheitspsychologie der Leipziger Schule und ihre Verzweigungen." *Neue Psychologische Studien, 15*(3), 1-67.

Werner, H. (1925). Studien über Strukturgesetze IV: Über Mikromelodik und Mikroharmonik. *Zeitschrift für Psychologie, 98,* 74-181.

Wohlfahrt, E. (1932). "Der Auffassungsvorgang an kleinen Gestalten. Ein Beitrag zur Psychologie des Vorgestalterlebnisses." *Neue Psychologische Studien, 4,* 347-414. [*Dissertation, Leipzig-1925*].

Wundt, W. (1917). *Leibniz.* Leipzig, Germany: Kröner Verlag.

1

Leibniz's Dynamic Holism*

Walter H. Ehrenstein
Dortmund University

Leibniz's philosophy is perhaps best known for its *principles* (of sufficient reason, continuity, differentiation, least effort, and pre-established harmony; see Ortega y Gasset, 1958) and for the idea that the rules of reasoning can be represented within a formal symbolic system to allow for computational or artificial intelligence (Davis, 2000). Yet, the emphasis placed on Leibniz's rationalism has to some extent obscured the robust role that Leibniz saw for sensory experience, observation, and experiments in establishing factual or contingent truths to complement necessary or axiomatic truths.

With respect to life sciences, Leibniz provided a remarkable framework for investigating complex, organic, and particularly mental phenomena by conceiving the surface organization of phenomena as dependent on a deeper order of underlying micro-processes so as to account for the emerging organization (Duchesneau, 2003). In particular, Leibniz postulated genuine units (monads) as autonomous and predisposed tendencies of living activity resulting in a multitude of original worldviews. Unity and activity were the concepts on which Leibniz's metatheory of being, his *dynamic holism,* essentially relied. Before going into this further, let us briefly turn to Leibniz's remarkable life and career with outstanding achievements apart from philosophy.

Biographical Sketch

Gottfried Wilhelm Leibniz (1646-1716) was born into a pious Lutheran family in the Saxon city of Leipzig, Germany, near the end of the Thirty Years' War. His father, Friedrich (1597-1652), was a professor of moral philosophy at Leipzig's renowned university, at which his son enrolled as a student already in 1661. In his bachelor's thesis "On the Principle of the Individual" (1663)

---

*Dedicated to Lothar Spillmann, neuro-perceptual pioneer, on the occasion of his 70th birthday.

1

Leibniz emphasized the value of the individual as a whole essence (*entitate tota*), not sufficiently described by matter or form alone. In 1666 he became qualified to lecture philosophy with a thesis "On the Art of Combination," which anticipates some basic principles of modern computation, emphasizing that all reasoning may be generated by an ordered combination of elements, be it verbal (words, numbers) or nonverbal (colors, tones). His application for the degree of a doctor of law was, however, refused because of his (too young) age. As a consequence he went to the University of Nuremberg, located at Altdorf, where his dissertation "On Perplexing Cases" procured him the doctor's degree of law at once followed by an offer of a professor's chair in 1667.

Leibniz, however, declined the offer for an academic career and instead entered the service of the nobility. It was the Baron of Boineburg, a minister of the Elector of Mainz, who first employed him as a lawyer and diplomat. His duties took him to Paris, where he stayed from 1672 to 1676. Soon after his arrival at Paris, he lost his protector by death and thus was free to pursue his scientific interests. In search of financial support, he constructed a calculating machine which he presented to the Royal Society during a short visit to London in 1673. His intense studies of mathematics culminated in his invention of the infinitesimal calculus late in 1675. Leibniz sought a permanent position in Paris, but his efforts were in vain.

In 1676 he entered the service of the Duke of Hanover and remained there for forty years until his death in 1716. Serving this major German noble house (that became the British royal family by the end of his service), Leibniz played a major role in the European politics and diplomacy of his time. Remarkably, he managed to combine his work as a courtier with intellectual interests and activities of the most varied kinds. He served as a librarian and was instrumental in founding the Academy of Sciences in Berlin, Vienna, and St. Petersburg. His intellectual merits excel in mathematics and philosophy. He invented the differential and integral *calculus* independently of Newton (1643-1727) and his notation is the one in general use since. He introduced the *binary system* on which modern computer architectures rely. With Descartes (1596-1650) and Spinoza (1632-1677), he is regarded to belong to the three great seventeenth-century rationalists, but only recently historians of philosophy took notice that his approach was markedly less rationalist than Kant (1724-1804) had suggested. Rather, Leibniz stood "on the interface between the holistic and vitalist world-view of the Renaissance, and the atomistic and mechanistic materialism that was to dominate the eighteenth and nineteenth centuries" (Ross, 1984:1). Besides, we owe Leibniz seminal contributions to a multitude of rather specialized topics in which he anticipated notions that surfaced much later in biology, cybernetics, geology, medicine, physics, psychophysics, and neuroscience; he also wrote on economy, ethics, ethnology, history, law, linguistics, and theology (see Aiton, 1985; Jolley, 2005). Many of his ideas were far ahead of his time to be taken up with great delay—sometimes not until today.

The access to Leibniz's work is difficult, since his contributions are scattered in journals, in tens of thousands of letters, and various unpublished manuscripts. Only two books, *Combinatorial Art* (1666) and *Theodicy* (1710) were published during his lifetime; two more books appeared posthumously—his *Monadology* (composed 1714) in 1720 and, in 1765 with huge delay, his *New Essays on Human Understanding* (completed 1705). To date, there is no complete edition of Leibniz's writings, hence a full account of his work is not yet possible. Much of what is published has been so only in recent decades. Leibniz wrote in three languages: French, Latin, and (least often) German; only a small proportion of his writings is available in English (see Gregory Brown's on-line bibliography: http://www.gwleibniz.com/).

A Universal Genius to be Recognized as Pioneer in Holistic Psychology

Leibniz's life was so rich of various activities with achievements in so many and distinct areas that he may be best characterized as *Universalgenie*, a "universal genius" (Ross, 1984). In taking every of his single achievements in the context of everything else he did, single contributions are indeed prone to rival with and to obscure each other. The eminent mathematician, logician, engineer, philosopher, and physicists he was, he is hardly identified as a psychologist. Thus, it may come as a surprise even to experts to recognize Leibniz as a still underappreciated "pioneer of psychology" (Fancher & Schmidt, 2003), who particularly anticipated key issues of Gestalt psychology and *Ganzheitspsychologie* (Ehrenstein, 1983).

In fact, Leibniz is rarely mentioned in current textbooks of psychology, although one of the founding fathers of modern psychology, Wilhelm Wundt (1832-1920), had devoted him a whole monograph (Wundt, 1917). While Wundt was able to appreciate Leibniz as a philosopher of mind, as the one who conceptualized minute sensations that led Fechner (1801-1887) to develop his psychophysics, and as a pioneer in cross-cultural psychology (e.g., his detailed linguistic and ethnographic studies of China and other cultures) he could not yet foresee Leibniz's role in a most recent field of psychology, that of *artificial intelligence* and *virtual reality*. "With his general conception that reasoning processes are reducible to mathematical-like computations, which in turn could be performed by machines, and with his anticipation of the binary notation that underlies the workings of modern digital computers, Leibniz deserves at least the title of intellectual grandfather to the modern movement of artificial intelligence" (Fancher & Schmidt, 2003: 12).

Even more astonishing is the neglect of Leibniz in the field of holistic approaches to psychology. We look for his name in vain in the representative texts such as of Ehrenfels, Koffka, Köhler, Krueger, Metzger, Uexküll, Volkelt, or Wertheimer (though see for some exceptions: Allport, 1955; Anschütz, 1953; Ehrenstein, 1947, 1965; Graumann, 1960; Huber, 1951). It is as if one had failed to see the forest for the trees. As we will see, the idea of Gestalt-like, supra-additive wholes is so central to Leibniz's thinking that one is easily led astray, if one, in the tradition of Kant, tends to disregard its key significance.

Leibniz's Search for Principles of True Unity

Initially, Leibniz was much impressed by the simplicity of the new atomic theory as set forth by the French philosopher Pierre Gassendi (1592-1655). His search for *real unities*, however, left him soon dissatisfied with its rather collective or accumulative assumptions of coherence. In his *New System of the Nature* (1695), he reports on his intellectual development that led him to adopt and conceptualize a holistic alternative.

> At first, when I had freed myself from the yoke of Aristotle, I had believed in the void and atoms, for it is this which best satisfies the imagination. But returning to this view after much mediation, I noticed that it is impossible to find *the principles of a true unity* in matter alone, or in what is merely passive, since everything in it is but a collection or accumulation of parts *ad infinitum*. Now a multiplicity can be real only if it is made up of *true unities* which come from elsewhere and are altogether different from mathematical points, which are nothing but extremities of the extended and modifications out of which it is certain that nothing *continuous* could be compounded. Therefore, to find these *real unities*, I was constrained to have recourse to what might be called a *real and animated point* or to an atom of substance which must embrace some element of form or of activity in order to make a complete being. It was thus necessary to recall and in a manner to rehabilitate *substantial forms* which are so much decried today, but in a way which makes them intelligible and separates the use which must be made of them from their previous abuse. I found then that their nature consists of force and that from this there follows something analogous to feeling and to appetite; and that therefore it was necessary to form a conception of them resembling our ordinary notion of *souls*. But just as the soul must not be used to explain the detail of the economy of the animal's body, so I judged in the same way that these forms ought not to be used to explain the particular problems of nature, although they are necessary to establish true general principles. Aristotle calls them *first entelchies*; I call them, more intelligibly perhaps, *primitive forces*, which contain not only the *act*, or the fulfillment of possibility, but also an original *activity*. (Leibniz, 1995: 116-117, emphasis in the original)

From his mathematical studies, in particular his method of the infinitesimal calculus, Leibniz knew how to analyze a complex variation (differential) and, conversely, how to gain a whole from a given value (integral). The idea of infinitesimal units that afforded such mathematical flexibility served to develop an alternative to the materialistic and mechanistic models. Leibniz asked for indecomposable units instead arguing that any material particle, no matter how small, can still to be subdivided further—hence, an ultimate material particle as a building block of the universe could be hardly obtained.

Furthermore, Leibniz's access to the then newly constructed microscope, by courtesy of Anton van Leeuwenhoek (1632-1723), afforded him to observe at first hand the amazing spectacle of microorganisms within a drop of ordinary pond water. This gave rise to a vision of a universe filled with hierarchies of organisms, to the conception that "each portion of matter may be conceived as like a garden full of plants, like a pond full of fishes"; it led Leibniz to adopt active or vital properties, force or energy, as primal entities.

Active Units and Interactive Dynamics

Leibniz faced two major contemporary cosmological accounts. Atomists such as Gassendi postulated discrete atoms, but had problems to explain their composition into continuous wholes. Conversely, Cartesians took spatial continuity as their point of departure, but failed to account for discrete objects out of it. In order to resolve this dilemma, Leibniz assigned elementary physical units to points in geometric space and interpreted these units as centers of force. Mathematically, the infinitesimal calculus allows for such an operation in that differential geometric points on space curves are assigned acceleration vectors which correspond to physical forces, if the curves are conceived of as motion trajectories. Thus, energy constituted the essence of matter and the world consisted of an infinity of centers of force, permanently expressed in motion. Leibniz's explanation of matter and space tried to avoid circularity in that his energy particles were themselves neither material nor, strictly speaking, even spatial.

Moreover, Leibniz challenged the conventional view of mechanical interaction. Although we tend to picture force as a *thing* which is transferred from one body to another, it is not a thing at all, but only a quality or state of things. Consequently, a force cannot literally be transferred from one body to another, any more than, say, a headache or color. Even in the case of balls ricocheting off each other on a billiard table their motions are permanently dependent on various other conditions, such as gravitational forces acting on them, properties of the table and its felting, air currents, and so on.

> In fact, the resultant motion of a particular ball is more like the expression of the solution to an infinitely complex equation, than like receiving the baton in a relay race. Leibniz was quite right to interpret the laws of mechanics, not as laws governing the amount of force transferred from one colliding body to another, but as elegant mathematical formulae governing the evolution of whole complex systems from their state at one time to their state at the next. (Ross, 1984: 86)

An important distinction in this context is that between *active* and *passive* dynamics. Things are active as far as their behavior is spontaneous and passive as far as it is determined by the constraints of the surrounding system. Accordingly, Leibniz assumes two different sources of an individual's dynamics: its spontaneous development or unfolding from within its own impulse or drive and its adaptation to the total system of which it is a part.

Monadology

Leaning on Aristotle's distinction of "sporadic" versus "monadic" ordering (in which several individuals belong to the same species versus in which each individual constitutes a species on its own) Leibniz termed the fundamental unit of his system a *monad* (Greek μόνας, meaning "unit"). Leibniz's theory of units, his *monadology,* is based on the primacy of the whole. Not only do monads share all attributes of non-additive wholes and sub-wholes, the entire universe relies ultimately on a central or supreme monad equated with God. Based on the undeniable reality and immediacy of one's own experience, Leibniz assumes graded consciousness or awareness as prime components. All monads are characterized by a charge of energy or impulse (an inherent urge to fulfill tendencies innate within themselves) that is accompanied by some degree of perceptiveness or awareness. They vary in strength and extent of their perceptive capacities and are organized within a multi-level hierarchy from *simple, sentient*, and *rational monads* to a unique *supreme monad.*

Simple monads with diffuse, subconscious percepts constitute the lowest level. Leibniz called these subliminal sensations *"petites perceptions"* (minute percepts) and compared them with the impression created by a single drop of water in a crashing surf. As a single drop it elicits an indiscernible, although obviously real, percept because in the aggregate with thousands and millions of other minute perceptions it produces the crashing sound of the surf.

Next in the hierarchy are the *sentient monads* affording basic conscious perception and self-awareness. Leibniz used for describing ordinary perceiving with the French verb *apercevoir* ("to perceive, to catch sight of, to foresee") and the higher form with the reflexive *s'apercevoir* ("to perceive oneself"), usually translated into English as "to apperceive." Sentient or apperceptive monads are followed by *rational monads* that allow for comprehending experiences by abstraction from perceptual phenomena and integration into conceptual or theoretical constructions—up to logical or mathematical reasoning. On top of—or most central within—this hierarchic order is a *supreme monad*, an all-comprising unit that is God.

Just as the simple perceptive capacities of an animal in response to its environment are put in shade by a human being who can further apperceive it with self-awareness and in terms of formal symbols, so are the apperceptive and conceptual capacities of humans overshadowed and subsumed by those of God—the supreme monad. Humans have access to only vague glimpses and partial insights into the overall grand scheme as formulated by the omniscient Creator. Here we are reminded of Ehrenfels' (1916) ideas concerning the cosmological implications of his Gestalt theory when he, without reference to Leibniz, speaks of God as the *AllGestalter* (see next chapter by Kissinger).

Leibniz assumed that this grand scheme was fitting to the most perfect possible principles of organization. Yet, not unlike William James' (1909) pluralistic universe, Leibniz allows for an "infinite number of simple substances . . . as if there were as many different universes . . . in accordance with the different points of view of each monad" (*Monadology,* § 57). Besides, Leibniz explicitly specifies that an optimal system's state ("as much perfection as possible") is characterized by a variety within order, this strikingly resembles Ehrenfels' (1916) independently found definition of the "level" of a Gestalt as the product of its degree of unity and the degree of multiplicity (variety):

> And this is the means of obtaining as much variety as possible, but with the greatest order possible; that is to say, it is the means of obtaining as much perfection as possible. (*Monadology* § 58, Leibniz, 1995: 188)

Even the lowest grades of monads are considered to be fairly autonomous in pursuing independent courses; yet, in their vast diversity they are nonetheless coordinated in that they are embedded within a general and reciprocal order.

> Thus there is nothing waste, nothing sterile, nothing dead in the universe; no chaos, no confusions, save in appearance. We might compare this to the appearance of a pond in the distance, where we can see the confused movement and swarming of the fish, without distinguishing the fish themselves.
> Thus we see that each living body has a dominant entelechy, which in case of an animal is the soul, but the members of this living body are full of other living things, plants and animals, of which each has in turn its dominant entelechy or soul. (*Monadology*, §§ 69-70, Leibniz, 1995: 190)

The principle of the harmony among the monads does not consequently belong to them, but it is the monad of monads, God, that affords an ultimate unity. What develops in an individual monad is at the same time compatible with all other developments. From a single grain of sand, Leibniz holds, the whole universe might be comprehended if we only knew the sand grain thoroughly. Monads are hence *pars pro toto* representations, reflecting the whole, but according to their respective dominant determinations and particular circumstances.

Leibniz's Holism Reassessed

Leibniz's monadology is not restricted to organic or mental aspects of life, but embedded within a more general cosmological view (see Rescher, 2006). It relies on indecomposable units as centers of force or activity, rather than on inert material elements on which formal principles are imposed; it thus equates substance with force and regards matter, space, time, and motion to derive from these primary forces. This view strikingly resembles that of modern physics, especially of *quantum field theory*, which supposes holistic structure for quantum systems and considers subatomic particles as wave-like energetic variations rather than material entities (Zee, 2003). Furthermore, in conceiving the activity of each monad to follow pre-set rules or programs peculiar to itself as well as applying to the whole, Leibniz echoes modern biology, especially *molecular genetics* (Gánti, 2003). Here we find an intriguing specificity of bodily organs in relation to their cells and, within each cell, nuclear acids or DNA from which the genetic information is passed to the proteins of which the body is largely comprised.

For Leibniz the *whole* is an *a priori* condition of reality. However he does not regard reality as static or absolute, but as variable and graded in that it obeys a reciprocal relation to holonomic function. It is still instructive to follow Leibniz's respective statements as, for example, in his letter to Arnauld of April 30, 1687:

> *I hold that where there are only entities by aggregration, there will not be any real entities.*. . . I maintain as axiomatic . . . that that which is not truly *one* entity is not truly one *entity* either. It has always been held that unity and entity are reciprocal things. . . . I do not mean that there is nothing substantial, or nothing but appearance, in the things which have no genuine unity; for I agree that they have always as much reality or substantiality as there is genuine unity in that of which they are composed. (Leibniz, 1995: 66-67, emphasis in the original)

And further, as if out of a current reader on Gestalt psychology, Leibniz already specifies gradual variation of organization in relating wholes to their constituent parts.

> I agree that there are degrees of accidental unity; that an ordered society has more unity than a confused mob, and that an organized body or a machine has more unity than a society – that is to say there is more point in conceiving them as one single thing, because there is more relation between the constituent parts. (Leibniz, 1995: 69)

The idea of gradual variation in holistic organization, of an organic hierarchy, nicely accounts for an infinite complexity of elements interacting at every level, while preserving a genuine autonomy. Each monad "mirrors" the universe, somewhat as the many flashes of light on a million ripples are in reality images of the sun. There is no more theoretical difficulty in supposing visual panoramas of the world to be multiplied in this way than in supposing the same film or program to be run off simultaneously on a million different television or PC screens. Furthermore, neuronal processing of information requires individual translation of impulses from the sensory nerves to generate an own private world-picture; there would be as many such pictures as there are living brains.

Perceptual as well as motor activities are highly organized relying on integrative dynamics of fairly autonomous agents. In particular, the noted Russian neuroscientist Nikolai Bernstein, based on his extensive biodynamic analyses, concluded that the major task of human sensory-motor coordination is to constrain the extreme number of possible body movements, which he characterized as kinematic and elastic, in terms of *degrees of freedom* (see Ganz et al., 1996).

Today, Leibniz might have expressed his theory in more neutral terms of *quantum field theory* or *molecular genetics* (see Auyang, 1999). But in his time, the vitalist and phenomenal model was the only one available for conceptualizing reality as something other than material, atomic, and inert. Terms like "life," "soul," or "perception" were all he had for describing coordinated energy and activity. Hence, we should take his more fanciful expositions, such as the last quoted almost poetic passage from the *Monadology*, metaphorically rather than literally (see Ross, 1984).

Conversely, we meanwhile know that perceptual and mental phenomena, rather than serving as mere metaphors indeed result from, and hence can serve as subtle indicators of, highly coordinated and interactive processes of our brains in response to changes in the environment and/or within the acting organisms (e.g., Ehrenstein et al., 2003; Spillmann & Ehrenstein, 2004). Consciousness is, as Liliana Albertazzi concludes in her metatheory of forms, not *blindly coupled* to corresponding psychophysical processes but *"similar* to them it its *essential structural properties*. This amounts to saying that emotion, perception and thought, as molar phenomena and unfolding processes, have the same *dynamically*-based structure" (Albertazzi, 1999: 296).

Leibniz clearly rejected mechanistic accounts of the mind (*Monadology* 17) pointing out that they would fail even if we had easiest access to the workings of the machinery. "Suppose that there were a machine so constructed as to produce thought, feeling, and perception, we could imagine it increased in size while retaining the same proportions, so that one could enter as one might a mill. On going inside we should only see the parts impinging upon one another; we should not see anything which would explain perception" (Leibniz, 1995: 181).

Certainly, Leibniz's quest for holonomic function, so poorly served by the mechanics of a mill, might be much more met by the integrative power of highly advanced and compact micro-circuitries of present-day computer chips or by the richness of genetic information contained in the DNA within every single organic cell of living beings. Still he might have rejected these impressive embodiments and instead referred to our perceptual and conceptual world as the richest source available to us for representing and understanding holistic functions. For example, perceptual phenomena, that are experimentally shown to be "illusory" in that they deviate markedly from the physical properties of the eliciting stimulus, provide excellent tools for the study of brain functions. They challenge neurophysiologists and computational modellers of brain function alike in that physics alone would fail to predict the perceptual phenomena as well as the brain processes that occur with them (see Ehrenstein et al., 2003; Spillmann, 2006).

Modern psychophysics and brain research strikingly echoes to Leibniz's phenomenalism in resembling holonomic organization, yet without reference to Leibniz, as in the concluding of a recent neuroscience review of vision:

Seemingly effortlessly, our brains pick up information, process it, and enable us to maneuver in a complex environment. We negotiate our world far better and faster than any robot without stumbling. Why? Because Gestalt factors, the interface between the world and the percept, guide us along. A large number of neurons is not decisive, nor is the speed of processing. Gestalt-like interactions makes the difference. (Spillmann & Ehrenstein, 2004: 1585)

More and more we advance to understand that highly integrated and amazingly complex neuronal structures allow for functional states that are appropriate to the uniting qualities and skillful performances of our cognitive and behavioral worlds. Consequently, neuroscience is revealing to us an ever growing richness of Gestalt-like functioning that comes close to what Leibniz's dynamic holism had envisaged long before.

References

Aiton, E.J. (1985). *Leibniz: A Biography*. Bristol: A. Hilger.

Albertazzi, L. (1999). "Form metaphysics." In: L. Albertazzi (Ed.) *Shapes of Forms*. Dordrecht & Boston: Kluwer.

Allport, G.W. (1955). *Becoming: Basic Considerations for a Psychology of Personality*. New Haven, CT: Yale University Press.

Anschütz, G. (1953). *Psychologie: Grundlagen, Ergebnisse und Probleme der Forschung*. (Psychology: Foundations, results, and problems of research). Hamburg: R. Meiner.

Auyang, S. Y. (1999). *Foundations of complex-system theories in economics, evolutionary biology, and statistical physics*. Cambridge & New York: Cambridge University Press.

Davis, M. (2000). *The Universal Computer: The Road from Leibniz to Turing*. New York: W. W. Norton

Duchesneau, F. (2003). "Leibniz's model for analyzing organic phenomena." *Perspectives on Science, 11:* 378-409.

Ehrenfels, C. von (1916/1948). *Cosmogony*. (Translated by Mildred Focht). New York: Comet Press.

Ehrenstein, W. (1947). *Probleme der ganzheitspsychologischen Wahrnehmungslehre* (Problems of a holistic theory of perception). Leipzig: J.A. Barth Verlag.

Ehrenstein, W. (1965). *Probleme des höheren Seelenlebens* (Problems of the higher mental life). Munich & Basle: E. Reinhardt.

Ehrenstein, W. (1983). "Über die Beziehung von Leibniz' Philosophie zur Gestalt- und Ganzheitspsychologie" (On the relation of Leibniz's philosophy to Gestalt psychology and Ganzheitspsychologie). *Gestalt Theory, 5:* 77-82.

Ehrenstein, W. H., Spillmann, L., & Sarris, V. (2003). "Gestalt issues in modern neuroscience." *Axiomathes, 13:* 433-458.

Fancher, R. E., & Schmidt, H. (2003). "Gottfried Wilhelm Leibniz: Underappreciated Pioneer of Psychology." In: G. A. Kimble, & M. Wertheimer (Eds.) *Portraits of Pioneers in Psychology V:* 1-17. Mahwah, NJ & London: L. Erlbaum.

Gánti, T. (2003). *The principles of life*. Oxford: Oxford University Press.

Ganz, R. E., Ehrenstein, W. H., & Cavonius, C. R. (1996). "Dynamic complexity of visuo-motor coordination: an extension of Bernstein's conception of the degrees-of-freedom problem." *Biological Cybernetics, 75:* 381-387.

Graumann, C. F. (1960). *Grundlagen einer Phänomenologie und Psychologie der Perspektivität* (Principles of a phenomenology and psychology of perspectivity). Berlin: de Gruyter.

Huber, K. (1951). *Leibniz*. Munich: R. Oldenbourg.

James, W. (1909/1996). *A Pluralistic Universe*. Lincoln & London: University of Nebraska Press.

Jolley, N. (2005). *Leibniz*. London & New York: Routledge.

Leibniz, G. W. (1995). *Philosophical Writings*. (Edited and translated by G. H. R. Parkinson). London: J. M. Dent.

Ortega y Gasset, J. (1958). *La idea de principio en Leibniz y la evolución de la teoría deductiva.* Buenos Aires: Emecé Editores. (English translation by M. Adams: *The idea of principle in Leibniz and the evolution of deductive theory.* New York: W.W. Norton, 1971).

Rescher, N. (2006). *Studies in Leibniz's cosmology.* Frankfurt: Ontos Verlag.

Ross, G. M. (1984). *Leibniz.* Oxford & New York: Oxford University Press. (Electronic edition, July 2000: http://etext.leeds.ac.uk/leibniz/leibniz.htm)

Spillmann, L. (2006). "From perceptive fields to Gestalt." *Progress in Brain Research, 155:* 67-92.

Spillmann, L., & Ehrenstein, W.H. (2004). "Gestalt factors in the visual neurosciences." In: L. Chalupa, & J.S. Werner (Eds.) *The Visual Neurosciences*: 1573-1589. Cambridge, MA: MIT Press.

Wundt, W. (1917). *Leibniz.* Leipzig: Kröner.

Zee, A. (2003). *Quantum Field Theory in a Nutshell.* Princeton, NJ: Princeton University Press.

2

Christian von Ehrenfels

Steven C. Kissinger
California Lutheran University

Biography of Christian von Ehrenfels

Christian von Ehrenfels was born in Rodaun, a village near Vienna, Austria, on June 2, 1859 (Smith, 1994). Christian was the oldest of five children. The Ehrenfels family lived on a country estate and, as was the custom of the time, the eldest child would take over the property. Therefore, Christian originally studied agriculture at the Hochschule für Bodenkultur (Fabian, 1996). During this time, his interest began to shift toward philosophy and he enrolled in the University of Vienna. There he met and studied under Franz Brentano (1838-1917) and Alexius Meinong (1853-1920), both with whom he would retain lifelong friendships. Ehrenfels became a professor at the German University of Prague in 1896 and continued to teach there until his death. Apparently, Ehrenfels was very popular with his students. He was admired for his personality and a variety of interests and talents. Ehrenfels excelled not only in philosophy, literature, and poetry but in music as well (Fabian, 1996). According to Ash (1995), these abilities along with his strong intellectual independence made him very attractive to students. Ehrenfels even considered becoming a writer and a poet at one point in his life (Fabian, 1996). Although he continued to be involved in philosophy and academic circles, it was his daughter, Imma von Bodmershof, who became a poet (Kitabevi, 2000).

Ehrenfels and His Love of Music

Ehrenfels was also passionate about music (which will be demonstrated in his groundbreaking publication of 1890 discussed later). Around 1880, he was becoming more and more disillusioned with religious matters and gave up his faith in Catholicism. Not comfortable in giving up faith all together, Ehrenfels turned to German music as his "religion" (Harrington, 1996). Inspired by

Richard Wagner, Ehrenfels wrote several stage plays[1], some of which were preformed in public (Fabian, 1996). A central theme of his works was the ability to rise above the harsh and dark realities of an earthly existence. In Kosmogonie (1916), Ehrenfels related his earlier ideas of perceptual qualities (to be discussed in more detail later) to psychic order that was to move humankind away from chaos (Harrington, 1996). This "chaos" was believed to be the randomness that originated in the development of the universe and human consciousness could supply the order needed to control the world and help to create a superior life therein. This attitude predominated the German culture of the time.

Ehrenfels and Human Nature

In his belief in the advancement of the human race, Ehrenfels supported Darwin's evolution theories and even supported eugenic breeding of superior males in polygamist relationships (Ash, 1995). In other words, fit males, with no bias toward any particular race, would breed with more than one woman thus producing superior children. Ehrenfels was opposed to the advances of technology that would prolong the lives of those he saw as "unfit" (Harrington, 1996). In spite of the uneasy tone of these statements, Ehrenfels favored mixed races (Smith, 1994). Of particular interest concerning Ehrenfels' attitudes and beliefs was his stance on anti-Semitism. In a period in Europe when anti-Semitism prevailed and led to the destruction of Jews in Germany, Ehrenfels vehemently opposed these actions (Ash, 1995). Presumably, his tolerance of different races and religions carried over to his only son, Rolf von Ehrenfels. In 1927, Rolf, who as a child was attracted to Eastern religions, accepted Islam and took Umar as his Muslim name (Kitabevi, 2000). In addition to the above interests, Ehrenfels wrote on topics such as sexual ethics and included Sigmund Freud in his long list of friends (Fabian, 1996).

Following World War I, Ehrenfels suffered a four-year long depression which prevented him from his work (Fabian, 1996). The specific cause of his depression is unknown but one can speculate that the effects of the war's outcome and the damage to the advancement of a better human condition lead him to despair. He did recover, however, and continued to write several plays. One of these plays optimistically involved the reconciliation of the German and Czech peoples. In 1929, at the age of seventy, Ehrenfels retired. In 1932 he died in his small castle in Lichtenau, Austria (Fabian, 1996).

Philosophical Foundations of Ehrenfels

Psychology in the late nineteenth century was essentially atomistic. That is, the mind or consciousness could be divided into individual components such as sensations and feelings. At least in terms of basic research conducted in the labs of Wundt and his followers, the goal was to understand conscious experiences in terms of the elemental components that made up such phenomena. Even though Wundt himself worked within a holistic framework that was part of the

German culture of that time (Kendler, 1987), it was Ehrenfels who, working in the Austrian tradition, brought forth challenges to the pure elementalists and set the stage for the Gestalt movement to follow. In 1890, Ehrenfels published the paper "On 'Gestalt Qualities,'" which by many is seen as the seminal work directly leading into the founding of Gestalt psychology and thus furthering the move toward a holistic analysis of the mind. Influenced by Mach, Brentano, and others, Ehrenfels' article would in turn influence Max Wertheimer to begin explaining the interaction of the elements of sensation and the active aspects of thought. In fact, it was Ehrenfels who first used the term "Gestalt" to refer to form qualities that were generated in addition to the sum of the elemental components (Smith, 1994). The ideas of Ehrenfels will be discussed later in this chapter following discussion of the preceding work and ideas of his time.

John Stuart Mill (1806-1873)

Although Mill was a British Associationist and definitely not in the Austrian school, Ehrenfels would certainly have been aware of his attitudes toward the study of the mind. Mill was most noted for his mental chemistry, a concept that predated an early move toward holism. In his theory, two or more mental ideas could combine or be associated creating an idea different from a simple addition of the basic ideas. Using an example with colors as perceptual elements, Mill stated that if one observes a spinning wheel divided into segments of different primary colors, the person would experience "whiteness" and not the individual colors. Therefore, a new color is being generated (Leahey, 1992). This concept was later rejected by Wundt who argued that the spinning colors, like two or more chemicals being combined, was a passive process that was not acted upon by the mind (Hergenhahn, 2005, p. 245).

Ernst Mach (1838-1916)

As early as 1865 Mach, working within an atomistic framework, proposed a question regarding "special forms." In his thesis he asked if these forms (or even melodies) were just a mere summation of elements or if something new was created in their combination (Hartmann, 1935/1974). It appears that he accepted the later based on several of his examples. For example, Mach stated that one sees a circle regardless of changes in its color, size, brightness, etc. Therefore, there exists a "space form" of "circleness." Similarly, if one discerns a musical melody, it should be recognizable regardless of its key or tempo (Hergenhahn, 2005: p. 419). This example of a melody will later provide a foundation for Ehrenfels.

Mach attempted to solve the problem of form qualities keeping within an atomistic viewpoint. He claimed that in addition to the elements present, there exists a new element that he called a muscular feeling that would become associated with the other elements (Smith, 1994). This new element existed outside of the actual perceived elements. When viewing a triangle, for example, one has a particular sensation originating from the muscles of the eyes that becomes associated with the elements of the three lines that make up the triangle. Whenever the elements are experienced again in a related form, these nervous system sensations of the muscle feelings are evoked resulting in the experience of a triangle (Mulligan & Smith, 1988). A shortcoming of this interpretation, however, is that it could account for special stimuli composed of elements presented simultaneously but not across time such as a melody (Smith, 1994).

Franz Brentano (1838-1917)

Franz Clemens Brentano, who entered the priesthood after receiving his doctorate in philosophy, became a professor at the University of Vienna in 1874. It was at this time that Ehrenfels became a student of Brentano's.

The essence of Brentano's psychology is what was known as "act psychology." Brentano, like Mach and others, was taking another step towards a holistic orientation. To him, mental events or acts are directed toward a stimulus. This stimulus then becomes part of the act (Thorne & Henley, 2001: p. 197). Brentano included three main categories of these acts: acts of presentation, acts of judging, and acts of desire. In all cases, these different acts are intentional processes above the basic perceptual elements leading to goal directed activity. At the time, Brentano's theory was an alternative to the content psychology of Wundt's and influenced a number of people including Meinong, Kuelpe, Freud, and Ehrenfels.

In spite of a movement away from atomism, Gestalt psychologists such as Wertheimer, would still view Brentano's work as elementalist. Leahey (1992: 200) states that the notion of intentionality separates the mind from the brain. That is, intention originates from mental states whereas individual neurons are matter and cannot by themselves have intentions. This separation of mind and body still fits into the atomistic philosophy.

Christian von Ehrenfels

Undoubtedly, the greatest movement toward a holistic approach was generated by Ehrenfels' work published in 1890 entitled "On 'Gestalt Qualities.'" Wolfgang Köhler wrote that:

> It was Christian von Ehrenfels who, preceded by an observation of Ernst Mach, called the attention of psychologists to the fact that perhaps the most important qualitative data of sensory fields had been entirely overlooked in customary analysis. (Köhler, 1947: p. 173)

Based largely on Mach's ideas concerning special form qualities, Ehrenfels would expand into the realm of time forms as well. In some ways it appears that Ehrenfels' proposals were not all that different from Mach's, and one is lead to be confused as to why Ehrenfels tends to receive the major credit for the foundation of Gestalt Psychology. There is, however, an important difference between the theories of Mach and Ehrenfels that will remove any doubt that Ehrenfels should be granted the credit in changing the philosophical views of the psychology of his time. As stated earlier, Mach's theory provided an explanation for spatial form qualities but did not provide one for qualities that occurred over time. Ehrenfels' theory expanded the Gestalt qualities to include temporal components thus providing a stronger and more inclusive theory. As suggested by Smith (1994), Ehrenfels' theory was more generalized thus giving it the ability to be applied to many more situations. Furthermore, many of the issues that later Gestaltists would investigate were already, at least in some form, discussed in Ehrenfels' essay (Smith, 1994).

Based on the limitations of the earlier ideas concerning Gestalt qualities, Ehrenfels wanted to provide a theory which could be generalized to complex perceptions that included all mental phenomena being either special or temporal. Such complex perceptions included ones that occurred across time. Such temporal perception could not be explained using Mach's muscular sensations approach. These temporal qualities necessitated the need for memory functions that aided in moving toward higher mental processing and away from the then popular atomistic explanations of consciousness.

Using a musical example, the basic tenants of Ehrenfels' theory are as follows. Imagine that one is listening to a common melody. The melody is composed of a series of individual notes of a particular frequency and duration and space, a certain distance apart in time. Upon hearing this sequence of notes, one immediately recognizes the particular tune. Based upon a purely atomistic viewpoint, one should hear nothing more than a series of tones. After all, that is what is being perceived by the nervous system. However, the emergence of a melody indicates that there is something in addition to the individual notes, that being a quality of a tune. Ehrenfels viewed this as a Gestalt quality that occurs along with the individual notes, therefore resulting in an experience that is more than just a mere sum of the parts. Again, this idea in itself varies little from those of earlier philosophers and even Wundt. To further the point that something greater emerges from a certain sequence of tones, consider the fact that if the basic elements (tones) are rearranged, the recognition of the melody is no longer possible in spite of the fact that the nervous system experiences the same elements as before.

What makes Ehrenfels' idea more profound is what occurs when a key change in the tune exists. That is, if a particular series of notes yields a certain tune, one can raise or lower the pitch of those notes and, providing the same relationship of intervals exists among them, the same melody is perceived. When this key change takes place, the entire series of elements may be completely different from the first presentation of notes yet the listener recognizes the same melody. Therefore, in addition to the individual elements, there exists a higher mental element, in this case, a "melody." This tonal Gestalt or "new positive element of presentation" is something different from a combination of the separate tones.

In essence, Ehrenfels is furthering the concept of a Gestalt quality to include a greater variety of stimuli. As with the spatial qualities, shapes for example, one can have a Gestalt quality referring to the relationship of elements across a temporal spectrum. Even though the crux of his seminal article deals with the establishment of temporal versus non-temporal Gestalts, he holds that Gestalts can be applied to such varied things as motion and face recognition. In addition, Ehrenfels like Mach stated that a Gestalt quality occurs automatically. That is, there is no active conscious processing needed to experience the Gestalt (Mulligan & Smith, 1988). This effortless act of experiencing a particular phenomenon as a Gestalt was an idea that was adopted by those working within both Gestalt psychology and *Ganzheitspsychologie*.

At this point, Ehrenfels discusses how fundamental elements such as tones and lines, give rise to a Gestalt, reinforcing the idea that a Gestalt is a perceptual component that is based on the relationship among the individual perceptual elements. He stated that individual Gestalt qualities *themselves* could serve as elements and create the foundation for higher order Gestalt qualities. A tonal example of higher order Gestalts is when one has the ability to recognize a composer of an unknown melody based upon its similarity to the composer's previous works (Boudewijnse, 1999). The underlying Gestalts need not be of the same modality, e.g., tonal, but are often cross modal as well, such as visual and auditory. Overall, these Gestalt qualities, according to Ehrenfels, make up the larger part of the consciousness by which we operate. Memories are largely formed from Gestalts rather than from retention of the aspects of simple elements.

Overall, Ehrenfels supplied the field of psychology with a general theory that could provide an explanation for the complex forms of human existence (Mulligan & Smith, 1988; Smith, 1994). His work lead directly into the establishment of the Gestalt psychology founded by Wertheimer. A major difference must be noted, however, between the views of Ehrenfels and those of the Gestalt psychologists. The Gestalt qualities according to Ehrenfels are not "wholes" operating on the basic elements, but rather additional elements, so to speak, that occur alongside the fundamental elements (Smith, 1994). Later, the people working within the framework of Gestalt psychology take the view that the Gestalts act upon the basic units of perception. This distinction still renders Ehrenfels as an atomist but without doubt bridging the gap that will lead into the formulation of Gestalt psychology.

Legacy of Ehrenfels

It has become evident that the work of Ehrenfels was one of the milestones that helped to establish the groundwork for the advancement of Gestalt psychology and *Ganzheitspsychologie*. The founder of Gestalt psychology, Max Wertheimer, took courses from Ehrenfels between the years 1898 and 1901, and they would remain in correspondence with one another long after Wertheimer became established at the University of Berlin (Ash, 1995). Of course, many others certainly contributed to the early Gestalt framework, but it was Ehrenfels who, as previously stated, built a theory that was indeed inclusive of many of the higher processes of the mind and yet retained an atomistic perspective. It would take the work of Wertheimer, Köhler, and Koffka to move toward a more holistic approach to psychology and away from the elementism studied by the Austrian School of philosophy. Of course, it was also the *Ganzheits* psychologists that used Ehrenfels' work in the advancement of their field even before the Gestalt psychologists. Through the work of Felix Krueger, in particular, the *Ganzheits* psychologists moved far beyond the later topics of Gestalt psychology and into an entirely holistic approach providing metaphysical explanations. This, in turn, influenced Ehrenfels' ideas about the power of Gestalt in his previously mentioned work *Kosmogenie* in which he speaks of the *AllGestalter* or God.

It is interesting to look at where the late eighteenth-century works have led to in modern psychology. Although the name of Ehrenfels is probably widely unknown in modern mainstream psychology, the principles and ideas he set forth over one hundred years ago are still very much a part of the current field of cognitive psychology.

Gestalt psychology and its antecedents continue to play an important role in the area of musicology. Psychologists in this field are rediscovering the early Gestalt ideas and still grapple with how the mind can accommodate transposition or the changing of keys of which Ehrenfels spoke (Ultriainen, 2005). Modern musicologists believe that the auditory system can interpret music in a form of constancy much like the visual system exhibits size and shape constancies (Matlin & Foley, 1997). Again, this is basically the same idea that Ehrenfels proposed over one hundred years ago.

Additional similarities to Ehrenfels' proposals in modern cognitive psychology lie in the area of pattern recognition. It is common today to speak in the terms of "bottom-up" versus "top-down" processing. Top-down approaches typically are based in a Gestalt interpretation. One such model in pattern recognition is the prototype matching theory. Generally explained by using alphabet letter examples, the prototype theory argues that one must first perceive a particular arrangement of lines, dots, etc. This pattern is then compared to a prototype existing in memory and if a similar one is found, the array is recognized as a particular letter. Again, the particular prototype can be seen as being similar to Ehrenfels' Gestalt quality. According to the prototype matching theory, a person can see a never before seen pattern and still compare it to a prototype and recognize the pattern as something meaningful, analogous to recognizing a melody after the key has been changed resulting in none of the original elements (see Sternberg, 2006 for a more detailed analysis of prototype matching theories).

Concluding Remarks

The most common criticism of the early approaches to understanding mental phenomenon was the notion that the process of breaking these phenomena down into basic elements creates an artificial abstraction. A holistic approach to the study of the mind was to come in the form a *Ganzheitspsychologie* of the late nineteenth century and Gestalt psychology in the early part of the twentieth century. Today, it is common to view the development of Gestalt psychology as an attack on the elementists' form of the discipline; however, it was the *Ganzheits* psychologists who were the first to establish this precedent. One cannot deny the importance of work of Christian von Ehrenfels in accelerating the movement towards *Ganzheitspsychologie*.

Note

1. For a list of his works see Ultriainen, 2005.

Acknowledgements

The author wishes to thank Dr. Mindy Puopolo for her assistance in the preparation of this chapter.

References

Ash, M.G. (1995). *Gestalt psychology in German culture, 1890-1967: Holism and the quest for objectivity.* United Kingdom: Cambridge University Press.

Boudewijnse, G-J. A. (1999). "The rise and fall of the Graz School." *Gestalt Theory, 21,* 2: 140-158.

Ehrenfels, C. von. (1890/1988). On "gestalt qualities." In B. Smith (Ed. & Trans.), *Foundations of gestalt theory.* Munich: Philosophia.

Fabian, R. (1996). "Christian von Ehrenfels" (1859-1932). In L. Albertazzi, M. Libardi, & R. Poli (Eds.), *The school of Franz Brentano:* 161-174. Dordrecht, Netherlands: Kluwer Academic Publishers.

Harrington, A. (1996). *Reenchanted science: Holism in German culture from Wilhelm II to Hitler.* NJ: Princeton University Press.

Hartmann, G. W. (1974). *Gestalt psychology: A survey of facts and principles.* Westport CT: Greenwood Press.

Hergenhahn, B.R. (2005). *An introduction to the history of psychology* (5th ed.). Belmont, CA: Thomson Wadsworth.

Kendler, H.H. (1987). *Historical foundations of modern psychology.* Chicago, IL: Dorsey Press.

Kitaberi, H. (2000). "Why did they become Muslims?" In *Hakikat Kitabevi.* Retrieved January, 20, 2006, from http://www. Hakikatkitabevi.com

Koehler, W. (1947). *Gestalt psychology: An introduction to new concepts in modern psychology.* New York: Liverwright.

Leahey, T.H. (1992). *A history of psychology: Main currents in psychological thought* (3rd ed.). Englewood Cliffs, NJ: Prentice Hall.

Matlin, M.W. & Foley, H.J. (1997). *Sensation and perception.* (4th ed.). Needham Heights, MA: Allyn & Bacon.

Mulligan, K. & Smith, B. (1988). "Mach and Ehrenfels: The foundations of gestalt theory." In B. Smith (Ed.), *Foundations of gestalt theory:* 124-157. Munich & Vienna: Philosophia.

Smith, B. (1994). *Austrian philosophy: The legacy of Franz Brentano.* Chicago: Open Court.

Sternberg, R.J. (2006). *Cognitive psychology* (4th ed.). Belmont, CA: Thomson Wadsworth.

Thorne, B.M. & Henley, T.B. (2001). *Connections in the history and systems of psychology* (2nd ed.). Boston: Houghton Mifflin.

Ultriainen, J. (2005). *Gestalt theory and musicology.* Retrieved on June 21, 2006, from http://gestalttheory.net/musicology/mbiblio.html

3

Genetic *Ganzheitspsychologie*

Rainer Diriwächter
California Lutheran University

It is no easy task to familiarize a readership with a doctrine that may not only presuppose a different philosophical outlook on how to study psychology, but which also stems from a different linguistic background (German) that poses several problems in how to adequately translate important terms and concepts. Moreover, currently the "scientific" way to investigate psychological phenomena (at least in mainstream psychology) is often considered valid only if done via quantitative methodologies, and researchers are quick to point out the lack of specificity with other approaches. That there are several fundamentally different experimental ways to study psychology has been thoroughly discussed some time ago by Albert Wellek (1947), and that the choice for what methodology—quantitative or qualitative—depends on the phenomena at hand has further been elaborated upon more recently by Diriwächter and Valsiner (2005).

The intent through this chapter is not to evaluate different methodologies; rather it is to provide the interested reader the opportunity to gain an overview of a "forgotten" approach to psychology. It has been a fairly long time that the discipline of *Ganzheitspsychologie* has laid dormant and rather untouched by recent advances in psychology. Nowadays it seems as if the British-elementaristic orientation towards understanding psychological phenomena has established itself as the predominant mainstream approach; yet it should not be forgotten that new breakthroughs can also occur by way of reexamining past neglected ideas.

While most psychologists have encountered the name of Wilhelm Wundt (1832-1920) in connection with having established the world's "first" official psychology institute (the "First School of Leipzig"), few modern day researchers are familiar with his writings. Even less is mentioned of the groundbreaking work done by his students, assistants, and other members of what became known as the "Second School of Leipzig," such as Felix Krueger, Hans Volkelt, Friedrich

Sander, or Albert Wellek. References to their achievements as well as to their contributions to the development of a unified theory of psychology are nearly non-existent in American psychological literature.

Thus, I shall introduce *Ganzheitspsychologie* by outlining its background, its main tenets, its methodology, and contrasting it with the parallel movement of the Berlin Gestalt psychology, of which arguably readers are more familiar. I shall further present current and ongoing attempts to revive *Ganzheitspsychologie* on its most famous experimental case: *Aktualgenese* (Microgenesis). It is my hope that future research (be it quantitative or qualitative) will take note of the benefits that *Ganzheitspsychologie* can provide.

What is *Ganzheitspsychologie*?

Ganzheitspsychologie[1] roughly translates into holistic psychology, but we retain the original term to indicate its link with the theoretical perspectives of the second Leipzig School of Psychology.

At the core of the *Ganzheits*-perspective stands the idea that the whole has a genetic and functional primacy towards its parts; therefore, within every living organism lies the "seed" of the whole, without which its elements are meaningless or artificial. This axiom is particularly relevant in the field of psychology, where science (in the German sense of *Wissenschaft*) traditionally has had to deal with intangible concepts, such as the mind or even the soul.

Scattered parts or static elements have little utility for psychology since only through their structural configurations, that is, through their dependence on *embeddedness* within a greater whole do they come to "life." One must only think of Delboeuf's (1893) "Illusion" (see Figure 3.1) to be able to exemplify this principle:

Figure 3.1

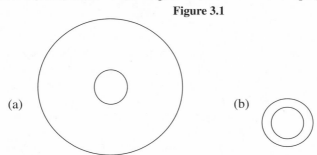

(a)   (b)

The inner circle of Figure 1(a) is typically perceived as slightly smaller than the inner circle of Figure 1(b). This is because we do not experience our environment or *Umwelt* in the sense of von Uexküll (1909, 1940/1982) as being comprised of elements (i.e., two circles: inner and outer) with no bearing upon each other. Rather our *Umwelt* is perceived as a whole configuration in which its components are dynamically linked in relation to each other. The inner rings are seen in relation to the outer circle: the bigger the surrounding field, the smaller the inner field. The images are seen as a holistic complex.

Hereby enters the fundamental notion—the all-important doctrine to which all schools of *Ganzheitspsychologie* turned—that *the whole is more (or different) than the sum of its parts*. This needs to be understood from the perspective of the experiencing organism.

> Certain relationships of independently variable composition of consciousness form (as an ensemble) qualities, that are different from the sum of qualities that the variables independently would claim for themselves. These qualities are called *complex qualities* (Komplexqualitäten). (Ehrenstein, 1934: 12)

For psychology, what develop^5 are organisms that are comprised of consolidated, yet ever transforming components that represent sub-wholes in and of themselves. Yet, the complex quality of the whole has a creative or novel character that is always _qualitatively_ different from its subparts. For example, a rectangle is experienced as more than just the sum of four individual lines. The elements become "lost" in the totality of the *Ganzheit* (the whole). Hence, the whole has an "over-summative" character that cannot be explained by merely adding up the individual components. In that sense, it is more (or different) than the sum of its parts. The idea that the whole has more than just an aggregate character and, instead, encompasses a dynamic whole that includes not only the immediately experienced, but also the totality of the dispositional and structural reality of a person's make-up is not unique to the second school of Leipzig. It has also been suggested (at least implicitly) in pioneering concepts like Ehrenfels' term of Gestalt quality (*Gestaltqualität*), Wundt's principle of creative synthesis (*schöpferische Synthese*), Dilthey's structural term (*Strukturbegriff*), and even in some sense through Freud's thesis of sensible determination (*sinnvolle Determinierung*).

For *Ganzheitspsychologists*, the dominance of the whole does not only apply to the experienced subject and the living individual, but also for social processes and configurations. Furthermore, since individual and social life is not seen as following pure mechanical laws, an alternative is to adopt an organic worldview (*organische Weltanschauung*). This way of thought follows a pattern along the lines of biological instead of technical or physical categories.

The Emergence of *Ganzheitspsychologie* as an Academic Discipline

Although numerous great thinkers, such as Kant, Hegel, Herder, and most notably Goethe, have contributed in some way or another to the discipline of holism, there seems to be a general agreement that it was Franz Brentano's (1838-1917) disciple, Christian von Ehrenfels (1859-1932), who took the necessary steps to enter holism into the field of science—although not with the vision of *Ganzheitspsychologie* in mind (Krueger, 1926/1953a; Volkelt, 1934/1962; Wellek, 1969).

In his classic study, Ehrenfels[2] (1890) showed that musical experiences have qualities that are not contained in their elements; for example, a tone sequence of a certain melody can be elevated (or lowered) but still maintain the qualitative nature of the melody. Ehrenfels' term *"Gestaltqualität"* (form-quality) pertains to the fact that there is an "over-summative" (*Übersummenhaftigkeit*) component to our psychological experiences that is not explainable based on the elements alone. A sound is "more" than just the sum of its tone-components. The melting of the components (i.e., individual tones) into a unit transforms them into something that is experientially novel and different from its parts.

A second, predominantly deductive approach was taken by Wilhelm Dilthey (1833-1911) who outlined a discipline that would stand in opposition to natural sciences, thereby becoming known as founder of the German *Geisteswissenschaftlichen Psychologie*. Dilthey's orientation was less towards empiricism; rather, it was to outline a program that would not be focused on dividing phenomena into elements, rather to focus on the linkages that comprise the structure of the totality of experience, hence calling for a genetic structural theory of life (Wellek, 1969).

However, Dilthey's approach had little common ground with the biological nature of organisms and neglected the teachings of Charles Darwin.[3] It was Hans Driesch (1867-1941), a zoologist and biologist, who grounded holism into biology (Kruger, 1926/1953a). His studies on the fertilization of sea-urchin eggs showed that the totality of development, to a certain extent, could still be maintained when extracting parts of its make-up. In other words, embryonic development continued despite the extraction of cells (e.g., after the zygote has split into two cells but also at the stages of four or more cells). The morphogenesis continued to proceed in ways that preserved the totality of its form. The totality was to be considered something that would be destroyed if parts of it were removed (p. 92).

Once the idea of holism was anchored both in philosophy as well as to a certain degree in biology, the stage was set for a new discipline of psychological thought—a discipline that would claim to be all encompassing. The paradigm of *Ganzheitspsychologie* includes all research programs whose units of measurement lie within irreducible totalities.

Körper und Seele: A Triadic Scheme

Krueger (1926/1953a: 41) once said that the idea of holism can be traced back as far as the early days of German mystical teachings. This brings back to mind the *Zeitgeist* of early psychology during which the "mechanism-vitalism-debate" so thoroughly dominated the discourse (see Hinterhuber, 2001; Siebeck, 1886). It can be said that what we today refer to as the "I," or any form of personology, was once referred to as the soul. Thus, psychology started out as the study of the soul (or *die Seelenlehre*), yet ran into increasing difficulties when trying to (a) define soul[4] and (b) explain the link between soul (*Seele*) and body (*Körper*). As Scheerer (1985) recounts, German medieval thinking (political and social) was dominated by the organism metaphor. The solution to alleviating the complication arriving through metaphysical concepts like the soul was solved via the route of Biopsychology. That is, by accepting a fundamental category of *organism* instead of the body-soul dualism, methods could be developed that address the subject as a whole (not a parted entity). More recently, Kleine-Horst (2001) suggested that we no longer discuss this issue in terms of dualism. Instead, the "manner of being" can be articulated in terms of "trialism" in which body-soul are *functionally* linked (see Figure 3.2).

Kleine-Horst (2001) suggests that out of a particular universal cosmic order (UCO) matter comes into existence. That inorganic matter (or universal cosmic matter—UCM) becomes hierarchically organized and develops into organic matter (vital matter—VM). We only need to look at the large quantities of H_2O contained in our own bodies to see traces of the universal cosmos within us. According to Eigen and Schuster (1979), we can explain the circular processes between nucleic acids and proteins (the "hypercycles") as the basis (but not the creation) of life. The larger cosmic cycle is also the foundation for a new primary hierarchy, that of life. The body of an organism can be seen as the derivation—the new hierarchy—that develops both phylogenetically as well as ontogenetically. That the body of an organism has functionality (vital functions—VF) should be undisputed. For example, on the second evolutionary level we can say that the heart (VM) has the function to keep the blood circulation

Figure 3.2
Partial schema of the 4-step "manner of being" model (Kleine-Horst, 2001).
Vertical axis indicates the trialism (Matter—Function—Phenomenal world).
Horizontal axis shows the four steps of evolution.

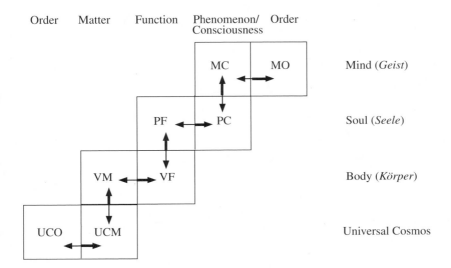

going (VF). Furthermore, the upper sublevel of VF becomes the basis for the lower sublevels of the next higher evolutionary level, especially of psychic functions (PF). The most "evolved" matter in our bodies, the neuron, has the function to *excite*, which in return leads to further excitation and so forth. This level comprises the basis for associations which on an experiential level can be seen as forming a Gestalt configuration (or a *Ganzheit* of *Gestalt-qualities*). The actualization of a percept, that is, the *experience* based upon the reception of stimulation from an object (stimulus) in the outer world which "clash" with our sensory organs, leave the realm of pure physical entity as the higher organisms apperceive the event not as a series of random stimulations, but rather as a *whole* (*Ganzheit*). The perception of Gestalts, a fundamental characteristic of higher beings, belongs to the realm of psychic functions (PF). The realization of the Gestalt-qualities is referred to as "psychical consciousness" (PC). As this hierarchical level is closely linked with the functionality of matter (VF), the laws of association are particularly strong here. Yet noticing Gestalt qualities is a phenomenological domain that has strong connections with the functional domain in the hierarchy.

What only few organisms have so far achieved (and achievement is *not* meant to indicate that phylogenetic evolution has a purposeful direction) is the capability of being able to reflect upon the Gestalt qualities that are circling in our psychical consciousness. This requires a developed mental system (or mental consciousness—MC) that takes the actuality of our environment (*Umwelt*) and allows for the manipulation of it in the abstract realm alone. When we refer to thought, we refer to mental consciousness. Yet thought does not occur independently. It draws upon its lower hierarchical configurations, as well as governing rules of mental order (MO), such as those internalized through the culture into which we are born. Thought systems such as our laws, systems of logic, arithmetic, and geometry are all configured through human mental consciousness. It is here where the reality of our lives is processed and this reality is always holistically oriented. It is not the "neurons" (VM/VF) which think, it is the higher level of the hierarchy that dominates over the lower ones, yet always through the use of its lower configurations. Thus, the cycle of the hierarchy comes to a full close. Taking this model to heart, we shall now turn to the discipline of psychology out of which it emerged: *Genetic Ganzheitspsychologie*.

Genetic Ganzheitspsychologie: The Second School of Leipzig

Felix Krueger (1874-1948) studied philosophy in Strassburg and Berlin as well as in Munich under Windelband, Dilthey, Lipps, Cornelius, and later on by Wundt in Leipzig (Hammer, 1993). After a two-year stay in Buenos Aires (1906-1908), during which he taught psychology classes and established a psychological laboratory,[5] followed several months of travel through Argentina, Chile, Uruguay, and Brazil. He returned to Leipzig again where he began to intensely study developmental psychology and what Wilhelm Wundt had been studying for decades: *Völkerpsychologie*—a social-developmental approach that made language, mythos, customs, and morals its primary focus of investigation (see Diriwächter, 2004a). It was also during this time that Wundt began to see his experimental approach that investigated elementary processes as relatively completed, thus wanting a new primary orientation for the Leipzig School of Psychology—one that would tackle the questions surrounding *Völker* and developmental psychology (Meischner, 1993). Upon Wundt's personal recommendation, Felix Krueger became his successor at the end of September 1917—thereby marking the end of the first school of Leipzig and starting soon thereafter a new direction that would make *Ganzheit* its core orientation.

That Krueger would make changes towards the general orientation of the Leipzig School was no surprise since he had already openly rejected Wundt's earlier approach back in 1915. One ground for criticism was that Wundt neglected to see that our perceptions and imaginations flow from feelings and most notably what the Germans called the *Gemüt*. It is a lengthy process to precisely translate the notion of *Gemüt*, and this would not greatly contribute to our discussion at this point, yet, generally speaking the *Gemüt* represents our disposition of feeling state (transitive and often of social nature) which is impacted by our consciousness and which impacts upon our character (for a comprehensive discussion on *Gemüt* see Rehmke, 1911). The concept of *Gemüt* cannot be found in elements or in Wundt's tridimensional theory of feelings[6] (discussed in more detail below), rather there is always a qualitative component to our feelings—one that addresses the person as a whole and needs to be dealt with in a descriptive manner. In order to see the forest, we must look beyond the individual trees.

Ganzheitspsychologie's Main Tenets: Holism—Feelings— Development—Structure

The main principles of *Ganzheitspsychologie* as advocated by the second school of Leipzig encompass the following four points, or theses (Wellek, 1950).

1. Holism (Ganzheit)

This is the overarching principle which carries in it all aspects and links that make us who we are. But what is the whole? Hans Driesch's definition stating that the whole is that of which one cannot take away a part without the whole losing its essence/entity (*Wesen*) has been criticized by Krueger (e.g., 1926/1953a: 92) on the grounds that such a view of the whole pertains to an ideal and further leads to a finite quantitative perspective[7] where the whole is the sum of its parts. *Ganzheitspsychologists* prefer to define the whole through the lack of obvious parts, that is, through the non-reducibility of the whole. Instead of focusing on assimilation (or disassimilation), *Ganzheitspsychologists*

⌐ define the whole in terms of the *processes* (or development—*Entwicklung*) of a
particular configuration (*Gliederung*). For psychology the most relevant aspect
is *the experience* and the functional and structural (*Struckturgefüge*) whole,
whereby the former has to be clearly distinguished from the latter two which
are mediated and removed from the immediate experience. It is important to
remember that the whole of the psyche is not based on logical correlations of
isolated, actual "parts" that are contained in the whole. "Parts" are not independent of one another and do not merely relate to each other, rather *they are
interwoven into each other*. Thus, it is not uncommon to observe experiences
that lack concrete configurations and are seemingly unstructured. In this sense,
a given (such as a feeling) can be qualified as a whole and differentiated from
what does not belong to that given and, thus, be examined based on immediate
similarities.

2. Feelings (Gefühle)

The experiential qualities of a totality are our feelings, or better put, feelings
are at the center of our experiences (see Krueger, 1928/1953c: 204). Feelings
are never secondary in the sense of simple accessories. That is, an experiential
feeling is never secondary in a time-bound sense, as it is always present. Feelings
are as primary as any sensuous intellectualizing. Undoubtedly, feelings can be
contingent upon our personal value system. Even more, the more completely
we describe a personal experience, the more vivid and stronger we find the
qualities of emotionality in its inventory. Or otherwise put, the less complete our
descriptions about personal experiences are, the more intellectualized the qualities become (Volkelt, 1934/1962: 51). Everything we experience is embedded in
a totality and the experienced qualities of this totality are our feelings. Hence,
to strip away feelings from human experiences (as is often done in psychology
research) is to reduce them to elements that are isolated, and thus artificial.

From the very beginning, the school of *Ganzheitspsychologie* demanded a
departure from the British-atomistic association tradition and a move to holistic
measurements. Wundt (e.g., 1922: 91-106) suggested the core dimensions of
feelings were not necessarily one, but could be three-dimensional (pleasant-
ness/unpleasantness, excitement/calm, and strain/relaxation. See Figure 3.3).
Through the process of creative synthesis (explained more fully below), the core
qualities of feelings would melt into the particular feeling the person actually
experiences. Simple sensory perceptions, such as taste or smell, can be seen as
one-dimensional. Generally speaking, feeling pain, according to Wundt, falls
along the unpleasantness dimension. However, a combination of pleasantness
and excitement may be detected in connection with color or sounds. For example, while the color red is perceived as exciting, the color blue is calming. The
dimensions of strain/relaxation can best be seen in areas where concentration
is involved, whereby concentration is accompanied by strain.

Figure 3.3
Wundt's (1922) three-dimensional theory of feelings

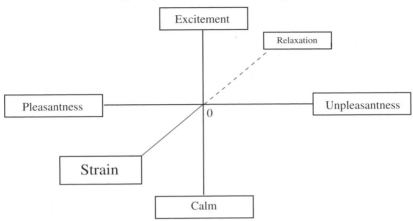

In the last few years before his death, Wundt emphasized that he preferred that his three dimensional schema be not understood as a classification system of elements, rather as a representation of what is being experienced (Sander, 1932/1962a: 127). That is, it served descriptive purposes of the dispositional aspects of a person's experienced state-of-being (*Gemütslage*). Feelings of seriousness or jolliness, as they may appear when hearing deep or high-pitched tones or as they emerge from dark or light colors, are perceived as unique qualities which may lie on the dimension of pleasantness/unpleasantness, as well as on the excitement/calm dimension (Wundt, 1922: 100). Wundt emphasizes that we must keep in mind that the feeling dimensions are not singular qualities; rather they are the direction that feelings take and which can be of an indeterminable amount of simple qualities. For example, the unpleasant feeling of seriousness is not only different from experiences of pain (e.g., when burning oneself), seriousness itself differs in qualities depending on the event in which that feeling takes place.

Our mental components, no matter what their origin or dependence on one-another, are connected through the unity of the *Gemüt*. This core disposition of feeling state—impacted by consciousness (both PC and MC) and which impacts our character—encompasses everything from thoughts to feelings (see Rehmke, 1911). It cannot be doubted that this very disposition is the result of a synthesis.

Valsiner (2005a) has suggested that the totality of feeling experiences can be understood from several levels (see Figure 3.4) that, using *Ganzheits*-terminology, comprise sub-wholes (or *Unterganze*). Several of these levels consist of semiotic mediation of affective phenomena and can be arranged in terms of increasing (or decreasing) generalizations. At the lowest level, we find the physiological subsystem that addresses the excitation and inhibition of feelings. It is

here that we begin to "feel into" (*Einfühlen*) the situation,[8] whereby the feeling
is anticipatory and preverbal. The transition between this lowest level and the
next higher one is the bodily basis for all psychological experiences of affective
phenomena. Within the next higher level we have developed a general immediate
"feeling tone" (*Gefühlston*) that is non-mediated and rather of an anticipatory
nature. However, as it progresses into the next higher layer, the transition is
made between *Gefühlston* and specific categories of emotions (such as "sad")
and, thus, it is here that cognitive appraisal accounts of affective processes are
localized. We see distinguished categories of emotions that can be verbalized
and are meaningful. Hence, the general immediate *Gefühlston* has become differentiated and generalized (e.g., to the meaning of "sadness"). The generalization process continues through the next higher level in which the sign-mediated
processes are led through self-dialogue into a generalized category of feelings
(e.g., "I feel bad"). At the highest level, the person enters an over-generalized
feeling field (a mediated *Gefühlston*) in which he/she "just feels" and finds it
difficult to put that in words. According to Valsiner, our most general meanings go through such processes, and it is here where we find meanings of our
aesthetic experiences such as love, justice, or the "Christmas Spirit."

Figure 3.4
Levels of human semiotic mediation of affective experiencing

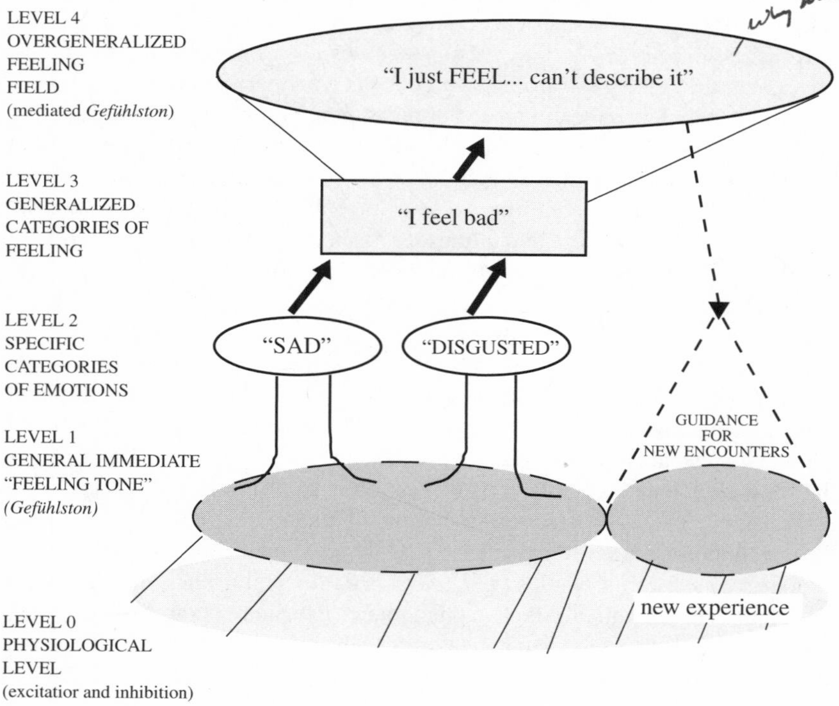

LEVEL 4
OVERGENERALIZED
FEELING
FIELD
(mediated *Gefühlston*)

"I just FEEL... can't describe it"

LEVEL 3
GENERALIZED
CATEGORIES OF
FEELING

"I feel bad"

LEVEL 2
SPECIFIC
CATEGORIES
OF EMOTIONS

"SAD"   "DISGUSTED"

LEVEL 1
GENERAL IMMEDIATE
"FEELING TONE"
(*Gefühlston*)

GUIDANCE
FOR
NEW ENCOUNTERS

LEVEL 0
PHYSIOLOGICAL
LEVEL
(excitatior and inhibition)

new experience

But more importantly, at the highest level of generalization we find a qualitative nature that is different from the lowest level of human semiotic mediation of affective experiencing. The over-generalized feeling field has qualities that are not contained in its lower levels, it is the *Übersummhaftigkeit* (over-summative) of which the *Ganzheit*-psychologists (e.g. Felix Krueger, Friedrich Sander, Hans Volkelt, Albert Wellek, and others) consistently have talked about, and it provides the grounds for future experiences. Thus, the higher levels of the hierarchical system of semiotic regulation of affect function set the stage for approaching new situations in one's encounter with the environment.

However, although the processes of the various levels are experienced via semiotic mediations, the experienced totality/whole (*das Wahrnehmungsganze*) of any level is immediate in its uniqueness. Krueger (1910) has long ago noted that the characteristics of the whole, which differentiates it from other perceptual-complexes (*Wahrnehmungskomplexe*), is not bound on having the person perceive the lower layers as separately given components (examining and judging them)—as such a dissection would inevitably destroy the uniqueness of the whole (e.g., the over-generalized feeling field in Valsiner's model).

3. Development (Entwicklung)

Humans and their experiences constantly transform and develop (see also Valsiner, 2000 for a thorough discussion). It is an axiom that humans never stay the same, or as William James (1893: 154) put it, "No state once gone can recur and be identical with what it was before." According to Krueger (1915: 166-171), in order to study the development of totalities, that is the *transformations of synthesis* (see below), the following three approaches must all be incorporated.

1. There needs to be a consistent questioning of the developmental changes that occur.
2. There needs to be a rigorous examination of how these changes are dynamically linked and integrated in a uniform whole with qualitatively different, interactive components.
3. The researcher needs to be aware of an overarching "drivenness" of the totality into a certain direction, whose changes are understood genetically and whose terminology is based on functional conditions that lead to the laws of occurrences (especially structural laws pertaining to the structure of the totality).

These structural laws and thus developmental laws, are the precondition of any form of analysis. *The dynamic whole with all its processes is the unit of measurement.* The totality is not just additive, that is to say, an amorphous unit. It is a synthetically living form, a structure that cannot be understood without its dynamic components, essential to life, stemming from present as well as past. In this, the *Ganzheitspsychologie* perspective is closely linked with Lev Vygotsky's cultural-historical perspective (e.g., the notion of "minimal Gestalt" as unit of analysis).

4. Structure (Struktur)

The fourth major thesis of *Ganzheits*-psychological thought pertains to structure. Structure consists of lasting joints, hierarchical layers, and holistically related forces—in other words, forces which are lawfully dependent on a totality and which give that totality its frame (Krueger, 1924/1953b: 135). The totality of a person entails both the structured buildup and developmental potential of his/her organs, that is biology, as well as non-physical capabilities (e.g., what we come to understand as consciousness or the human psyche). Both physical and non-physical are linked together into a dispositional whole (thus, the organic approach). Such a structure represents a uniform or undivided complex (*einheitlicher Komplex*) of constant conditions that underlies all human expressions. We can, however, look at partial structures (*Teilstrukturen*), such as perceptions, memory, or productive thought. Partial structures are dispositional states of affairs, which nonetheless display in various degrees their inner layers and linkages. In general, the dispositional whole can be subdivided into (a) *organism* (e.g., the unity of mind and body), (b) *community*, (c) *culture and civilization*, and (d) *cosmos* or nature (Wellek, 1950: 12). In this sense, structure is *not* to be equated with experiences; rather *it represents the conditions in which experiences emerge.*

Implicit in these four main tenets of *Ganzheitspsychologie* is that they are always related, that is, interwoven into each other. Hence, the overarching principle is that of holism, which carries in it all aspects and links that make us who we are. Krueger (1926/1953a) believed that before we can look at an organization of any kind (e.g., experiences or personality) we must first thoroughly *describe* (in their entirety) the given *qualities* of the conscious experience and if given include the greater complexities (*Hauptkomplexe*) to which this experience belongs (p. 115).

Methodology of *Ganzheitspsychologie*

Levels of Analysis: Not accumulation of elements, but synthesis through transformations

1. Creative Synthesis: from elementary processes to wholeness.

Under the principle of creative synthesis I understand the fact that psychical elements, through their causally related interactions (Wechselwirkungen) as well as the resulting consequences thereof, create connections which may be psychologically explained through their components, but at the same time those connections contain new characteristics which are not contained in the elements. (Wundt, 1894: 112)

For Wundt, creative synthesis was the necessary link between the lower mental processes (i.e., sensory perceptions) and the higher processes that give our life meaning. The higher ones were the foundation of *Völkerpsychologie*. However, it needed to be understood that *Völkerpsychologie* (at least in theory) was not self-standing; rather it was intimately connected to the lower processes, that is, physiological psychology (Wundt, 1917).

Sensations, according to Wundt, are the product of isolated abstractions. They become the end result of psychological analysis when components of a totality can no longer be reduced, that is, they are the elements which precede consciousness/awareness. Although such elementary processes can be temporarily examined in isolation, it needs to be reiterated that they too are constantly connected with other components that lead up to the wholeness of experiences. While it may well be possible to further abstractly differentiate sides/aspects of the elements (sensations), it comes at a cost: the destruction of the experiential totality. A psychology which takes these elements as the starting point of analysis, from which they build up to create the immediate experience, will always find it impossible to show the complex state of affairs (*Tatbestände*) from these elements alone (Sander, 1922: 57).

It may be helpful to use one of Wundt's (1894: 113) own examples on how this worked. When looking at our sensory perceptions, every conscious perception *(Wahrnehmung)* can be divided (*zerlegt*) in elementary sensations. However, our perception is never just the sum of these sensations. Instead, through the connections of these sensations something new is created, with unique characteristics that were not contained in the sensations alone. In other words, while we can abstract elements from a phenomenon, attempting to put these elements together again will not result in the original phenomenon. For example, through numerous light-impressions (*Lichteindrücken*) we create spatial forms (*räumliche Gestalt*). No matter how nativistic our philosophical orientation is, this conscious perception is something creative as opposed to the sum of all the light-shades/impressions, which is the substratum (*Substrat*) of the perceptive act. For Wundt, this principle is valid for all psychical causal relationships, it guides the mental development from the first to the last step.

2. Creative Synthesis Transformation.

Volkelt (1922: 88) points out that for Wundt, synthesis had a double meaning: First, synthesis is the reversal of psychological analysis, that is, the task in which psychologists take the abstracted products of their analysis and place them together again. It must be noted that the object of synthesis (the totality) is the starting point of analysis and abstracted components need to be reintegrated into the original totality.

The second meaning for synthesis according to Wundt was that it is a real genetic process of "melting" originally *unrelated* elements. As mentioned above, when we are looking at an object, we may say this object consists of numerous elements (i.e., the light-shades/impressions reflected on our retina) however, we do not perceive this object in terms of its elements, rather it is the object in its totality—a *Gestalt*—upon which we reflect. The genetic process of melting of unrelated elements goes unnoticed and our psychological processes thus begin at the level of synthesis. Nevertheless, although unnoticed, the finalized synthesis has undergone a genetic process.

The finalized synthesis is precisely the point that Wundt's students (e.g., Krueger, 1915, 1922; Sander, 1922; Volkelt 1922) pick up on. Any attempt to incorporate the products of elementary processes into a totality (*Ganzheit*) requires the person to leave the method of summation of properties and acquire the process of *qualitative description* of the experienced phenomenon from the perspective of the totality.

Psychic (*seelische*) development does not proceed from scattered/unrelated elements to a synthetic whole, rather it proceeds from one whole to another. Psychical synthesis is never created entirely new, rather it is merely transformed relationships (Volkelt, 1922). Hence, Wundt's principle of creative synthesis, which states that originally unrelated elements are connected to a totality, needed to be dropped and replaced by the principle of creative synthesis transformation: primitive totalities transform into more developed totalities (or old syntheses are transformed into new ones).

If we give up the genetic elemental-synthesis (the melting of unrelated elements) and replace it through the genetic totality (*Ganzheits*) transformation, then the creative character of development is no longer hindered: each higher totality is in relationship to the totalities out of which it emerged: a creative novelty.

How Would a Holistic Methodology Work in Empirical Practice?

The methodology of the Leipzig *Ganzheitspsychologie* profited from the experimental approach of Külpe's "Würzburg School" (Wellek, 1954). However, the approach of the Leipzig circle went beyond the much emphasized thought psychology (*Denkpsychologie*) of the Würzburgers that often alienated or underemphasized the importance of emotionality contained in participants' statements. Feelings are a central tenet of *Ganzheitspsychologie*, and thus, feelings were under no circumstances to be left out of psychological experiments (or studies). To think is to feel!

In this sense, the Würzburg approach could be expanded by putting particular emphasis on the aspects pertaining to a person's feeling states. The focus on holistic integrative processes of the psychological (internal) and the external worlds were central for Külpe's concept of realization (*Realisierung*), which considered the centrality of volitional processes as integrating forces of the psychological system (Külpe, 1912, 1920, 1923). For *Ganzheitspsychologie*, more attention needed to be paid to the transformations (i.e., development) of these processes pertaining particularly to feeling states.

Furthermore, in order to proceed with any form of human analysis, we must be aware of the following differentiable aspects of analysis that must be kept separate (Kruger, 1915, p. 75-80).

1. *The analysis of components.* Here "components" refers to the non-reducible parts of a totality, which are necessarily totalities of their own. These sub-totalities are inevitably standing in relation to each other and cannot be fully segregated from one another or from the greater totality without losing their meaning.

2. *The analysis of conditions.* This second approach (which is always conceptually abstract) goes beyond the immediate experience, rising analytically over everything that was ever a part of a single psychological experience and could ever be held in its components. Conditions are always conceptualized; empirical conditions (which as we know all science seeks) are abstracted from compared events of the past, which are terminologically abstracted in and of themselves (that is, they are bound to the limitations that our language allows for interpretation).

The latter also describes causes. Causal analysis is only a specific case of the analysis of conditions. This is based on the idea that, from comparing past and present events, we can more or less establish laws by which these events happen with the expectations that these laws will apply in the future as well. But since there is always a chance that these laws contain faults, all analyses of conditions are more or less hypothetical.

This is especially applicable to psychology where, strictly put, the primary reality of the immediately given takes place within a person's phenomenal world. This is also where we touch on the roots of what Wundt (1919) believed was supposed to be the focus of psychological analysis, the "immediate experiences." In order to make sense of it, he drew upon his *Völkerpsychologie* which elaborated and went beyond the simple psychological processes (see Diriwächter, 2004a).

The *Ganzheitspsychologie* school of thought, however, went much farther in its analysis than the separation of higher and lower psychological processes. For them the history of a person, that which he/she experienced not only immediately prior to a certain event but also much further back in time, was essential to any present experience. Humans are intricately interwoven in their community, which in return is but a mere subtotal of the society and larger culture we live in. This cannot be quantified, rather it always needs to be qualitatively analyzed and integrated with empirical observations.

Thus, the *Ganzheitspsychologie* comparative method proceeds from the analysis of components of a psychological phenomenon to the analysis of conditions within different contexts. These phenomena are then compared across contexts: through consecutive abstractions, one arrives at universal developmental laws. Humans are developmentally integrated in the web of history, society, and ongoing events that continuously change ongoing conditions. As the structure of one's life necessitates development, *Ganzheitspsychologie* naturally encompasses both structural and developmental psychology. In fact, Volkelt (1922: 104) mentions that Wundt's (1912: 4) use of the term "developmental psychology" (*Entwicklungspsychologie*) in his *Elemente der Völkerpsychologie* was in direct response to Krueger's "lobbying."

Gestalt Psychology—A Subdivision of *Ganzheitspsychologie*

There is often confusion about the differences between *Ganzheitspsychologie* and *Gestalt* psychology. The differences are plentiful and I, thus, find it important to briefly distinguish these two German approaches. The Berlin Gestalt school came to being after Carl Stumpf (not without hesitation) was "lured" away from Munich in the spring of 1894 by Wilhem Dilthey and Friedrich Althoff. Carl Stumpf (1848-1936), a disciple of Franz Brentano, was to set up a psychological seminar[9] that would support and supplement his lectures and his research on acoustics. By 1900, Stumpf's psychological seminar turned into the Berlin Psychological Institute. By 1912, it was the physically second largest psychological institute in Germany that could boast the largest overall budget (see Ash, 1995), thus presenting itself as a formidable rival to the institute at Göttingen[10] or the Leipzig School of Psychology that was being run by Wilhelm Wundt at that time.

The definite start of the Gestalt movement is generally linked to Wertheimer's famous experimental paper on the "Perception of Apparent Movement" that appeared in 1912 through which Wertheimer, who had also studied with Christian von Ehrenfels, showed that explanations based on learning (previously believed by Wundt and Helmholtz) were not plausible to explain experiences like the *phi-phenomenon* (Hartmann, 1935/1974). Instead, the concept of *psychophysical isomorphism* was introduced that Köhler (1929/1970) described as follows: "Experienced order in space is always structurally identical with a functional order in the distribution of underlying brain processes" (p. 61).

The Gestalt psychologists believe that sensory data are modified by the structured fields of electrochemical forces contained within the brain (a nativist perspective), but that the data also modifies these structured fields within the brain. In this sense, the brain activity transforms sensory data and further gives the data characteristics it would otherwise not possess, thus, the whole (the electrochemical force fields in the brain) exists prior to the parts (the individual sensations), but not without being transformed through the parts. In this sense, it is a bi-directional developmental process that should be analyzed from a top-down approach (versus bottom-up) due to the functional and genetic primacy of the whole.

Naturally, not all Gestalt psychologists focused on the Gestalt grounding in a certain locale of the body (i.e., the brain). One may want to think of Köhler and Koffka's dealings with emotional qualities, drawing upon Heinz Werner's research on physiognomic perception (see Ash, 1995), or how Kurt Lewin's research impacted the social sciences (see Cartwright, 1976). Nonetheless, the rivalry as to which approach has priority (Gestalt versus *Ganzheit*), as well as social stigmas (see Scheerer, 1985) led to an intense "battle" between *Ganheitspsychologists* and Gestalt psychologists. The most vehement criticism on Gestalt psychologists can probably be pointed to their lack of differentiation between Gestalt and Structure. The Gestalt psychologists predominantly focused on the immediate given of physical happenings, and that they engaged in a form of physicalism (*Physikalismus*) that was usually pointed to the Gestaltists' neglect to seriously investigate feelings and actual developmental processes. Thus, the Gestalt approach was not truly genetic (developmental) in its orientation.

As mentioned earlier, for the *Genetic Ganzheits*-psychologists, not only form, but especially feelings were important, which always had to be analyzed simultaneously. Phenomena and experiences are not carriers of development; rather it is the person, his/her structural makeup that does the "job." Gestalt qualities, as advocated by both the Berlin and the Leipzig schools of psychology, were therefore to be seen as a special case or subgroup (*Unterart*) of the complex qualities (Volkelt, 1934/1962: 48). In other words, for *Ganzheits*-psychologists Gestalt psychology was a subdivision of *Ganzheitspsychologie*, but the term Gestalt (form) implied certain boundaries that were limited to phenomenological aspects of experiences and hence it did not encompass the entire spectrum of the whole *(die Ganzheit)*. They did not account for the lasting dispositions that overlap with the present moment. Gestalt psychology lacked a distinct historical perspective.

Life at "Work": Orthogenesis and Aktualgenese

The notion of development is one of the few key *Ganzheitspsychologie* characteristics that have been exported to the United States, most notably by Heinz Werner (1890-1964), who in 1933 was forced by the Nazi regime to leave Germany and who would eventually chair the Department of Psychology at Clark University in 1949 (for a thorough review of Heinz Werner's life and work, see Valsiner, 2005b). As early as 1919, Werner had made contributions to *Genetic Ganzheitspsychologie* in Felix Krueger's book series *Arbeiten zur Entwicklungspsychologie* in which he examined the origins and development of metaphors within indigenous tribes.

However, more relevant for this discussion is Werner's contributions to developmental psychology—that is, the hierarchical transitive notion (synthesis-transformation) of *Ganzheit* from the Leipzig School is comparable to the stages of differentiation, articulation, and hierarchical integration of Werner's (e.g., 1957) orthogenetic principle. Similar to Werner's theory, the sub-totality of the *Ganzheit* must first be differentiated from the totality of the *Ganzheit*, which is diffuse at first. However, for the *Ganzheits*-psychologist, it was the totality in and of itself that was of primary interest. The stages of relative globality were necessarily and dynamically linked to those that did not lack differentiation,[11] and Werner's genetic levels of opposition are interesting insofar as they contribute towards differentiation of sub-totalities.

It is precisely this differentiation of totalities, their abstraction from a diffuse globality, which provides a basis for analysis. When we are immersed in a novel situation, we must first abstract what is known from the unknown, that is, differentiate, articulate, and then reintegrate the event we are encountering—for this is the way of true *microgenesis*.

Sander (1932/1962a, 1940/1962b) characterized this principle through the concept of *Aktualgenese* (actual-genesis). *Aktualgenese* was first articulated by Erich Wohlfahrt (1925/1932) in his doctoral dissertation (under Sander) where he demonstrated that through continuously increasing the stimulation of our visual senses, a step-wise development of percepts evolves that are first holistically (*Ganzheitlich*)-diffuse forms, but continues over a series of more differentiated pre-Gestalts (*Vorgestalten*) until it reaches the veridical *Endgestalt* (final-Gestalt). The slowing down of the time continuum, that is, the successive manipulation of the stimulation (be it visual or auditory) allows us to capture that part of the "moment" which usually goes unnoticed. Thus, the term *Aktualgenese* (or Microgenesis as Heinz Werner called it) is used to reference the development in the "here-and-now" (see also Diriwächter, 2004b, 2005a). This development runs parallel to the phylo- and onto-genetic development. We must remember that time itself represents the dimension along which we measure a particular developmental progression. It indicates the trajectory through which we see the path of an ever-unfolding Gestalt. However, the Gestalt of a particular morphogenesis (whatever kind it may be) is not time itself, rather the *entirety* of the phenomenon under investigation. On the microgenetic level, we can speak of two types of genetic developments—*hologen* (those forms that develop out of initially diffuse wholes) and *merogen* (those forms that show characteristics of seemingly unrelated "parts" which combine to produce a meaningful End-*Gestalt*) (see Sander, 1928/1962c: 111-112). The latter comes close to the singular event in the Wundtian sense of creative synthesis; the former assumes continuity out of something previously developed (synthesis-transformations).

The structural, relative robust union of the mind-body-totality vis-à-vis the physical requirements of our environment represents a conditional complex for the actuality of experience and the formation of actions. A person's experience transforms from diffuse to clarity during *Aktualgenese*. If this transformation is slowed down via a tachistoscope (for optics) or via acoustic instruments (for tones)—by going through a step-by-step process in which unclarity and irregularity are first evoked, and then going increasingly to a state of clarity or regularity—we come to see the structural dynamics as a necessary condition for perception in which dynamic qualities of the totality (such as affect) are being experienced. It is believed that irregularity or unclarity lead to feelings of distress or unrestfulness (Sander, 1932/1962a: 311). Our structural forces[12] tend to press an experienced phenomenon to optimal clarity. That is, the union between subjectively experienced relationships with the objectively given relations. It would be a grave mistake not to look at the intermediate steps of the process in which we gain this veridicality.

The *reale Ganzheit* (real whole) can be empirically shown by highlighting the experienced totality, the functionality, and structure of the whole. The *ideale Ganzheit* (ideal whole) is comprised of a formal (definition based) whole (that can be seen through logical evidence of content) and value orientations (*Wertganzheit*) that have apriority (in the sense of the platonic idea). These ideas follow Krueger's (1918/1953d) system of the whole (*Systematik der Ganzheit*) and take the unfolding processes empirically full into account.

Present Day Research on *Aktualgenese*

The methodology to uncovering *Aktualgenese* requires description since research participants express in different ways the process they are undergoing. It would be erroneous to force participants (i.e., via questionnaires) to express their experiences in predetermined categories for the sake of standardization (for further discussions about the shortcomings of such an approach, see Diriwächter & Valsiner, 2005; Diriwächter, Valsiner, & Sauck, 2004; Valsiner, Diriwächter, & Sauck, 2004).

Recently, the phenomenon of *Aktualgenese* (Microgenesis) has been re-examined at Clark University's research laboratories (see Diriwächter, 2005b). In one experiment, a picture was presented[13] by having it go through a series of stages ranging from blurry (i.e., the research participant is not able to determine what the nature of the picture is) to optimal clarity. Overall, participants reported feelings of unrestfulness at the stages where the picture was unclear until they underwent a "release" (an "*Aha-Erlebnis*") during the final stages of optimal clarity.

But more interestingly, the whole dynamics of *Aktualgenese* change if music is introduced while presenting the same series of pictures that transform from blurred to clarity. If one introduces a calming musical piece, such as Johann Pachelbel's "Canon," even during the first, most blurred picture, subjects seem to shift their focus away from the unclear picture to the clearly distinguishable musical piece. We hereby again see a transformation away from the unclear (picture) to what is optimized (the musical piece), and further comments by the participant are geared towards synthesizing music and visuals in a way that brings them to a non-negative feeling state. There is a "pull" away from the diffuse towards a unified and meaningful whole via the immediate experience of *Aktualgenese*.

Similar findings have been made when replicating and expanding upon Sherif's (1935, 1937) study involving the autokinetic effect. When music is introduced to the perceived movement of the light-dot, subjects seem to report more agitation, presumably because the autokinetic movement does not necessarily correspond with the melodic harmony of the musical piece being played. The lack of coherence between auditory and visual stimuli often leads participants to project negative physiognomic meaning into the situation or concentrate predominantly on one of the two stimuli (either auditory or visual) regardless of what the instructions were. There is one notable exception, however, when the music has fast tempo with a dominance of drumbeats (such as with music of "techno" style); subjects report a surprisingly high correspondence between perceived light movements that seems to match the rhythm of the music. The forceful nature of techno music seems to lead to a physiognomic synthesis with the light. Participants often express surprise at how well the two match, even when they know that the light, in fact, is not moving at all.

The "pull" towards a synthetic and dynamic whole in all our experiences is thus something that can be further expanded upon from the old *Ganzheitspsychologie* studies of the Leipzig circle, which predominantly focused on *one* sensory experience (i.e., only visual or only auditory). The principle upholds also when two sensory experiences are introduced simultaneously (i.e., visual *and* auditory), albeit the nature of *Aktualgenese* is different and harder to determine. Yet, it seems that the fundamental principle still stands: Humans strive for clarity and Ganzheit!

Currently, there are efforts underway to bring back to psychology the centrality of microgenetic development. A collection of microgenetic studies ranging from the analysis of visual perception, daydreams, violence and affective regulation, to the actual research process of data interpretation are scheduled to be published with subsequent critical commentaries (see Abbey & Diriwächter, 2008).

Some Final Thoughts

We are still a long way from the days when *Ganzheitspsychologie* dominated German psychology. The decline of *Ganzheitspsychologie* can be linked to the dark era in Germany that culminated in World War II and left several *Ganzheitspsychologists* dead or missing; entire libraries burned to the ground (countless *Ganzheitspsychologie* studies have been lost forever); and, eventually, through the occupation and the establishment of American (and Russian) methodology in German psychology (see Wellek, 1954). Yet the reasons for why the discipline of *Genetic Ganzheitspsychologie* has come to a near halt are numerous. Neither the destruction of Germany during World War II nor some incriminating and unfortunate remarks by certain followers of *Ganzheitspsychologie* (see Harrington, 1996) can or should be pinpointed as the sole reason for why *Genetic Ganzheitspsychologie* has lost its place in mainstream psychology. What remains to be said is that modern scholars are largely unfamiliar with *Ganzheitspsychologie*, thus leaving few people willing to fill the thinning ranks of those who once followed the ideas developed at the second school of Leipzig.

I hope that this text was able to show that there are important, yet often neglected, alternatives to present-day approaches to studying "mental" phenomena. The importance of taking into account the developmental processes (on all levels of existence) should not be understated. It is through such a morphogenetic lens that we can conceptualize our ever-transforming experiences. Feelings guide our every moment in life, but it is not the feelings alone that are central to our everyday experiences, rather it is the feelings we project into things, the physiognomic meaning we give to what we experience (Wellek, 1950, 1954, 1969). It is especially this physiognomic perception that impregnates all empirical findings, even the most "rational" lives of us humans.

Genetic Ganzheitspsychologie is descriptive in nature, yet not bound to physicalism (as Gestalt psychology is) and deals with what is most meaningful to all of us: Our experiences in life. If we come to see that we are holistic creatures by nature and that the complex quality of this holism reaches beyond the individual elements to something qualitatively novel, then we may finally come to understand that human development means transformation of wholes through instant-by-instant processes we label as *Aktualgenese* or *Microgenesis*. In short, we are given a discipline that is truly genetic, that is, developmental in every aspect of its perspective.

Through the *Ganzheitspsychologie* approach we may begin to look through new lenses at current as well as classic psychology studies such as those done by Muzafer Sherif, Stanley Milgram, Solomon Asch, and others in order to strengthen (or weaken) the possible conclusions drawn therein. Science is not, as we once believed, a discipline that is free of a particular *Weltanschauung*. And so I, like many before (see Diriwächter, 2004a), invite the research community to provide renewed attention to a discipline that can offer answers where our present-day, mainstream approach may be faltering. Let us not forget that the aim of publications in psychology journals is not to accumulate a large flux of studies without any serious reflections upon the methodology used and with seemingly little or no theoretical integration. The aim is to provide empirical evidence to a particular theory *while fully aware of the underlying philosophical outlook* and the implications thereof. As we know, a particular empirical study can never provide answers beyond the conditions of the study. That context is finite, whereas our complex lives reach well beyond the limits of any study making causal inferences. The age-old *Ganzheitspsychologie* principle still stands valid today: "*Das Ganze ist mehr (oder anders) als die Summe seiner Teile.*"[14]

Acknowledgements

The author wishes to thank Jaan Valsiner, Lothar Kleine-Horst, Walter Ehrenstein, and the CLU "Brown Bag" members for their helpful feedback on earlier versions of the manuscript.

Notes

1. *Ganzheit* here is defined as the whole or the totality.
2. See Chapter 2 of this book for a more thorough discussion by Steven Kissinger on the life and work of Christian von Ehrenfels.
3. See also Chapter 11 of this book where Camilo Khatchikian provides a more thorough discussion on biology and holism—and Chapter 12 by Rosemarie Sokol and Philip Rosenbaum for a discussion on evolutionary theory and holism.
4. Something that arguably present day researchers find equally difficult to do with the notion of "personality" or "mind."
5. See Taiana (2005) for an interesting interpretation of personal correspondence between Felix Krueger in Buenos Aires and Wilhelm Wundt in Leipzig. The theoretical conflict between the French-thinking Associationist camps in Argentina and Krueger's German philosophy-bound approaches are highlighted, as well as the general national boundaries surrounding psychological approaches and laboratory uses.
6. Yet it needs to be acknowledged that Wundt's theory of feelings has remained far superior to the one-dimensional theories along the lines of positive/negative (see also Diriwächter, 2003; Krueger, 1918/1953d).
7. It needs to be emphasized that there is no general rejection of quantitative methodology per se implied. In fact, it was Krueger, who together with his English friend Charles Spearman (1863-1945), introduced correlations into German psychology (Krueger & Spearman, 1907), where for the first time a "General Factor" to which all correlating achievements can be traced back to was established (a concept that Spearman would later continue to develop).
8. Here we can emphasize that to feel into a situation is to become *one* with the situation (*"Einfühlen ist Einsfühlen!"*).
9. Alongside Hermann Ebbinghaus' (1850-1909) predominantly private labs.
10. Under the leadership of Georg Elias Müller (1850-1934).
11. See also Valsiner's (2005a) model of affective experiencing described above.
12. For a list of twenty-five visual "structural forces," see Kleine-Horst, 2001.
13. Via Microsoft Power Point.
14. *The whole is more (or different) than the sum of its parts.*

References

Abbey, E. & Diriwächter, R. (Eds.) (2008). *Innovating Genesis: Microgenesis and the Constructive Mind in Action.* Charlotte, NC: Information Age Publishing.

Ash, M. G. (1995). *Gestalt psychology in German culture, 1890-1967: Holism and the quest for objectivity.* New York, NY: Cambridge University Press.

Cartwright, D. (1976). *Field theory in social science: selected theoretical papers by Kurt Lewin.* Chicago, IL: University of Chicago Press.

Delboeuf, J. L. R. (1893). "Sur une nouvelle illusion d'optique." *Revue scientifique,* 51: 237-241.

Diriwächter, R. (2003, June). *What really matters: Keeping the whole.* Paper presented at the 10th Biennial Conference of International Society for Theoretical Psychology, Istanbul, Turkey.

Diriwächter, R. (2004a). "Völkerpsychologie: the synthesis that never was." *Culture & Psychology, 10*(1): 85-109.

Diriwächter, R. (2004b, August). *Learning from Ganzheitspsychologie: Overcoming the "blind spot" of complexity in psychology's methodology.* Paper presented at the 28th International Congress of Psychology, Beijing, China.

Diriwächter, R. (2005a, March). *Aktualgenese: Development in the 'here-and-now.'* Paper presented at the Clark University Multidisciplinary Conference, Worcester, MA.

Diriwächter, R. (2005b). "Ganzheit & Feelings: An investigation into the process of psychological synthesis." *Dissertation Abstracts International, 66*(10) (UMI No. 3189853).

Diriwächter, R., Valsiner, J., & Sauck, C. (2004, November). "Microgenesis in making sense of oneself: Constructive recycling of personality inventory items [49 paragraphs]." *Forum Qualitative Sozialforschung / Forum Qualitative Social Research* [On-line Journal], *6*(1), Art. 11. Retrieved on December 1, 2004, from http://www. qualitative-research.net/fqs-texte/1-05/05-1-11-e.htm

Diriwächter, R. & Valsiner, J. (2005, December). Qualitative Developmental Research Methods in their Historical and Epistemological Contexts [53 paragraphs]. *Forum Qualitative Sozialforschung / Forum: Qualitative Social Research* [On-line Journal], *7*(1), Art 8. Retrieved on December 30, 2005, from http://www.qualitative-research. net/fqs-texte/1-06/06-1-8-e.htm

Ehrenfels, Ch. von. (1890). "Über Gestaltqualitäten." *Vierteljahresschrift für wissenschaftliche Philosophie, 14:* 249-292.

Ehrenstein, W. (1934). *Einführung in die Ganzheitspsychologie.* Leipzig, Germany: Verlag von Johann Ambrosius Barth.

Eigen, M., & Schuster, P. (1979). *The Hypercycle: A principle of natural self-organization.* Heidelberg, Germany: Springer Verlag.

Hammer, S. (1993). "Felix Krueger." In H. E. Lück and R. Miller (Eds.), *Illustrierte Geschichte der Psychologie* (pp. 103-105). München, Germany: Quintessenz Verlags GmbH.

Harrington, A. (1996). *Reenchanted Science: Holism in German Culture from Wilhelm II to Hitler.* Princeton, NJ: Princeton University Press.

Hartmann, G. (1974). *Gestalt Psychology: A survey of facts and principles.* Westport, CT: Greenwood Press. (Originally published 1935).

Hinterhuber, H. (2001). *Die Seele: Natur- und Kulturgeschichte von Psyche, Geist und Bewusstsein.* Vienna, Austria: Springer-Verlag.

James, W. (1893). *Psychology.* New York, NY: Henry Holt and Company.

Kleine-Horst, L. (2001). *Empiristic theory of visual gestalt perception. Hierarchy and interactions of visual functions.* Köln, Germany: Enane. Retrieved on November 11, 2006, partially available from http://www.enane.de/cont.htm

Köhler, W. (1970). *Gestalt psychology: An introduction to new concepts in modern psychology.* New York: Liveright. (Originally published 1929).

Krueger, F. (1915). "Über Entwicklungspsychologie: Ihre sachliche und geschichtliche Notwendigkeit." *Arbeiten zur Entwicklungspsychologie, 1. Band - Heft 1.* Leipzig, Germany: Verlag von Wilhelm Engelmann.

Krueger, F. (1953a). "Über psychische Ganzheit." In E. Heuss (Ed.), *Zur Philosophie und Psychologie der Ganzheit: Schriften aus den Jahren 1918-1940* (pp. 33-124). Berlin, Germany: Springer Verlag. (Reprinted from *Neue Psychologische Studien, 1*(1), 1926).

Krueger, F. (1953b). "Der Strukturbegriff in der Psychologie." In E. Heuss (Ed.), *Zur Philosophie und Psychologie der Ganzheit: Schriften aus den Jahren 1918-1940* (pp. 125-145). Berlin, Germany: Springer Verlag. (Reprinted from *Bericht über den 8. Kongress für experimentelle Psychologie,* 1924. Jena, Germany: Fischer).

Krueger, F. (1953c). "Das Wesen der Gefühle." In E. Heuss (Ed.), *Zur Philosophie und Psychologie der Ganzheit: Schriften aus den Jahren 1918-1940* (pp. 195-221). Berlin, Germany: Springer Verlag. (Reprinted from *Archiv für die gesamte Psychologie, 65:* 91-128, 1928).

Krueger, F. (1953d). "Die Tiefendimension und die Gegensätzlichkeit des Gefühlslebens." In E. Heuss (Ed.), *Zur Philosophie und Psychologie der Ganzheit: Schriften aus den Jahren 1918-1940* (pp. 177-194). Berlin, Germany: Springer Verlag. (Reprinted from *Festschrift zu Johannes Volkelts 70. Geburtstag*: 265-286, 1918, München, Germany: Beck).

Krueger, F., & Spearman, C. (1907). "Die Korrelation zwischen verschiedenen geistigen Leistungsfähigkeiten." *Zeitschrift für Psychologie und Physiologie der Sinnesorgane, 44*: 50-114.

Külpe, O. (1912-23). *Die Realisierung: Ein Beitrag zur Grundlegung der Realwissenschaften*. Vol. 1(1912), Vol. 2 (1920), Vol. 3 (1923). Leipzig: S. Hirzel.

Meischner, W. (1993). "Die Leipziger Schulen." In H. E. Lück and R. Miller (Eds.), *Illustrierte Geschichte der Psychologie* (pp. 101-102). München, Germany: Quintessenz Verlags GmbH.

Rehmke, J. (1911). *Zur Lehre vom Gemüt* (2nd Edition). Leipzig, Germany: Verlag der Dürr'schen Buchhandlung.

Sander, F. (1922). "Wundt's Prinzip der schöpferischen Synthese." In A. Hoffmann (Ed.), *Wilhelm Wundt - Eine Würdigung* (pp. 55-58). Erfurt, Germany: Verlag der Keyserschen Buchhandlung.

Sander, F. (1962a). "Funktionale Struktur, Erlebnisganzheit und Gestalt." In F. Sander and H. Volkelt (Eds.), *Ganzheitspsychologie*, (pp. 303-320). München, Germany: C.H. Beck'sche Verlagsbuchhandlung. (Reprinted from *Archiv für die gesamte Psychologie, 85*, 1932).

Sander, F. (1962b). "Gestaltwerden und Gestaltzerfall." In F. Sander and H. Volkelt (Eds.), *Ganzheitspsychologie*, (pp. 113-117). München, Germany: C.H. Beck'sche Verlagsbuchhandlung. (Originally presented in Athens, 1940).

Sander, F. (1962c). "Experimentelle Ergebnisse der Gestaltpsychologie." In F. Sander & H. Volkelt (Eds.), *Ganzheitspsychologie* (pp. 73 - 124). München, Germany: C.H. Beck'sche Verlagsbuchhandlung. (Originally presented in 1928 at the 10. Kongress der Deutschen Gesellschaft für Psychologie in Bonn).

Scheerer, E. (1985). "Organische Welt-anschauung und Ganzheitspsychologie." In C. F. Graumann (Ed.), *Psychologie im Nationalsozialismus*, (pp. 15-53). Berlin, Germany: Springer-Verlag.

Sherif, M. (1935). "A study of some social factors in perception." *Archives of Psychology, 187*.

Sherif, M. (1937). "An experimental approach to the study of attitudes." *Sociometry, 1*(1/2): 90-98.

Siebeck, H. (1886). "Das Verhältnis von 'Leib und Seele.'" *Zeitschrift für Völkerpsychologie und Sprachwissenschaft, 16*(1): 1-34.

Taiana, C. (2005). "Conceptual resistance in the disciplines of the mind: The Leipzig Buenos Aires connection at the beginning of the 20th century." *History of Psychology, 8*(4): 383-402.

Uexküll, J. von (1909). *Umwelt und Innenwelt der Tiere*. Berlin, Germany: Verlag von Julius Springer.

Uexküll, J. von (1982). "The theory of meaning." *Semiotica*, 42(1): 83-87.

Valsiner, J. (2000). *Culture and Human Development*. London, GB: Sage Publications.

Valsiner, J. (2005a). "Affektive Entwicklung im kulturellen Kontext." In J. B. Asendorpf (Ed), *Soziale, emotionale und Persönlichkeitsentwicklung*. Göttingen, Germany: Hogrefe.

Valsiner, J. (Ed.) (2005b). *Heinz Werner and developmental science*. New York, NY: Kluwer Academic/Plenum Publishers.

Valsiner, J., & Diriwächter, R. (2005). "Qualitative Forschungsmethoden in historischen und epistemologischen Kontexten." In G. Mey (Hgbr) *Qualitative Forschung in der*

Entwicklungspsychologie. Köln, Germany: Kölner Studien Verlag.

Valsiner, J., Diriwächter, R., & Sauck, Ch. (2004). "Diversity in Unity: Standard questions and non-standard interpretations." In R. Bibace, J. Laird, K. Noller, & J. Valsiner (Eds), *Science and medicine in dialogue* (pp. 385-406). Stamford, CT: Greenwood.

Volkelt. H. (1922). "Die Völkerpsychologie in Wundts Entwicklungsgang." In A. Hoffmann (Ed.), *Wilhelm Wundt-Eine Würdigung*, (pp. 74-105). Erfurt, Germany: Verlag der Keyserschen Buchhandlung.

Volkelt, H. (1962). "Grundbegriffe der Ganzheitspsychologie." In F. Sander and H. Volkelt (Eds.), *Ganzheitspsychologie*, (pp. 31-65). München, Germany: C.H. Beck'sche Verlagsbuchhandlung. (Reprinted from *Neue Psychologische Studien, 12*, 1934).

Wellek, A. (1947). "Das Experiment in der Psychologie." *Studium Generale, 1*: 18-32.

Wellek, A. (1950). *Die Wiederherstellung der Seelenwissenschaft im Lebenswerk Felix Kruegers.* Hamburg, Gemany: Richard Meiner Verlag.

Wellek, A. (1954). "Die genetische Ganzheitpsychologie der Leipziger Schule und ihre Verzweigungen." *Neue Psychologische Studien, 15*(3), 1-67.

Wellek, A. (1969). *Ganzheitspsychologie und Strukturtheorie* (2nd Ed.). Bern, Switzerland: A. Francke AG Verlag Bern.

Werner, H. (1957). "The concept of development from a comparative and organismic point of view." In D. B. Harris (Ed.), *The concept of development* (pp. 125-147). Minneapolis: University of Minnesota Press.

Wohlfahrt, E. (1932). "Der Auffassungsvorgang an kleinen Gestalten. Ein Beitrag zur Psychologie des Vorgestalterlebnisses." *Neue Psychologische Studien, 4*: 347-414. [*Dissertation, Leipzig-1925*].

Wundt, W. (1894). "Ueber psychische Causalität und das Princip des psychophysischen Parallelismus." *Philosophische Studien, 10*(1): 1-125.

Wundt, W. (1912). *Elemente der Völkerpsychologie-Grundlinien einer psychologischen Entwicklungsgeschichte der Menschheit.* Leipzig, Germany: Alfred Kröner Verlag.

Wundt, W. (1917). "Völkerpsychologie und Entwicklungspsychologie." *Psychologische Studien, 10*: 189-238.

Wundt, W. (1919). *Vorlesungen über die Menschen- und Tierseele* (6th Ed.). Leipzig, Germany: Verlag von Leopold Voss.

Wundt, W. (1922). *Grundriss der Psychologie* (15th Ed.). Leipzig, Germany: Alfred Kröner Verlag.

4

Felix Krueger and *Ganzheitspsychologie*: History of Psychology in Japan before and during World War II

Miki Takasuna
Tokyo International University

Tatsuya Sato
Ritsumeikan University

We cannot remember how we came upon the term "Gestalt psychology" while studying psychology, but we can recall the first time we found Felix Krueger (1874-1948) and the term *Ganzheitspsychologie*. Later, while reading a German textbook on the history of psychology (Lück et al., 1984), we wondered if there was any difference between the two. We subsequently found a few Japanese books and dictionaries that offered some description of Krueger and *Ganzheitspsychologie*. We provide these here.

Ganzheitspsychologie has been translated as "wholeness psychology" in Japanese (*Zentaisei-Shinrigaku*). *Ganzheit* is translated in English as "wholeness, entirety, entireness, or totality." *Ganzheit* has fewer synonyms in Japanese than in English. Since *Zentaisei* is the combination of *Zentai*, the whole, and *sei* means nature or being, it is a literal translation of "whole-ness." As such, we use the same word *Zentai* for the Japanese translation of totalitarianism (*Zentai-shugi*; literally "whole-ism") when we refer to totalitarianism as seen in the Nazi regime. This linguistic limitation regarding to the application of *Zentai* to different contexts of "the whole" has often lead to misunderstanding when considering the history of psychology in Japan.

Ganzheitspsychologie in Japanese Dictionaries

Heibonsha's *Psychological Dictionary* (new ed., 1981), one of the largest psychology dictionaries available in Japan, retained an entry entitled *Ganzheit-*

spsychologie. The definition was originally written for the older edition of the same dictionary (published in 1957), which was written by the late Yoshikazu Ohwaki (1897-1976). Ohwaki studied psychology in Germany from 1929 to 1931, mainly at Narziss Ach's Institute of Psychology in Göttingen.

Ohwaki described *Ganzheitspsychologie* as follows: *Ganzheitspsychologie* refers to F. Krueger's psychology. It rejected a parquet-like elementary psychology, such as traditional association psychology, and focused on the wholeness of mental life, which was similar to the Gestalt psychology of W. Köhler and others. However, Krueger's *Ganzheitspsychologie* never fell into the physicalism of natural science, nor did he try to give it a dynamic explanation by relying on a physiological field, as was done with Gestalt psychology. (Ohwaki, 1957: 428; 1981: 517-518; English translation from Japanese by Takasuna)

Another short description of *Ganzheitspsychologie* was written by an anonymous author and is found in the *Seishin Dictionary of Psychology* (1981):

> *Ganzheitspsychologie* refers to Krueger's psychology, which emphasizes the wholeness of mental processes. This area of psychology, which belongs to *Geisteswissenschaft*, incorporates history, culture, and society. Since *Ganzheitspsychologie* attaches importance to development as well, it is also designated as developmental psychology. Each developmental stage should have a structure as *Ganzheit*; less articulation is found in children's stages than in adults' stages. As one grows, articulation proceeds, and the structure becomes more complicated. Moreover, it is better to understand development by grasping the aspects of *Ganzheit*, since development is determined much more by culture, society, and history. (Anonymous, 1981a: 273; English translation from Japanese by Takasuna)

Although we could not determine the author of this article, Ohwaki was not included in the list of contributors to the Seishin dictionary. Both dictionaries highlighted Krueger's regard for the importance of the developmental factor and his opinion of an infant as unstructured, having fewer constituent parts. However, these two dictionaries were exceptional. Other more recent dictionaries such as *The Yuhikaku Dictionary of Psychology* (1999), perhaps the most popular psychology dictionary in Japan, referred neither to *Ganzheitspsychologie* nor to Krueger, whereas all the other psychology dictionaries in Japan included the entry "Gestalt psychology."

Since Japanese psychology has been heavily influenced by American psychology, we were not surprised to find no entry for Krueger in *The Corsini Encyclopedia of Psychology and Behavioral Science* (Craighead & Nemeroff, eds., 2001). However, *The Encyclopedia of Psychology* (2000) did indeed carry Krueger's entry. Interestingly, though it was written by the German psychologist Ulfried Geuter, the term *Ganzheitspsychologie* was not incorporated in the article. After comparing the concepts of Krueger's psychology with Gestalt psychology, Geuter pointed out that "[the] development of Krueger's ideas was determined by the political discourse of his era" and that "[being] a German nationalist, Krueger did not accept the idea of self-determination of the individual" (Geuter, 2000: 463). He thus concluded that Krueger "firmly believed in the role of leadership, faith among the followers, and *Volksgemeinschaft*" (Geuter, 2000: 463).

The Seishin dictionary also carried a separate entry for "Krüger [sic], Felix Emil" in which an anonymous author assumed that "it was because of the totalitarian trend of thought prevailing at that time that Krueger advocated his *Ganzheitspsychologie*" (Anonymous, 1981b: 498). This was a typical perfunctory explanation of wartime psychology written in the 1960s through early 1980s in Japan, which attributed every psychological study done during WWII to a kind of *Zeitgeist*.

Japanese Psychologists Study in Germany during the 1920s and 1930s

Psychology was one of the typically Western disciplines imported into Japanese society immediately after the Meiji Restoration in 1868. From then until the outbreak of WWII, more than one hundred Japanese students as well as young associate professors, went abroad to study psychology either in Europe or the United States. Whereas Yujiro Motora (1858-1912), the first Japanese psychologist, went abroad to earn a Ph.D. in 1888 under G. Stanley Hall (1844-1924) at Johns Hopkins University, no Japanese students obtained a Ph.D. in the field of psychology from any German university. A Japanese philosopher, Umaji Kaneko (1870-1937), did achieve a Ph.D. under Wundt in Leipzig in 1903 (Kaneko, 1903), but he only attended Wundt's lectures on philosophy and did not attend those on experimental psychology. This observation was recalled by Masakazu Tsukahara (1872-1946) who came to study psychology in Leipzig in 1902 (Tsukahara, 1937).

There were a number of young lecturers and associate professors who went to the United States, Germany, and other European countries to study psychology because, at that time, studying abroad was one of the prerequisites for becoming a full professor at a national Japanese university. In total, more than fifty psychologists visited Germany during the first half of the twentieth century. Tanenari Chiba (1884-1972), Mantaro Kido (1893-1985), Kanae Sakuma (1888-1970), and Usao Onoshima (1894-1941) were among the young scholars who studied in Germany in the 1920s. Chiba, who went to Leipzig in Germany in 1921 just after Wundt died, wrote the following in his autobiography:

> I was nominated as a research student abroad in September 1920. It was just after WWI, and the prevailing atmosphere was such that there seemed to be nothing to learn in a country like Germany, which had lost the war. Most of the students at that time went to the United States. . . . But I assumed that such a situation would not discourage the German folks . . . and I decided to study in Germany. (Chiba, 1972: 190; English translation from Japanese by Takasuna)

During his two years in Europe, Chiba stayed mainly in Leipzig, Germany, where he was lucky to discover the Wundt Collection (see Takasuna, 2001, for details). Most of the books and journals Wundt once owned were sold around 1921 to a bookstore called Lorenz. Chiba decided to purchase the collection for Tohoku Imperial University, where he was appointed chair of psychology. Krueger, who took over Wundt's chair in 1917, asked Chiba to donate some of the collection's books (especially on *Völkerpsychologie*) to the University of Leipzig. Following the purchase, Chiba did just that. Krueger expressed his gratitude by according a warm welcome to all Japanese visitors thereafter. Unfortunately, these journals and other books were ultimately destroyed during WWII bombing raids.

Kido also went to Leipzig in 1922. In a letter dated November 17, 1922, he reported on the activities and lectures delivered at Leipzig by Krueger, Wilhelm Wirth (1876-1952), Otto Klemm (1884-1923), and Hans Volkelt (1886-1964) (Kido, 1923a). He did not seem to be impressed by Krueger's or Wirth's lectures, but he liked the philosophy lectures given by Volkelt. Toward the end of 1923, Kido was visited by Sakuma and Onoshima who arrived in Berlin in 1923, having boarded the same ship from Japan. Sakuma published an experimental study on perception with Kurt Lewin (1890-1947) during this time (Lewin & Sakuma, 1925), and Onoshima published his paper a few years after Sakuma's appeared (Onoshima, 1928). While Sakuma occupied the psychology chair at Kyushu Imperial University in Fukuoka immediately after he returned to Japan in 1925, Onoshima first became a professor of Mito High School in 1921-1929 and then eventually began his career as a functionary of the Ministry of Education in 1937. Curiously, his devotion to Gestalt psychology later caused a dispute in the teaching of psychology at Japanese high schools (see below). Although Japanese psychologists knew of Gestalt psychology by the time Sakuma and Onoshima returned to Japan, those two psychologists were angry that some Japanese textbooks had mistakes in their description of Gestalt psychology. Consequently, Sakuma and Onoshima then wrote several books on the topic and became the representatives of Gestalt psychology in Japan.

Although Wundt retired in 1917 and died in 1920, German universities including Leipzig and Berlin continued to be a mecca for Japanese psychologists throughout the 1920s and 1930s.

Ganzheitspsychologie and Japanese Psychologists

When did Japanese psychologists first become aware of Krueger's *Ganzheitspsychologie*? A record of a psychology gathering at Tokyo Imperial University noted that Professor Yoshizo Kuwata (1882-1967) reviewed Kruger's 1926 paper on November 13, 1927, which suggests that the concept of *psychische Ganzheit* (mental wholeness) was introduced to a Japanese academy relatively soon after the publication (Anonymous, 1927).

In an above-mentioned letter (Kido, 1923a), Kido described Krueger's specialty as developmental psychology and mostly focused on evaluating Krueger's concept of complex quality (*Komplexqualitäten*). Kido attended the eighth meeting of the German Society for Experimental Psychology held in Leipzig in April 1923 and made a full report of it (Kido, 1923b). This was the meeting where Krueger spoke about *Ganzheitspsychologie* and emphasized that "Gestalt phenomena are connected with an experienced *Ganzheit*, but the reverse is not true" (Krueger, 1926: 23). The difference between complex quality and Gestalt quality was that the latter referred only to the intellectual aspect, and the former included broader aspects, especially feelings. Kido also admitted a similarity in terms of methodology between Krueger's developmental psychology and the biological philosophy that Hans Driesch (1867-1941) advocated. Later, Kido began using the term *Ganzheitspsychologie* instead of developmental psychology to label Krueger's psychology after publication of the paper *"Über psychische Ganzheit"* (Krueger, 1926), which was found in the first volume of *Neue Psychologische Studien*, the journal Krueger edited.

During the second quarter of the twentieth century, several Japanese psychologists were still studying at the University of Leipzig. One of them was Katsujiro Iwai (1886-1937) who left Japan in 1928 and stayed in Germany for two years. Iwai conducted experiments with children, and he reported his results at the twelfth meeting of the German Society for Psychology (the first Japanese to present at this meeting) held in Hamburg in April, 1931. His full paper, posthumously published in *Neue Psychologische Studien* (Iwai & Rüssel, 1938), reflected Volkelt's influence.

Ichiro Fukutomi (1891-1946) was an associate professor at Keijo Imperial University. In 1933, Fukutomi arrived in Germany to study in Leipzig for one year beginning in the spring of 1934. After his stay, he concluded his paper on the δ-phenomena and attached a foreword as follows:

> In order to investigate the facts of mental reality and mental events as well as their lawful necessity, in 1931 to 1932 I undertook and carried out an independent study of apparent movement, especially of the δ-phenomena, without prejudice against a specific theory. Prior to this, I examined the various psychological theories and concluded from my findings and my own stance on psychology that the issues in question can be exhaustively explained only from the *ganzheitlich* point of view, especially from Krueger and his colleagues. However, as I was only able to know about Krueger's fundamental ideas and characteristics from reading his publication, I went to Leipzig to learn more.
>
> During my stay at the University of Leipzig's Institute of Psychology, I became convinced that my understanding of the fundamental thoughts of *Ganzheit* theory proved true and that I needed to translate my small thesis into German, as I had completed it by the end of my stay.
>
> Although my agreement with the theory of *Ganzheitspsychologie* is emphasized in the theoretical conclusion of this paper, I stand by the dynamic-genetic point of view represented here, not only for the problems presented, but also for the field of psychology in general. (Fukutomi, 1938: 269; English translation from German by Takasuna)

Kido, Chiba, and Onoshima wrote separately about *Ganzheitspsychologie* in their own books (Chiba, 1949; Kido, 1968; Onoshima, 1930) and as described, Ohwaki wrote an article about it in Heibonsha's dictionary. Iwai and Fukutomi each published extensive papers in German, but unfortunately, none survived the war. It is surprising that with the number of Japanese psychologists who met Krueger in Germany, the names of Krueger himself and his term *Ganzheitspsychologie* have been lost in Japan's current history of psychology these sixty-plus years later.

Ganzheitspsychologie and Gestalt Psychology

Regardless of the above-mentioned study by Fukutomi, who described the problem of Gestalt theory in fine detail, and based on our overview of the history of psychology in Japan, our impression is that the Leipzig school of *Ganzheitspsychologie* was not always recognized and was in fact not fully differentiated from the Berlin and/or Graz schools of Gestalt psychology. This could be partly due to the late arrival of Gestalt psychology in Japan.

Because of WWI, virtually no Japanese scholars studied psychology in Europe during 1914-1918. At the earliest, direct information about Gestalt psychology was first reported by Sadaji Takagi (1893-1975), who visited various universities in Europe during 1920-1921 at a psychology gathering at Tokyo Imperial University in 1921 (Oyama et al., 2001). Takagi first studied psychology in 1919-1920 at Cornell University in the United States when Edward B. Titchener (1867-1927) was the psychology chair. Titchener's concern with Gestalt psychology must have influenced Takagi; thus, the acknowledging Gestalt psychology by Japanese psychologists was an indirect result of American influence.

While we cannot know exactly to what extent Takagi's lectures influenced his audiences; considering the above-mentioned atmosphere, which was described as "such that there seemed to be nothing to learn in a country like Germany, which had lost the war" (Chiba, 1972); Takagi's report must have impacted some psychologists such as Kido, Sakuma, and Onoshima to study Gestalt psychology in Germany.

Since there was only a short time between the acknowledgment of Gestalt psychology and the arrival of *Ganzheitspsychologie* in Japan, many Japanese scholars thought the former was a derivative of the latter and, therefore, lumped them together. We can conclude other reasons as well. For example, there was the review by Taro Takemasa (1887-1965), who stayed in Germany and studied chiefly at the University of Rostock under David Katz (1884-1953) from the summer of 1931 until the spring of 1933. Unlike Chiba and Ohwaki who belonged to Imperial universities, Takemasa was a professor of the Tokyo Higher Normal School and taught the students who were to-be teachers of junior high schools. When he reviewed the concept of *Ganzheitspsychologie* in 1933, he pointed out "despite that *Ganzheitspsychologie* or *Strukturpsychologie* of the

Leipzig school advocated the totality of mental function earlier than Gestalt psychology . . . it did not gain much of a reputation. This may be due to poor publicity and its less aggressive nature of negation. . . . However, I wish that the concepts of the Leipzig school of developmental psychology, together with those of Lewin and Katz, should be adopted for the educational psychology in Japan" (Takemasa, 1933: 801).

The younger post-WWII generation of psychologists thought that Krueger was merely jumping on the bandwagon of new holistic trend with his *Ganzheitspsychologie*, as described in the above-mentioned entry of Krueger (Anonymous, 1981b). That Krueger became the chair of the German Society for Psychology in 1933 (the beginning of the Nazi regime) may reinforce the impression that he adapted his psychology to the political situation. However, his early retirement in 1938 was never reported in the main Japanese journals of psychology.

Another factor that may have overshadowed the *Ganzheitspsychologie* theory was the boom of Gestalt psychology, which prevailed all over Japan. Kurt Lewin visited Japan in 1933 and lectured in Tokyo and Fukuoka (following his visit to Japan and Russia, he emigrated to the U.S. in the same year). Lewin's influence was already observed in the establishment of a study group called "*Lewin Klasse*" (Lewin class) around 1931, which was later renamed the "Thursday Group" since students were afraid of mistaking the handwriting "Lewin" for "Lenin" (Sagara, 1984). Lewin was glad to hear of the existence of such a group.

Dispute on High School Psychology Curriculum

The debate for Gestalt and/or *Ganzheit* psychology also influenced the high school psychology curriculum in Japan. To understand the relationship between theoretical psychology and education, we must first consider the history of education prior to the 1930s. One of the events that symbolized Japanese education from the Meiji era forward was the Imperial Rescript on Education (*Kyoiku Chokugo*) issued in 1890. This rescript strongly conveyed the message that the goal of education was to nurture its Imperial subjects (Japanese people under monarchy). The principles of this rescript influenced almost all young pupils until 1945, the year of Japan's defeat in WWII.

It should be noted here that totality or *Ganzheit* was one of the key words that appeared in Japanese education in the 1930s and 1940s. Japan had seceded from the League of Nations in March 1933, and in November of the same year, the National Socialist regime of Germany followed suit. Because of the alliance between Germany and Japan, Gestalt psychology and *Ganzheitspsychologie* held a rather special status in Japanese educational psychology from the late 1930s to early 1940s. The influence of Nazism was observed all over Japan, and a form of "totalitarianism"—not only in a political context, but also in the general meaning of holism—was admired. The German word "Gestalt" was somewhat hard to understand for non-psychologists, so *Zentaisei* (totality, *Ganzheit*) was used more frequently.

In 1937, a guideline for the General Mobilization of the National Spirit (*Kokumin Seishin Soudouin*) was officially adopted by Japan's Cabinet to generate a positive popular attitude toward cooperation in the national effort. The guideline influenced many aspects of Japanese people's lives—such as the promoting of savings and the delivery of metal ware. As such, the guideline became a part of the school education system, which included high school (in the old Japanese system, high school was equivalent to today's college; Japan's present educational system was established in 1949). Consequently, the high school curriculum was reformed under the influence of government policy to include the guideline for the General Mobilization of the National Spirit.

When Onoshima became a functionary of the Ministry of Education in 1937, he undertook the responsibility of reforming the curriculum and, in 1939, attempted to change the curriculum. Onoshima's proposal to emphasize Gestalt psychology in high school psychology courses was denounced by many university professors and finally discarded (Sato, 1999). This dispute reflected a kind of generational gap among psychologists. Onoshima was a leader of the young generation of psychologists who were bored by or who lost interest in the old structural trend of psychology in Japan. From the younger generation's view, psychology was fractionated and outdated. Thus, these up-and-coming psychologists were captivated by the German contemporary theory. In this dispute, Onoshima used the concept of totality derived from Gestalt and/or *Ganzheit* psychology in order to support and strengthen the national policy. Yet this theory was contrary to the older generation's view, and they held the positions of power at the university. They could not accept the Gestalt theory as a brand new idea and support Onoshima's ideas on curriculum reform. They may have feared that Onoshma's intention was to not only reform the curriculum but also to reform the regime of Japanese psychology. Of course, nobody today knows whether Onoshima had such intentions or not, but many young psychologists around that time expressed in various venues that they were excited to learn about new German theories such as Gestalt theory which would create a new overall scientific psychology of the twentieth century (Sato, 2002).

National School (*Kokumin Gakko*) System and Education

Although the high school curriculum reform was not realized, the reform of elementary schools was called for as the war progressed. In accordance with the aims of properly training (*Rensei*) Imperial subjects, elementary schools were reorganized as National Schools (*Kokumin Gakko*) in 1941. As a functionary of the Ministry of Education, Onoshima's role was to change the educational system into the one that met the demands of the times. Children were considered immature and unorganized creatures. The aim of education for them was, therefore, to form *Taisei*. *Taisei* was a Japanese word which corresponded to "organization" or "system." *Shinteki taisei* (mental organization) was one of the most used terms in psychology from the 1930s to early 1940s. This concept of organization often corresponded to Gestalt and/or *Ganzheit*.

Seki (1944) insisted that the structure of the National School (*Kokumin Gakko*) curriculum should reflect the organization (*Taisei*) of Japan's way. He wanted the subject content of the National School to have an organizational structure that was composed of five subjects: Japanese, science and mathematics, physical training, performing arts, and vocational training. These subject areas were to comprise the larger articulation of the National School education view. Thus, the subjects did not exist as specific to the National School education system, but as part of a bigger view of education determined appropriate for the road of the empire. National School education was considered the whole, with each subject its articulation.

Another functionary of the Ministry of Education was Koichi Masuda (1898-1982) who graduated from the Department of Psychology at Tokyo Imperial University in 1923. He insisted on psychology's important role and presented a keynote address "Issues on psychology and the new system of education," during the eighth annual Meeting of the Japanese Psychological Association in 1941. According to Masuda, it was important for psychologists to investigate child psychology issues as they related to children's education in the National School system (Masuda, 1941). In his talk, Masuda related that child psychology implied *Ganzheitspsychologie*, which showed Onoshima's influence in the new education policy. Onoshima also published a few books on personality psychology, which were influenced by Gestalt psychology (e.g., Onoshima, 1933).

Implications

Based on our research, it is difficult to judge whether the Japanese political system, either before or during WWII, should be labeled totalitarianism or not. Unlike Italy and Germany, there was no single strong leader in Japan. However, in the 1930s at the latest, Japan had many features of a totalitarian state, especially after the Manchurian Incident (1931). Following three large successive wars (Sino-Japanese, Russo-Japanese, and WWI), liberal ideas and an intellectual atmosphere arose in Japanese society. But after the Great Depression emerged, the national government (specifically as WWII approached) minimized its scientific viewpoint of education (Sato, Namiki, Ando, & Hatano, 2004). For example, the concept of individuality was completely ignored under the ultra-nationalistic system because all children were seen as equal to each other under the Japanese emperor (*Tennou*). Instead of a single dictator such as Adolf Hitler, a small group of military leaders dominated Japan's government. Military leaders, government officials, entrepreneurs, scholars, and other citizens tried to ride the tide. *Zentai* was a good term because of its ambiguity; many disciplines could prepare materials related to *Zentai*. In the case of psychology, both Gestalt and *Ganzheit* were useful concepts.

Contrary to the impression Kido made in Germany, *Ganzheitspsychologie* was not considered part of developmental psychology in Japan. After WWII, a new trend in developmental psychology prevailed in Japan, and most of the younger psychologists leapt to be a part of it. Although the Japanese Association of Child Study was organized as early as 1902, developmental psychology was not yet a big branch of psychology, and there were only a few textbooks in the field before WWII in Japan. After the war, educational psychology including developmental psychology became a required subject for schoolteachers. The field expanded quickly, and for three decades beginning in the 1960s Jean Piaget (1896-1980) was one of the great promoters of child psychology. Let us take *The History of Developmental Psychology* (Murata, 1992) as an example; it consisted of almost five hundred pages and was apparently the largest textbook in this field ever published in Japan. Murata (1992) referred to the Piagetian theory in various sections in six chapters and allotted one chapter to the works of Kurt Lewin and Heinz Werner (1890-1964). However, he did not write a single sentence on *Ganzheitspsychologie* or Krueger. Both Lewin and Werner sought refuge in the U.S. after the establishment of a Nazi government in 1933; they published books and papers in English, and were capable of influencing Japanese psychologists after the war.

When reconsidering Felix Krueger and *Ganzheitspsychologie*, we found that it was difficult to separate the psychology theory from its social-cultural background. In Germany, key figures of Gestalt psychology were dismissed from national universities because of their political views and/or racial circumstances. In Japan, the distinction between Gestalt and *Ganzheit* concepts was rather vague, and both Gestalt psychology and *Ganzheitspsychologie* were misused to fortify totalitarianism. Consequently, it is still to be clarified how the misuse of *Ganzheit* and Gestalt emerged and proceeded in Japan.

Acknowledgements

This study was supported by a Grant-in-Aid for Scientific Research (#15330138) from the Ministry of Education, Culture, Sports, Sciences and Technology in Japan. The authors appreciated the comments and suggestions given, especially by Rainer Diriwächter.

References

Chiba, T. (1949). *Contemporary psychology*. [In Japanese] Tokyo: Kyodo Shuppan.
Chiba, T. (1972). "Following the soul." [In Japanese] In *Complete works of Tanenari Chiba, Vol.4* (pp.157-280). Tokyo: Kyodo Shuppan.
Craighead, W. E. & Nemeroff, C. B. (Eds.) (2001). *The Corsini encyclopedia of psychology and behavioral science*. 3rd ed. New York, NY: John Wiley & Sons.
Fukutomi, I. (1938). "Über das δ-phenomenen und die subjective Bedingtheit der Scheinbewegungen." *Neue Psychologische Studien*, 9: 267-349.
Geuter, U. (2000). "Krueger, Felix." In A. E. Kazdin (Ed.), *Encyclopedia of psychology. Vol.4.* (pp.462-463). New York, NY: American Psychological Association and Oxford University Press.

Iwai, K. & Rüssel, A. (1938). "Der Umgang des Kindes mit verschieden geformten Körpern im 9.-12. Lebensmonat." *Neue Psychologische Studien*, 7, 153-181.

Kaneko, U. (1903). *Moralphilosophie Adam Fergusons: Inaugural-Disseration zur Erlangung der Doktorwürde der Hohen Philosophischen Fakultät der Universität Leipzig*. Leipzig: Reinhold Berger.

Kido, M. (1923a). "Letters." [In Japanese] *Japanese Journal of Psychology (Tokyo)*, 1(2): 282-288.

Kido, M. (1923b). "Reports on the meeting in Leipzig and the current trend of modern German psychology." [In Japanese] *Japanese Journal of Psychology (Tokyo)*, 1(3): 435-448.

Kido, M. (1968). *History of issues in psychology*. [In Japanese] Tokyo: Iwanami Shoten.

Krueger, F. E. (1926). "Zur Einführung. Über psychische Ganzheit." *Neue Psychologische Studien*, 1: 1-121.

Lewin, K. & Sakuma, K. (1925). "Die Sehrichtung monokularer und binokularer Objekte bei Bewegung und das Zustandekommen des Tiefeneffektes." *Psychologische Forschung*, 6: 298-357.

Lück, H.E., Miller, R. & Rechtien, W. (Eds.) (1984). *Geschichte der Psychologie. Ein Handbuch in Schlüsselbegriffen*. München: Urban & Schwarzenberg.

Masuda, K. (1941). "Issues on the psychology and the new system of education." [In Japanese] *Japanese Journal of Psychology*, 16: 100-101.

Murata, K. (1992). *The history of developmental psychology*. [In Japanese] Tokyo: Baifukan.

Nakajima, Y. et al. (Ed.) (1999). *The Yuhikaku dictionary of psychology*. [In Japanese] Tokyo: Yuhikaku.

Ohwaki, Y. (1957). "Ganzheitspsychologie." In Heibonsha (Ed.), *Heibonsha's psychological dictionary*. (p.428). [In Japanese] Tokyo: Heibonsha.

Ohwaki, Y. (1981). "Ganzheitspsychologie." In Heibonsha (Ed.), *Heibonsha's psychological dictionary. New ed.* (pp.517-518). [In Japanese] Tokyo: Heibonsha.

Onoshima, U. (1928). "Über die Abhängigkeit akustischer Intensitätsschritte von einem umfassenden Tonverband. " *Psychologische Forschung*, 11: 267-289.

Onoshima, U. (1930). *Twelve lectures of modern psychology*. [In Japanese] Tokyo: Baifukan.

Onoshima, U. (1933). *Personality psychology and child studies*. [In Japanese] Tokyo: Chubunkan.

Oyama, T., Sato, T., & Suzuki, Y. (2001). "Shaping of scientific psychology in Japan." *International Journal of Psychology*, 36: 396-406.

Sagara, M. (1984). "Around the Thursday group." [In Japanese] *Bulletin of Human Science*, 6: 90-97.

Sato, T. (1999). "New psychology curriculum arises from a dispute during pre-WWII Japan." *History of Psychology and Psychology Studies*, 1: 19-29. [In Japanese]

Sato, T. (2002). *The acceptance and development of psychology in Japan*. [In Japanese] Kyoto: Kitaoji Shobo.

Sato, T., Namiki, H., Ando, J., & Hatano, J. (2004). "Japanese conception of and research on human intelligence." In R. Sternberg (Ed.), *International Handbook of Intelligence* (pp.302-324). Cambridge University Press.

Seki, K. (1944). *The study of Gestalt psychology*. [In Japanese] Tokyo: Teikoku Shuppan Kyokai.

Takasuna, M. (2001). "The Wundt Collection in Japan." In R. W. Rieber & D. K. Robinson (Eds.), *Wilhelm Wundt in history: The making of a scientific psychology* (pp.251-260). New York, NY: Kluwer Academic/ Plenum Publishers.

Takemasa, T. (1933). "On Krueger's *Ganzheitspsychologie* (1)." [In Japanese] *Educational Psychology Review* (*Kyoiku Shinri Kenkyu*), 8(11): 800-812.
Tsukahara, M. (1937). In memory of Dr. Kaneko. [In Japanese] *Riso*, 76: 86-89.
Anonymous. (1927). "Reports." [In Japanese] *Educational Psychology Review* (*Kyoiku Shinri Kenkyu*), 2(1): 72.
Anonymous. (1981a). "Wholeness psychology." In Sotobayashi, D. et al., (Eds.), *Seishin dictionary of psychology* (p.273). [In Japanese] Tokyo: Seishin Shobou.
Anonymous. (1981b). "Krüger, Felix Emil." In Sotobayashi, D. et al. (Eds.), *Seishin dictionary of psychology* (p.498). [In Japanese] Tokyo: Seishin Shobou.

5

Ganzheitspsychologie in Heidelberg

Dietmar Görlitz[1]

Rudert to His Students

As a student new to Heidelberg's holistic psychologists, I experienced a strange sort of language from one of those psychologists, Johannes Rudert (1894-1980), a founding teacher and assistant to Felix Krueger in Leipzig. The tall professor tended to bow over his lectern and read small handwritten lecture notes. He also used language accompanied by gestures in order to try to reach his audience. He looked straight at us. He turned directly toward the person to whom he was referring thereby creating a singular atmosphere of close involvement in what was happening. Everybody felt directly affected. It was the same with a personal conversation with Rudert. As a new student, we would stand in front of him and explain what had led us to study psychology. The new student, encouraged by the relaxed and cheerful nature of the professor, would recount to Rudert—with no sense that he was being obliged to do so—his entire scholastic and professional life up to that time with candidness. This directness would occasionally lead to a non-negotiable recommendation that the student go and chose another subject, or at the very least certainly not come to study psychology in Heidelberg. It could also lead to the recommendation, which was in fact the case for the writer of this account, that the intending student shift the focus of his studies away from Sigmund Freud and his mechanical compulsion interpretation of motivation.

The concept of *Ganzheitspsychologie* in Heidelberg was related to and supported by the individual. This was not just the case with the ever-present *Ehrenfels* criteria, according to which the sum was more than the total of its parts. As Krueger's student, Rudert was deeply convinced (even more so than Krueger) that the individual was ineffable, and he respected the individual or "Person" in all her/his fundamental unfathomability. What remained recognizable was only recognized by one person considering another person directly. The purpose of this was certainly not some form of "strategic inscrutability" in dealing with and deciding about others. "More to the Point," as far as personal meetings were concerned, there was no question of shying away from explaining exactly why one had chosen psychology. That additionally served to give a special tone to introductory interviews with Rudert. Thus it required a good deal of courage on the part of the applicants who had been rejected, despite their rejection, to take part in the small and manageable seminars and to face up to Rudert's disapprobation. He never became loud in that respect. It was almost as if he were without anger. Despite the need to be close to others and engage in dialogue with them (especially his students who were not young at that time) Rudert remained unreachable.

Faculty parties, made easier by the ample dimensions of the Heidelberg Institute (which was a several-story-high villa in the middle of a richly adorned garden) played their part too. At these parties the status and origins of the guests did not matter, in fact, they were changed in the course of the often clumsily carried out lawn games. Rudert was there at these events and did not withdraw from them, on the other hand, neither did he help to set the tone of them. What helped to secure a sense of wholeness between teachers and students was the almost schoolboy-like readiness on the part of the other participants. The key was the certainty in advance, that as a student, you were a witness to something of value. You were not being drawn into something in any kind of priestly manner and not ceremonially—although, as a matter of fact, Rudert had come to psychology via the study of theology. The attraction lay rather in a muted vitality nurturing a language of its own.

Gestures, Feelings, and Expressions

Rudert used a pointing hand, which was stretched out as a typical gesture, encircling and spreading to encompass what was meant. This gesture was to enable us, his audience, to understand a given thought. This floating, hovering certainty was suited for the repeated expressions and basic ideas of what at Heidelberg represented the teaching of *Ganzheitspsychologie*. These concepts were without the exclusive defining quality of abstract conceptualizations. At the same time, the view of the world was not one in soft lines. There was no loss of substance here, no blurring. Along with all that were the words—words which are difficult to translate into another language without losing their content—words such as *Sphäre* (spheres) or *Mitgemeintes* (intended as well), *Anmutungen* (appearances or seemingness) or *pathische Ergriffenheit*, (pathos-filled emotion) and *Reimplikation* (reimplication). What could re-emerge on an earlier ontogenetic level was, according to Rudert, a key element resounding through the life of a healthy soul.

We experienced time and time again the role and significance that feelings possessed in Rudert's "household" of the "Person" and what really characterized feelings in holistic language usage. This approach set the Heidelberg psychologists apart from the (Berlin) holistic psychologists whose definite mutual dislike and distrust worked more like a silhouette of earlier hostility. One disciple became great. His passion for the acuteness of concept analysis led him to seek to make a clean sweep of what was the entire field of then contemporary psychology. This was Robert Kirchhoff, who became a university lecturer under Rudert. Hans Driesch's concept of order lay at the core of Kirchoff's thought, while at the core of Rudert's was morphology and Goethe's theory of form, which he repeatedly drew on as a source. He did this in order to present to us students a realizable model from which to learn.

Goethe and Other Stylistic Hallmarks

There is no doubt that Rudert knew that he was at one with every classic writer in the German language in recognizing and acknowledging excellence out of the past and putting that excellence to use (Manfred Osten reminds us of this in a recent essay).[2] In terms of respect for the manifest and the phenomenal, Goethe's color theory was significant. Apart from that, Rudert utilized outstanding examples of European novels and essays to introduce the larger-than-life figures he presented. He did this in order to teach his students the necessary art of characterization, an art which proved its usefulness in our final examinations. Using both our own and others' test diagnostic materials in the course of exams lasting for several hours, a picture of the visible person under consideration had to be "drawn." An evaluation of said "drawing" placed considerable demands on the examinee. Time, which otherwise in Heidelberg moved slowly, was important when it came to exams. Rudert was patient with a slowly unfolding educational path or life plan, which at first could only be seen in outline. Goethe, whom Rudert so much admired, had in his time termed *"Veloziferisches"* (luciferian velocity), which described a principle which held, so Goethe claimed, his age in thrall.[3] This was a concept that was reflected for us in the life and educational style practiced by Rudert and his holistic psychology. The fact was that time and the far-reaching influence of the past were corrective in his thoughts, which was, recalling Goethe again, on intimate terms with "the memory of the excellence of mankind."[4]

Rudert's students heard an exemplary performance of *"Faust"* over the course of many semesters. This was done in order to discern what was human from the figures in *Faust* and to develop a new way of listening sensitively to patients. Nevertheless, neither Rudert nor the kind of psychology which he represented wished to have much to do with representations of horror or dismay. Not even the personally endured experience of two world wars (in World War I he lost the use of a hand) was for Rudert argument enough to illuminate the dark side of personalities and systems. His approach in that respect was close to a then prevalent "memory culture," which withheld the prospect of the terrible from young people in order to safeguard itself. Maybe Rudert's first class work on the significance of the human voice system was a mild pointer to the murderous and murdering speeches of Adolf Hitler, the speeches we were protected from hearing, the speeches which were the foundation of that man's dictatorship.[5]

Sources, "Poison Closets," and Consent

Goethe, writing more than a century before in July, 1830, stated: "We would still be living in barbarism were it not for what has come down to us in various forms from antiquity."[6] This legacy, along with those writings from the past, was on our seminar desks. The philosopher Gadamer, with whom Rudert was on friendly terms, taught as an expert on Plato an area he had particularly well prepared. Rudert took individual extracts from ancient writings; for example, from *Theophrastus*; for the purposes of character study and then drew conclusions as to what such sources could teach us. To return to the sources with a concomitant disdain for what was commonly accepted as relevant was the impetus and agenda of the phenomenologists—whom the Heidelberg psychologists happily and often quoted.

In the new language familiar to us, we were given to understand that the environment, the context, from which and within which a pattern emerged lost its vividness and importance once one had focused attention upon the person's work. Certainly, there were scientific books, principally by German speaking psychologists, which attained the highest respect; for example, Ludwig Klages, with his orientation towards a philosophy of life, with his notion of the opposing principles of Spirit and Soul, and his elitist justification for claiming a hierarchy of form rose above the success of structures. We, the older students, grew out of the seminars into a "consensus of the adepts," if not in so many words—as the adjudicators of the criterion of knowledge and truth in this lively Heidelberg circle as it came to be known. This came to involve an exclusion of the younger students of certain lines of pursuit of information, information which was stored in the so-called "poison closet" of the faculty library. For the Heidelberg holistic psychologists the "consensus of the wise" did not mean a consensus of souls; it was rather through the exchange of ideas, an approach to an agreed path of understanding, not in any way a doctrine of the "eyes of innocence" but rather the effort to reach a consensus of non-prejudice.[7]

A "Dialectic Triad"

The new student would begin with a concentration on the subject and place his own impressions and the realization that they should be taken seriously, but not blindly. In the course of dialogue with others, the student's impressions would be reflected upon, so as to enrich and, where necessary, correct them. This process of investigation was used to approach all subject matter—whether in diagnoses, or in the psychology of expression, or in defining complete qualities confronted in psychological work. Rudert and his circle called these *Ganzheit* qualities "characters of impression" (*Eindruckscharaktere*) or "qualities of seeming" (*Anmutungsqualitäten*). He based, on their supposedly subjective character, a highly significant method of confident definition and interpretation; but understanding and interpretation were never for him neither concluded nor closed. The learning process took place through discussion and comparison with others and was an on-going procedure, a work in progress.

It was the methodic tableau of the dialectical triad (*dialektischen Dreischritt*) that Rudert attempted with all the patience it took to portray to even the youngest among us. *Triad*, that is to say—not as his assistant Robert Kirchhoff was prone to stress: *one* method is *no* method—but the approach to a person understood in terms of single, methodical steps, following systematically one after the other. The holistic element is present from the beginning, followed by layers of analysis, which would make it possible to bring out a more facetted complete picture in the last stage. Anyone more than a little familiar with the history of German speaking psychology will be reminded of the first two of the three steps described above—of the great Karl Bühler in Vienna—who in his early radio experiments stressed the distinction in a procedure for arriving at conclusions between one which reacted to resonance and one which reacted to individual indicators. These are the two procedures which listeners used in order to understand, or better said, to assess the personal characteristics of the persons whose voices they heard. Rudert brought these two steps together and brought in a third holistic step; this three-step dialectic or triad could be employed far beyond the terms of reference of voice analysis.

Guests in the House and Influential Authors

Converging lines of thought were thus echoed and accepted in the small circle of teachers of psychology around Rudert; but we are not speaking here of sheltered lives or an "island of the blessed." Rudert's own memory harbored gruesome and hard times,[8] as is shown by the fact that the most important congress of German psychologists, which took place every two years, was well attended in the late fifties when it took place in Heidelberg. Its fame is documented in the high number of invitations to speakers from outside institutions, among the most prominent being no less a personage than Charlotte Bühler, then from the USA, who used to accompany her husband, Karl Bühler, in his advanced years. Also among the invited were students from Konrad Lorenz's study group; Rudert along with his students visited Lorenz in person in Seewiesen. There were also professional colleagues of the biologist Adolf Portmann from Basel, at that time an influential person with his view on early human development. Particularly warm were the exchange visits with the psychologists around Albert Wellek, the pugnacious characterologist, whose views are reflected in *Polarität im Aufbau des Charakters* (Polarity in Character Building) which also contacts with Bonn. Friedrich Sander—who had also been a student of Krueger—taught Sander's daughter who was studying for her doctorate with us. We became very familiar with her father's work through the replication of microgenetic perception tests, the building up of forms and diminishing of forms by presenting optical stimuli from various angles or temporal sequences. But the conveying of such thought about actual/microgenesis in processes of development was not in the foreground of teaching or discussion, even though Heinz Werner's psychological development theory was regarded with respect.

There were many influential authors who were guests, and not just occasional guests, at Heidelberg. I am not entirely sure, but I seem to recall seeing Niko Frijda from Holland there. Always important for the psychology of expression (and at the time decisively so) was his phenomenon-ordered thought, his scrupulous reflection on facial expression and physiognomy—which was to become an essential formative element in the re-founding of the psychology faculty in the Technical University of Berlin by Robert Kirchhoff, who came from Heidelberg. For Kirchhoff too, the psychology of expression was the core of sensible psychological research—which is what the faculty in Heidelberg taught, although of course psychology under Kirchhoff worked from other perspectives than those at Heidelberg. Without doubt, however, for Rudert the great Dutch psychologists were Buytendijk and Huizinga. In the presentation of material of Rudert's holistic teaching, it is necessary to be more precise about the significance he gave to human play and the way people play. It was expected of us, as students who had not exhausted the possibilities posed by the anthropology of Friedrich Schiller, to conclude an analysis of play with reference to Buytendijk's work—and more than that, when our subject was expression and development, Buytendijk helped by teaching from examples out of the lives of animals or from the first smile of a child. It was at that time we were made acquainted with Johan Huizinga and his artistic, expressive work on a dying, an epoch entitled *Herbst des Mittelalters* (The Autumn of the Middle Ages), without other historical lines of thought shaping material or the contents of the teaching. That could have brought about a dispute with Philipp Lersch, if it were not for his work marked by phenomenological and layer theorized dominated called *Aufbau der Person*, (Construction of the Person). It was available in several editions at that time and obligatory reading for us students as well as the expression and system analysis in *Gesicht und Seele*, ("Face and Soul") which presented the research that sought fruitful signs of expression in human facial expression. But in relation to Lersch's *Vom Wesen der Geschlechter* (On the Natures of the Sexes), it was a work which we accepted uncritically—a piece of writing in which the traditional allocation of male and female roles were presented as a phenomenon rooted in nature.

History and Culture

History was not thematically studied and history did not just stop for Rudert at the level of occasional historical anecdotes. For example, the illustration which remains embedded in our memories is taken from the age of *sensitivity* in the eighteenth century—that a letter writer was not ashamed to admit to his correspondent that he had wept *a plate-full of tears* occasioned *in view of the shattering event.* And it was this period of history, with all its intensities of feeling, which Rudert made visible for us. This was at a time in which Heidelberg was still in a period marked by the aftermath of war, a time when the writer of these lines was still a student, and also a time when Rudert attended the 22nd Congress of the German Society of Psychology (DGfP) in 1959. After he had already been working for it for seven years, he commented ruefully that after 1933 National Socialism had eradicated no branch of science more thoroughly than it had psychology—the step-by-step reconstruction of which in Germany was in some small way reflected by the work of that very congress (Rudert, 1959:152). This was pronounced in a place that had escaped the destruction of war, namely Heidelberg, this city was spared by the Allies in their bombing raids, for which Graumann and Klüpfel many years later in their History of Psychology at the University of Heidelberg specifically thanked the Allied forces (in the Introduction to Klüpfel and Graumann, 1986).

Heidelberg's *Ganzheitspsychologie* held a central place at a time when German psychology was re-emerging and finding itself again. Phenomenology and a critique of the analysis and comprehension of expression colored the first day of the congress. That does not mean to say that the organizers were taking inappropriate advantage of the fact they were "playing at home." The theme treated was complemented by a critique of expression, analysis, and the rules of its practice; this was in order to not undermine Rudert's foundation for an alternative draft of a psychology of the natural sciences so that an "organ" (the perception of expression for the psychologists who had studied traditionally) could be examined critically and one might thereby "judge its contribution, its suitability for uncovering the truth" (Rudert, op. cit). This in no way meant that the strict in-depth examination of psychological themes and conclusions by means of statistical methods as opposed to "fine-tuned phenomenological case study" (Rudert, op. cit) was dispensable. For Rudert methodological orientation (the emphasis of methods in general) was, not only for him but for this Heidelberg congress, an important message.

Heidelberg was decorated by the fall weather, as Rudert characterized the city at the time of the congress, and by the muted joviality. Something quite different from a noise of tourists in holiday mood filled the rooms allocated to psychology and reflected the mood of *Ganzheitspsychologie,* as it was taught by Rudert in Heidelberg. His earlier discourse on character and feeling-disposition (*Gemüt*) in 1948 had persuaded Willy Hellpach (not really Rudert's predecessor, who was living in Leipzig, at that time in the Soviet Occupation Zone) to apply for a chair at Heidelberg (1950). Feeling-disposition (*Gemüt*) was the bridge, so to speak, which led over to Heidelberg. The spirit of a balanced character is not loud, does not have its own tendency to "break out," but at the same time it is neither weary of life, nor apathetic, nor bored, nor does it try to retreat from the world. (We youngsters were not in a position to understand then how much of Nietzsche[9] and his judgment of "German high spirits" was revealed in all this). With his sensibility for the *Ganzheit* and for an orientation towards values—"*Gemüt*" (Character and Feeling-Disposition) was for him the "place of connection," the "value resonance." Rudert was someone who turned towards the world, more illuminator than brooder, and in that role he found in history a way of bearing witness to figures—historical figures who were omnipresent to him because of the timelessness of their values. Hardly ever did he draw our attention to vileness in history, and these historical figures found their place in his lectures. He compensated for a war disability by training to become ambidextrous. Rudert published little. If teaching is to be "an enticing into the realm of culture," as he put it in one of his lectures on educational psychology related to the art of education in early childhood, then it certainly held good for his own teaching. It also holds good for his view of psychology as a source of historical witnesses in which the fictive reality of the poetic and the historical reality in the figures of past centuries were of equal worth one to another, citing as he did—although not mixing—texts taken from Shakespeare or Martin Luther.

Expression and Projective Procedures

The high standard of education that Rudert demanded allowed enough room for the perambulations of the imagination—the forming of other possible worlds in an unfolding projective process out of figures (*Sceno),* figurative sketches (as in the *Wartegg Drawing Test*), or scenic pictures (*CAT* or *TAT*). Expression was always the appearance, that which became visible in a person's inseparable *Ganzheit* and in the thematic components that are always person-bound. The traditional areas of facial expression and physiognomy belonged to this, so did gestures and gesticulations. In fact, movement of every kind, including pose and gait, and, essential for the psychology of expression, the manner and nature of speaking, vocal expression (with lines of reference stretching far back into history, a comprehensive collection of which has been published by the author of this essay—cf. Görlitz, 1972). Not included, despite what has been so widely claimed to the contrary, is graphology. Rudert's position on the analysis of handwriting was conciliatory in contrast to Kirchhoff's uncompromising rejection. Like many other things, working with handwriting was certainly a highly revealing form of work. Handwriting was a projective kind of work; one which Karl Bühler, writing on crisis-determination and crisis-order in "The Crisis of Psychology" (Bühler, 1927) alongside experience and behavior, picked out and called the third aspect of the crisis prone subject that was "psychology."

"Superintendents," teachers of this important aspect of study of the person and figures free of the personal, were initially only available to us through the literature, for instance, that of the adept collector of cultural-historical figures, Franz Kiener, on clothing and fashion (Kiener, 1956). A decisive figure for the disciplines represented at Heidelberg and not just in the controversial field of graphology, was that of Ludwig Klages. His books, with their pronouncements on a philosophy of life, in both the demands they placed in terms of complexity and sheer readability taxed us students mightily. But Klages was indispensable. Kirchhoff's critical opposition to Klages did not reassure us; in fact, it brought a belligerent element into the university atmosphere, compelling people to decide. But the aim of our text here is to consider the role of the Heidelberg Institute in forming complementary orientation to the psychology of expression and not the role of individual guests. If the work on expression (on the expression of others), taking into consideration all careful phenomenological description, remained nevertheless a *diagnostic* of expression, then this diagnostic aim also applied to the individual creation of handwriting and drawing. Strangely enough, the focus was not on the actual object but was on a kind of interpretation which was introduced into the perception and clarification protocols of the test subjects as they arose in Rorschach's pilot tests, in *Murray's Thematischem Apperzeptions-Test* (TAT) (Thematic Perception Test), in Wartegg's drawing test, or in August Vetter's[10] *Auffassungs-Deutungstest* (Opinion-Clarification). There was a battery of diagnostic procedures, which was presented to the students in the form of an intensive training stretching over several semesters, the use and proven applications of which constituted a key element in the final examinations which followed after eight to ten semesters.[11]

That was a collection of *Diagnostica* that suited the *Ganzheitspsychologie* represented by Rudert particularly well since its respect for the other person was deeply rooted in its characterology. This was, for him, not only research into character but accepting the limits to the means of recognition—to quote again: *"individuum est ineffabile"*—meant that other persons had a story of their own to be told but not necessarily to be preferred. Hence, Rudert's mild scorn was aimed at William McDougall's compiled lists of instincts, which was popular at the time (his scorn did not embrace, be it noted, the standardized intelligence tests composed by the likes of Wechsler or Amthauer).

More on the "Dialectical Triad"

Those test procedures depended on or required the "dialectical triad," which Rudert claimed for psychology—for him, the postulate of an approach always appropriate to the given subject. "Triad" suggests something circular—something which recurs in a reflected exchange of kinds of assessment, i.e., if one went to work on the expressions and formations of a person or if the person were himself a partner at the meeting. It meant grasping the whole without describing an evaluation or prejudice, and the whole did not necessarily mean only allowing the surface of the subject to become visible. The described Ganzheit, at first highlighted at the level of impressions, could be thereafter analyzed more exactly in terms of hallmarks. That is less puzzling than it may sound. Coming from a distance of half a century and recalling it in modern writing has made it up-to-date again (for a comprehensive collection on qualitative methodology, see Mey, 2005). We students grew up with this relaxed earnestness of appearances, with a critical trust in all that was perceivable and audible, but perhaps we were still too immature to understand what Rudert's structure orientation—or let us say rather his reliance on structure—so profoundly meant.

In every "dialectical triad" the suppositions or "seemingness" (*Anmutungen*) which the observer or the one passing judgment would have in view of a given perceptible state of affairs is of central significance. So rapidly and without prejudice did they adapt themselves, so reliably and with confidence were we trained to rely on them, so difficult is it to convey them in context to a modern readership. Let us put it like this: *Suppositions* or *Seemingness* mean that taken as a whole something is indeed a whole, whereby the whole gives the appearance of permanence over time, communicating to its perceivers and concurring with them about the appropriateness of a given linguistic formulation. The questionable factors, which convey a sense of permanence to someone, may be present in anything—such as portraits or photographs or a realization over time, as with vocal characteristics. Much in the complex formulation for the basic phenomenon of subject-centralized *supposition*—for which the term "character impression" (*Eindruckscharakter*) can also be used—is contained in other things, in the *concordance,* or the agreement, of those involved. They were at least experienced enough to provide a state of facts about a thing or subject, having to be aware of their open and unprejudiced resonance, and the affect which the other had on them. Statistical analyses of the data underline trust in the (subject-centered) objectivity of the procedure. How strange that this process methodology of the "dialectical triad" in the later publication of Rudert's work about a pair of characteristics specific to vocal expression was not accorded particular attention in the *Handbook of the Psychology of Expression* edited by Robert Kirchhoff (1965). We, then assistants in Berlin, were co-editing this publication and saw in the method an indisputable legacy of our psychological-scientific identity—a legacy which clashed with Kirchhoff's ill suppressed impatience and his acute concept analysis to the extent that we overlooked its mistakes and did not realize how overblown it was in Rudert's texts of the time (1965), and we certainly did not think to suggest that the author might make corrections.

Of Two Kinds of Expression and More

Let us pass over an analysis of the handbook chapter, which deals with the qualities of "sound" and "noise" in vocal expressions exemplifying expressions of mood, with copious documentation and sensitive analyses. It is instead another aspect of Rudert's teaching, which accorded equal importance to the psychology of expression, characterology and educational guidance that is strikingly contemporary. I imagine that when the American reader thinks of the term "expression," he or she thinks primarily, if not exclusively, of the expression of feelings. All the effort in the field of the psychology of expression by the holistic psychologists at Heidelberg pointed in another direction. As already noted, Rudert's thought was indebted, although not uncritically, to Krueger's concept of structure (*Strukturbegriff*). Following Krueger, Rudert shows, in the above-mentioned chapter, expression in two of its crucial aspects, put briefly: expression of feeling (*Gefühlsausdruck*) and expression of character (*Wesensausdruck*), upon which pathogenetic and character-genetic points of interest could be established in the person. He kept his interest in lasting character traits of the person, but *Rudert*'s last contribution in the sixties shows certain hesitancies in the presentation of this aspect. What remains is the primacy of the expression and the comprehensibility of its features for others and the significance for oneself remained. But the all-important role given to vocal expression as key witness of characterological features and/or intentions had become less self-evident. For him it was necessary to have historical testaments, for example, the speeches of Hindenburg, the speeches of the President of the German Reich, or test findings to support the vocal evidence.

This was another kind of Ganzheit, in the sense of complementary favoring of sources, than that which we had experienced as students in the recording studios of the Psychological Institute of Heidelberg in earlier times. When we heard time and again the voices of *Faust* or *Gretchen* or *Mephisto* in the *Faust* recorded by Gründgens in Düsseldorf. Then there stood before us in flesh and blood, persons, and ever more persons, persons with all the curiosities of character and gulfs of being. To be sure, these were *stage* characters, who had prepared prearranged texts. I recall the actor, famous at the time, Will Quadflieg; the *Mephisto* was played by Gründgens himself in texts which, thanks to our school education, we all recognized as Goethe. Rudert assured his pupils that one had to become familiar with the forms (vocal forms in this case) of larger-than-life characters in order to become sensitive to confrontation with figures from everyday life that bore every relevance to the everyday. And, to our amazement, Rudert would insist it was the great advantage of such stage performances that they were worked out (in this case by Goethe) and performed (in this case by the actor of *Faust*).

Authenticity and the Authentic in Expression

In his concern for expression, as in all areas, Rudert got to the essence of the subject concerning our doubt as young students about the authenticity of what we saw and heard. It did not interest Rudert to acknowledge inauthenticity. He was seeking to develop the possibilities of the method as far as possible. In so doing, he was thinking systematically and genetically. I have never since heard lectures in the world of academia of such richness and dedication as Rudert's. When he said, in the course of a lecture on the psychology of the manifestation of expression, "Life means standing happily in the light,"[12] he was laying down the style of his presentations, marked as they were by his dedication and replete with a wealth of memorable expressions. It was not only in this lecture that he made ample use of a comprehensive collection of sources—not to forget those which were new at the time, such as M. Scheler, K. Bühler, Ph. Lersch, W. Hellpach, L. Klages, E. Kretschmer. and the older ones like J.J. Engel, Ch. Bell, C. G. Carus, G. B. Duchenne, Th. Piderit, Ch. Darwin, and C. Lange.

Johannes Rudert always saw the person as layered, so that a consideration of the person at different levels seemed to him entirely natural, and something to be borne in mind in all talk of and about expression. So critical talk of a lack of authenticity, that something was only played up to an audience, or that an expression was phony (which we see in others or show ourselves to others) was not a criticism which moved him in the slightest. The position of the demanding distinction between expression and presentation had been in need of clarification since the publication of J.J. Engel's "Ideas on a Facial Expression" (*Ideen zu einer Mimik*) in the late eighteenth century. This is a rich theme in the framework of which so much about formation and extreme formation, regard for others, and layering all have their role to play, but here is not the place to examine it.

Feelings in Expression

For Rudert and those with him, expression is an intense concept. Rudert was assisted by the distinction already referred to between the expression of feelings (*Gefühlsausdruck*) and the expression of character (*Wesensausdruck*), both of which were genetically and ontogenetically sub-classified. Under the subtitle "Pathognomic Expression" (referring to Descartes and his characterization of feelings as passions) Rudert named as four of its major elements the expression of feeling, the expression of drives (*Triebausdruck*), the expression of human emotion, and the expression of character. It must be said that a mere listing of points of call, so to speak, conceals more than it reveals of Rudert's thought—a thought which was not confined by definitions or categories but that brought different categories all together. This was something which began to set generations of students apart from one another. Kirchhoff, the most important of those who took another view though less influential on the generation of students in Rudert's time, rose to meet the challenge of creating order in psychology, above all the psychology of expression, by giving its data a dependable and distinctive location. "Order by location" was his motto. This was intentionally scientific and at the same time mundane in its choice of words. If, metaphorically speaking, Kirchhoff's instruments were the knife and the plumb line, then Rudert's tool was the paintbrush—his need was not a need for location but for the effect of illumination intended in language and encountered before it. Rudert did not dispute nor admit that, to quote an old saying, "his own had insulted him."[13] It was for us to live with the rift.

The lack of a systematic agreement in the field of expression did not bother Rudert and did not deprive those who heard him lecture of the fullness of expression nor of the wealth of knowledge of expression. In his lectures, lines of thought originating centuries apart from each other flowed together—as when, for example, he would pause to consider one or pointed to the manifold nature of another and, in doing so, showed his students how to recognize expression. The person was many layered and so was his appearance in expression. He saw the notion of the person in the abundance of his relationships, in the way in which he lived in space, and the manner in which he included the spatial in his expression.[14] The chapter on the symbolism of space (*Raumsymbolik*) belongs to the most important section of his lectures on expression where he considers human expression of feeling as the third version of pathognomic expression. Creating and maintaining a frame of reference means identifying thematic centers. These centers may also change over the course of one's life (the writer as writer now and student in Heidelberg then) and, depending on who heard Rudert, will turn out differently. But still there is no question that on reading Rudert's lecture notes, as far as dealing with the human expression of feeling is concerned, one gains the indisputable impression that essential dimensions of the human "being in the world"[15] are recognizable in his dealing with the human expression of feeling. That is not a feeling which is hidden away, that is to say within the body of the grown human being, whose surface shows itself to be moved in parts further removed from the center (and also helped feelings towards expression as in the case of sympathy) (Görlitz, 1960). Rudert's fixed points of departure were aimed at expressing wholeness, that the form of expression in appearance is whole, that *wholeness* pertains between expression and the expressed, and that we always had to reckon with a *Ganzheit* between expression and the being (*Wesen*) which was seeking to express itself. He added that, concerning the notion of human expression of feeling, one should always (in the social situation) work from the point that there was a circular process between expression and impression. Symptomatic was "a permanent back and forth, an impression which the expression makes and which works back upon me"[16] but an expression as well, which is controlled according to the familiarity of the communicating partner. There were feelings, which were only shown to some persons and others shown in general or, as Rudert put it, "made known." The style of expression and the means of expression were examined in-depth and were vouched for by names such as Karl Bühler,[17] Philipp Lersch, and Th.Piderit as well. Not only through them—Rudert always thought ontogenetically—"levels of internalization" became clear and there would form a no longer diffuse ego of feeling (*Gefühls-Ich*).

As this writer, after nearly fifty years, goes through the notes taken during his time at Heidelberg, it becomes clear to him that the concepts of feeling, expression, and person are precisely what we are looking at—much more so than just respect for the intensity of what was being taught through written and spoken words. Perhaps there is only one example from an earlier time—a time before that of *Ganzheitspsychologie* in Leipzig. The following is *one* example in which the feeling of a person had been accorded so much importance in terms of face and form. That is in the writings of Robert Musil. There are, dating from

1912, two supposedly minor short stories by Musil, which Fred Lönker (2002) has represented to the modern reader patient enough to understand them. The protagonists are two women whose character defining fullness is so colorfully portrayed and so aware of what it is to be human that the characters work not as fictional individuals but as bearers of the hallmarks of a genus.

Rudert used that as the occasion to make his ontogenetic orientation take concrete form, which only some individual terms of expression seem dated, in eight conclusions: the lack of a defining gap between expression and feeling in genetically earlier times; the construction of the genetically higher upon earlier levels—an event to which thought committed to a theory of levels must necessarily subscribe; the change of function from one means of expression to another in the "hands" of an economical nature; the continuation of basic forms of elementary life under other names—he was thinking here of hunger and love and their sublimations[18]—and that to cite just the first four conclusions, which from a distance offer "close-ups" of feelings and the potential of how they will form all the way to their inherent meaning. "Only then," claimed Rudert, "is one in a position to talk of a complete feeling, when it permeates the whole person, and all levels within that person. The consideration of resonance is appropriate where what is genetic primacy is just expressive movement, whereas where it is expressive action, we are considering, then, we are dealing more with a symbolic or metaphorical relationship."[19] That swiftly led him to come to decisive conclusions about feelings where, comparing man and animal, he sought to highlight aspects of characteristically human feelings central to which was the peculiarity of their relationship to the situation they were in. This also what pertained to mood, representative in our feelings, whose form is defining and charters an *inner world,* which distinguishes our moods from the moods of animals. The relationship of feelings to the situation in which they find themselves provides the feelings with opportunity, in fact, the basic mood of a continually oscillating relationship between a coloring of the world and inwardness of feeling. Feelings never play their part merely within.

Expression and Presentation

It is no coincidence that as Rudert's thought continued in the context of the human expression of feeling that considerations about expression and presentation arose. This basic problem, which has concerned the psychology of expression from early days, is one which J.J. Engel (1785/86) came to grips with in "Expression and Painting" and "Imitative and expressive gestures," in which Karl Bühler paid tribute to in his definitive *Ausdruckstheorie* (Theory of Expression) (Bühler, 1933: 36ff.). Kirchhoff, who was from Rudert's Heidelberg circle, explained that the problem of the right referential frame of reference of both, that is to say of feeling and presentation, had not been settled since Engel's time (Kirchhoff, 1957: 207ff.). Firstly, there was the figure of Klages who had played a very considerable formative role in psychology in Heidelberg. Kirchhoff reached his position out of a confrontation between Klages and Bühler, appropriating Klages' criterion for the non-directness of represented expression. Rudert's formulation (op. cit.) was lengthier; he criticized Klages' expectation of visible success for the conveyor of the expression. This is to be expected, for at this point a dispute over language becomes inevitable. In this respect too Karl Bühler formed the thematic terms of reference for us in Heidelberg. If expression is a school of thought for psychology, then so in particular is a discussion over the concept of representation. Here again Rudert argued his case with documentation of development from phylo- and ontogenesis, and here perhaps for the first time he also came up face to face with art and artistic formulation, which embodied for him another form of representation. Thus, he skirted around the critical terms of reference for relationship, enriched them rather with considerations about the feeling-framed ego and its genesis, with postures and their meaning in represented expression, giving the theme a certain emphasis but without sharpening defining contours.

But he kept the *world* in view—the social world of human interaction—the conveying of which, borrowing from his other work, is not exhausted by laughing, smiling, and crying but is also demonstrated in given ways of behavior, such as notions of how to manage people, what it is to be courteous, and how to adjust. The position of *Achilles* in Homer's *Iliad* has only the excuse of poetic invention, for "one is as hated as the very gates of Hell who hides the sense of what he speaks and speaks not what he thinks,"[20] but it shows too the struggle going on at the time of myth and tradition and shows that "creation lies. Wherever one looks, there is deception."[21] This world is one of lies, deception, and deadly cunning, as it was put in a recent text (von Matt, 2006), and if *Mephisto* were a reliable actor he would present it with these words to dramatic effect. Rudert is not so graphic but rich in source material when borrowing from Konrad Lorenz's examples of mimicry in the animal world. Thus, Rudert argued that deception and adaptation as deeply rooted in living creatures.

This opens up in human social interaction, the broad spectrum of politeness and etiquette, for which the writings of Norbert Elias could have been or could have become instructive. I do not think that the *process* of civilization became a theme for us in those days in Heidelberg to that extent, nor was the subject of etiquette, which we observed scrupulously in our own lives (Rudert's Institute demanded), festival occasions included, definitive codes of comportment. Lying far back in the past are those days which are yet still near to us. The days in which, before the French Revolution Johann Jakob Engel wrote on the psychology of expression (*Ausdruckspsychologie*) (1785/86) or when Louis Sébastien Mercier (1781-88/1979) studied life on the streets, in the houses of Paris with all the rules of proper etiquette (*Schicklichkeitsregeln*) which appear so strange to us today.[22] More recently Antal Szerb has written on the subject.[23] The theme has often to do with action and its regulation by the rule of convention—by cultural codes of comportment and custom. In such a case, expression receives two applications, one placed before representation and one before *action*.

Action and Doing and the Characteristic Value of Appearance

Expression—as documented by the psychologists of expression of the early days—lived from drawings and pictures and was inseparable from them. The veracity of the visually portrayed had its own problem. It was mutable, in a process of development, a process which was frozen in the pictorial representation. But expression needs must unfold over time. Pictures are frozen effects. If we could not start with the chance and opportunity of working from an intensified expression, be it in mimic or gesture, and encapsulate as in a "snapshot" all the special features otherwise lost in the running of time that are caught in such "moments," then only Karl Bühler could attenuate the doubts facing anyone researching expression. Bühler extracted in the course of the procedure particular parts which he judged to be especially important for psychological diagnosis and for the psychology of expression. In his words, these were the initial procedures to action (*Handlungsinitien*) at the start of a process of action and the ongoing *fruitful moments,* which were of key significance in the perception and understanding of expression.

We find here that expression had in the early days not only a problem with conserving records—a problem which film and photographs and phonographic recordings on vinyl and tape helped to solve (The Heidelberg Institute created a copious archive administered by the technically very competent Joseph Schön, Rudert's assistant at the time). The problem was more fundamental than that. Expression is realized through a process, stretching across time like action, and indeed expression is itself often a highly important aspect of action. Robert Kirchhoff's approach was phenomenon-oriented and concept-analytical. Nobody in our Department of Psychology was more actively dedicated to providing a sufficient understanding of expression than he was. He taught how to distinguish between *pragmatic and semantic procedures of action,* the former best understood perhaps as action as doing action to a specific permanent physical end, whilst the latter (especially in language) convey meaning. (It should be noted that the emphasis on and differentiation of forms of action are particularly important for vocal expression and expression conveyed through speech.[24])

Karl Bühler turned to the questionable relationship between expression and action with intellectual verve and very thoroughly, and in doing so, commented on the cases of Charles Darwin and Ludwig Klages with particular care (Bühler, op. cit.). These were sources which the Heidelberg psychologists were drawing on too. The method of thought, as already mentioned, had demonstrated to be one which relied on stressing differences (Kirchhoff, 1957: 192 ff.) or in pointing out earlier expositions by Rudert—according to which "the theory of expression has to account for . . . the relationship between expression and action"[25] and argued that one should not be content with Klages' formula that expression is a metaphor for action. Rudert places the emphasis elsewhere in this key material, though Darwin's principles of expression, which for Bühler were only *regulae ad directionem ingenii* (rules of thumb), are worthy of specific if not uncritical mention—as well as countering his principle objection that "the expressive moment" is missing from these principles. That the inventory belonging to expression was genetically composed out of primary actions, composed by Darwin and subsequently supported by Bühler, was for Rudert already out-of-date. "A universal reduction really yields nothing." Appearance has its own value, fulfilled in expression and is not to be reduced to a matter of action. For him, expression was every bit as much a primary source as action and, along with action, various traits which stem from it. The expression of feeling, as presented by Rudert, appears many facetted and provisional to today's reader. Along with the expression of character and on the same footing, the expression of feeling was *one* of the elements close to the heart of the psychology of expression at Heidelberg. He collected so much around him and still managed to leave so much out, for example, provision for *vegetative* expression—if not laughing and crying and how smiles unfold. Missing too is a regard for music, so important at the university, music which is not part of us but which moves us, and which we listen to with deep emotion, "resounding processes of feeling and passion" (Nietzsche). At least the performance of music would have been a special facet of *Expression and Situation*, how situative conditions can provoke feelings and manifestations of expression, even when they are not representing them themselves.

Let us not forget that expression, for Rudert in his holistic approach to manifestations of interpersonal encounters, was neatly ordered. There it was then, after his expositions on smiling as an "innate form of increased manifestation" with the special cases of the smile of embarrassment and the "smile of being caught out" and touching at the same time on laughter and crying, had been pursued further,[26] weighty, and rich development, the *expression of character* (*Wesensausdruck*), which was embedded in ontogenetic relations and developed out of them. Rudert linked this to two forms of expression, as characterized in pre-puberty, puberty, and maturity, and which finally comes to characterize the adult: the controlled and employed expression conveyed at different levels of shyness and shame. To put it more simply: the control of expression is a key requirement of mature expression, one which in addition is able to opt for a choice of expressions and only falls into inauthenticity through a lack of commonly agreed principles.

That always meant *expression of character*, as when Rudert stresses the situation surrounding the first impression, when people give off something totally specific, a "coloring of character" (*Wesensfärbung*). There too "character is an apparent truth." The part is enriched in its own dimensions in the subsequent structuring of this apparent truth when Rudert tackles the accompanying presence of model and ideal. After the child has continued far "into the immediacy of his being" in the time before puberty, a time of self-reflection, another appearance, a strange one, offers itself to girls and boys—strange also in regard to how it can serve as model and ideal. What both model and ideal have in common is the style of expression which the adult person's comportment offers, anticipating and full of hope like the trace of that "which will become within us, crystallizing in the person to a core of fundamental feelings" from positions, forms of behavior, and connections. There is also a shadowy nocturnal side, crippled and depraved, in the tendencies out of which character develops.

Rudert regrets, and supports his reasoning with ample references to diverse authors, that still so little has been researched concerning the means of expression used in presenting the expression of character itself. For him, this applies to *physiognomic* expression, to morphology, and to the stature of the body; and his considerations go back very far to the time of the *pseudo-Aristotles*.

Character Sketches in the Diary and the Proportion of Belief

If we leave the psychology of expression as shaped at Heidelberg in order to add notes to Rudert's view of character and personality, we still do not forget expression completely. Like other great representatives of his field, Fritz Heider for example, Johannes Rudert—who was living in Leipzig at the time—kept not a psychological but certainly a *"characterological"* diary. Starting in July of 1948, on the pages open before me (from 1949) comments keep recurring which are to do with vocal expression, for example, the "courting of the voice" and often about peculiarities of a concrete person—quite possibly someone out of Rudert's day-to-day social environment (Rudert, 1948/49). Action, a powerful theme and the antonymic challenger to expression, leads us to personality, then to characterology as shown by Rudert in a festschrift for August Vetter (Rudert, 1968) . Here he tries to make the part played by belief in human action apparent. He is concerned there, (again genetically disassociating himself from "naive belief in oneself . . . as a lowest level of human action,") (Rudert, op. cit.: 139) with *clarified* forms of belief. Belief such as "the belief as had and held to, a person who knows that he believes and why he believes" and how this permeates human action (op. cit.: 140) whereby action is not the one and only source of his assurance; how certainty supports belief; and how inspiration and intuition play a role. By way of example, Rudert retells a dispute between Luther and Melanchthon during the Augsburger Reichstag. And in behavior based on belief, he highlights as its defining extremity the readiness to accept destiny, even in the highest instances, which he took from Shakespeare's works. The muted pathos of the presentation makes the person become aware of the determining situation and its structure. The title of the Festschrift for Vetter, *Reality of the Middle* ("*Wirklichkeit der Mitte*"), encompasses what is meant. To approach thought with regard to structure was not considered obvious, nor was it uncontested in the Heidelberg circle. Again, it was the younger people who led the attack to which Kirchhoff (1954) gave a tangible form. At a time before his sobering review of expression in a dispute decades later (Kirchhoff, 1975), the entire vigor of his thought (without seeking to dissolve the "community in spirit") (Kirchhoff, 1954: 265) was concentrated on the contestable tendencies to ontology in what was then a very influential field of psychology. The purpose was, notwithstanding all "indirect homage," subjecting structure as a basic concept of Leipzig *Ganzheitspsychologie*, as in Krueger and Wellek, to a critical analysis. As in his later work, critique was shaped by a theory of order. That shook the conviction of several "impartial attitudes" towards apparently plain facts.

In listening to Rudert we nevertheless learned about character and person, to think of structure as the essential given of a person, and maybe in connection with a quotation from Goethe—as a "molded form, which develops itself in the course of its life" (*"geprägte Form, die lebend sich entwickelt"*). We also learned of the levels which constitute a person genetically and determine him in ever-changing proportionality. The manifold nature of personal understanding, in whose action and behavior Rudert demonstrated through what he called the "covert nature of propelled intentions" (*"Kulissenhaftigkeit der Antriebsziele"*), inspired indeed by psychoanalysis. The repeated reference to G.W. Allport clarifies, again genetically, "the functional autonomy of motive." But the person does not dissolve in this; the person retains his core, if that can be another expression for "structure." This applies to premonitions, outlines of what they can become, more surely as dream image or protective illusions. Friedrich Nietzsche offered to Rudert the great example of a "disclosed psychology (*"entlarvenden Psychologie"*), but he would have concurred with him in the earnestness of the characterization of Richard Wagner, "renouncing the fumbling, the straying off, the flourishing of little minor shoots, and within the most bizarre projects contained in his artistic plans, a single inner rightfulness holds sway."[27] That brings the awareness of the dominating passion to a level whence it determines development which, for Rudert, was also feasible and open to formulation in simpler versions,[28] just as he would surely have concurred with Nietzsche's judgment that in even in the briefest of moments we may encounter that which is higher than ourselves, whose holiness outweighs all distress.[29]

Operating Powers

There is not enough space here to actualize for today's readership Rudert's understanding of development beyond these indications. They belonged as the "psychology of development" with emphasis on childhood and youth and as "psychology of personal age" with regard to the course of human life—very much to his lecture cycle. They were themes which found their practical application in educational advice centers (as they were then called) headed by his wife, the psychologist Ruth Rudert, who was one of the first to work in this branch of psychology with its commitment to helping people (for many years at Ludwigshafen am Rhein, near Heidelberg) (R. Rudert and R. Stein, 1959).

Maybe Rudert also built up a feeling for the pedagogical in the carefully prepared lectures on "educational psychology." In the two available pieces of writing, which were only separated from each other by two years, the material he received was intensely worked over.[30] The ontogenetic orientation and the order which was derived from it: small child and primary school age, childhood and school; retreated into the background. He placed major importance instead on calling forth and analyzing the so-called "education operating powers," to which belonged not only morals and customs but also abstraction and overcoming. At that point he liked to choose very practical and material turns of phrase, such as "the charity of the solid barricade" (*"die Wohltat der festen Schranke"*) (for the self-developers), which in some cases lasted over decades. "The limit in itself is a delight," Peter von Matt in another context wrote about the anthropology of clothing and disguise (von Matt, 2006: 84), but Rudert saw in barriers not so much compulsion as the transmitted orientation for those who press against them while respecting their function. An inherent order to life he saw as an educational moment providing orientation and support within the framework and values with which one would grow up. The morally wicked and the lord of misrule threw a dim light on this scene, although Rudert later in the course of a lecture at the *Studium Generale* of the University of Heidelberg read out a list under the heading "What is Man?" dimensions *"On the Psychological Truth of People."*[31] He had already earlier dealt in a considered piece of writing with the way in which *character and fate* were allotted (Rudert, 1944). He had attempted to make more profound distinctions and most difficult of all for him, to highlight those fates which damage the "inner core" of a person and destroy their system of values. He had complained of and had demanded "blindness as being sunk in the passage of their own being." The construction of the core of a personality was "sacrificed to the dark powers of the ineffable" (Rudert, op. cit.: 20 & 25). This idea of fate was comprehensible enough to a generation, the destiny of whose values Sebastian Haffner (2002) insistent like few others, described from the perspective of his affected and involved experience as a young adult from a good middle-class family.[32]

At the time of this attempt to elucidate the interwoven character of person and fate, Rudert was already a professor at Leipzig, with which title he signed his contribution to the *Potsdam Lectures*. That was in no way a release from responsibility or a loading of responsibility onto a notion of inescapable fate (and there were no grounds to oppose his reappointment to his old post after the end of the war). There was soon his own monograph on the orientation of aims in education, their targeting, and reasoning (Rudert, 1956). And in a tribute in honor of August Vetter, a festschrift for the man who from the aspect of his view of humanity and his value orientation was very close to him, Rudert developed his ideas further about the requirements and stipulations taken from the metaphor for life of the *way* for a "psychagog's"[33] need to act. He separated *maturity*, regarded critically as the term used to describe the aim of the psychagogy of its time, from "the way, (as) an old analogy of human life" (Rudert, 1966: 429). He separated it as an operating term of supportive action, an operating term in which the normative and the factual are especially closely connected, permeating one another in the certainty of being on the right way. The person affected will find this operating term not as something rationally considered, rather it is measured in terms of feeling. Guiding feelings are the determining factors reaching to soundness of feelings. Those are factors which Rudert seeks to help the advisor to respect. (He had managed to win Ludwig Pongratz for the Heidelberg circle. Dream and dreaming constituted a whole, once the medium of divine experience, as in the texts of the Bible; now, as a profane but wise source of expression, it can help to develop an understanding of the person.)

Educational Psychology as Human View and Field of Application

Understanding, with all the force of human wisdom, was something richly fulfilling for him when it came to what concerned educational psychology and conveying it to his students, who covered more than half a generation. There he noted from the start,[34] the direction for use taken by all educational psychology which was worthy of the name, and along with Meumann, extracted from the history of this subject the contribution made by American psychology, whose experimental direction had also seemed to him worthy of critical attention. For Rudert, the life of the soul was very much richer than allowed for and in its conditions so awesomely manifold, that it did not lend itself to being reduced to facile analyses of conditions. Every individual is different and that had to be taken into account by every educator. The fact that no two individuals are the same gives the lie to every conceptual formula. That unavoidably places limits on how far any calculation or prognosis of success can go. The life of the soul of each individual is possessed of an irrational element, which condemns all hope of a perfect system of education before it begins. Also, the necessity of seeing in human development the given *and* the given-up, leads to insoluble problems for educational psychologists. For this reason, psychology for Rudert cannot be reduced to a science of facts.

The themes which are then dealt with follow along the lines of an ontogenesis of an orientation according to levels and layers with fine concepts working like searchlights on the theme of education, for example, "educational rapport" (which has been watered down in modern jargon to "mother-child interaction"). Other themes included order, accustomization, and imitation, which are seen as equally important in life development, although less original, as well as the beginnings of commandment and ban gaining their own characteristic traits. As in the discussion of "suggestion" and "ruling through expression," the most winsome conveyor of which is called charm, educational theory draws on this to this day, (albeit it has another name) that educational effectiveness must be aware that it has to address people at all levels, which the more sober kind of education fails to do. Remarks on authority and the unsuccessful forms thereof on the ego in formation, on punishment, and the way of the child (under educational guidance) to what is objectively valid, can be here as little elucidated as can Rudert's overall view of the educational research and learning of the time. To say that there should be "enticement to soar higher" within the learning process is definitely not just a pretty turn of phrase. And Rudert is clear in his position here too, "person is only recognized through person." That is a fact which cannot be ignored.

Variations on Pedagogical Themes

The focus of attention changes, not the themes, when Rudert in a new exposition contributed to educational psychology.[35] That which before had been stressed, but only as a parallel observation, was now a criterion for the composition of the entire material. Only a little varied in its terminology, the *Pedagogical Rapport* is the determining frame of events which encompasses all development periods up to puberty. That necessitates something for which Rudert pleads in many ways—action on what he calls the "culture of the apprehended," respect for fruitful breaks. The pedagogical rapport lives from an affirmation of the *Other* in the reciprocal relationship between the *Becoming* (the young person) and the *Giver* (the older person). Included in what is to be conveyed is certainly for him what has been handed down through culture—a "psychology of mental content" (*Psychologie geistiger Gehalte*) being an essential component of educational psychology. Epochal moments keep gleaming through in the treatment of the themes which do not just color or change the tone of the pedagogical rapport. Rudert demonstrates this in the forms of appearance assumed by authority in the past with remarks on National Socialism's breaches of tradition and its distortions.

In his second leading criterion for theme ordering called *the educational steering of strengths,* also termed *pedagogical-psychological energetics,* a possible relation to historically changing situations is found in the insistence that human urges and their ordering are "elastic," not rigid, as they are (according to Rudert) represented in psychoanalysis—a science to which he nevertheless pays tribute owing to a high regard for the importance of the unconscious. He distinguishes at this point—we are quoting here—moments of operation, not just conscience, or punishment and obedience, but also that which one can do on one's own— in abreaction and overcoming as guiding help, overcoming here understood as a "total and integral reforming" (*ganzheitliche Neuformung*).

Again and at this point strongly stressing the totality, Rudert deals with the social group as an educational factor (thinking here of the family and the children's group[36]) learning in its classical forms as a "holistic gestalt teaching" ("*Ganzheitgestaltlehre*"). In opposition to the predominating opinion in the English-speaking world, it does not guarantee the emergence of the human person and is not the driving factor of all its processes of appropriation. Much grows out of and within encounters, in which something announces itself within people, thereafter to come into being. Conscience and principles are formed in this way—here he is following another author (Guyer). What is needed is to lighten the way, for the self-developing is straining to form without leading to the making of people who are over-formed—people for whom form is everything and background nothing. Learning plays a role here, a learning with all the notes of freedom and productive moments. But here once again, "learning must be an enticement into the field of culture."[37] And expressly, "to stake out our moral barricades sensibly and to respect them from our inner serenity"—that weighed more heavily and incurred a commitment to more than the backdrop of old Heidelberg would leave one to suppose.

Traces and Pictures

We have gone through private notes[38] and books for this purpose, some of which were printed. The books out of Rudert's private library were handed over to the writer of this chapter by Ruth Rudert (still working on and nurturing contacts in the institute as her husband's legacy) and these materials are now to be found at the Psychological Institute of the University of Leipzig, where Rudert once worked. "Life means leaving traces" was written on a note put up on the notice board in the hall of the Heidelberg Institute of Psychology in the summer when this chapter was being written. It has Rudert's hallmark and refers to the uniqueness of his work.[39] When he began in 1917, he had a wound and handicap, which hindered him in writing and he documented the (neuropsychological) consequences on himself in the first volume of the *New Studies in Psychology* (*Neue Psychologische Studien*). It is the same volume to which Felix Krueger contributed a chapter on *Ganzheit*, which was also a pole of Rudert's thought. There was no "counter type" like that created by E.R. Jaensch, which was placed at the service of Germany's dark regime of the 1930's, closer rather to what led Stendhal to the remark on keeping the ego holy and pure.[40] However unrealizable it may sound, this was for Rudert a remark of great, although not unquestionable, value. Nietzsche, the de-mystifier, praised himself in his "Out of a Psychologist's Casebook" (*Aktenstücken eines Psychologen*) as ahead of psychologists in not drawing, as they did, conclusions about an originator of a work from the work itself.[41] If that protects, nevertheless despair remains in Nietzsche because he and his psychology offer no such surety. Myths about heroes of psychology have nothing to do with it—a theme productively and vividly developed by Jaan Valsiner (Valsiner, 2004). Is the whole more than the sum of its parts? Is what is worth leaving behind the portrait and not statues of the body (Warnke, 1984)?[42] Thus, Heidelberg and its ruin of a castle leaves traces which reach much further back (Hensen & Ludwig, 2005) than those which can only bear witness to a short history of psychology. But there are pictures, or rather portraits, where one practices the art of understanding the person and subject of attention more from a holistic than analytical view. "If you can call it a story, it has no real beginning or end," to quote Dylan Thomas.[43] How remarkable it is that *Ganzheitspsychologie* nevertheless seems to continue into the present, essentially in the consciousness of methods being used, which adds to the quality of approach of the younger generation. Thus the Berlin Institute, historically linked to Heidelberg, when drawing from the source of its new wisdom, draws on inspiration from the old (Mruck & Mey, 2005).

Acknowledgments

This text was translated from German to English by Michael E. Walker. We gratefully acknowledge and thank Mindy Puopolo and Ellen Diriwächter for their help with the translation process and California Lutheran University for funding this translation. The author warmly dedicates this work to his dear friend and colleague, Jaan Valsiner, a proven expert in German psychology. The author thanks his companion from Heidelberg in the Berlin years. Thanks for the cautious and patient help in all technical aspects of this work to Carme and Niklas from the younger generation.

Notes

1.	The author studied psychology (together with philosophy and medicine) at Heidelberg University from the winter semester 1956/57 to the winter semester 1962/3, psychology under Johannes Rudert, Robert Kirchhoff, and Ludwig Pongratz. The author now lives in Berlin.
2.	Osten (2004: 21).
3.	As a prejudice of the speed obsessed and acceleration tendencies of his (Goethe's) time (quoted Osten, op.cit.: 25), metaphorically "blind flying", as recent writers have termed it, for example, Norbert Bolz (2005).
4.	Osten, op.cit.: 33.
5.	That is not far from the blotting out of every reflection of that epoch, as Bohrer demonstrated analytically in the case of a group of Germans in the post-war period (Bohrer, 2003, quoted Osten, op.cit.: 30). For Adolf Hitler's evaluation of the spoken word and his violence in releasing social revolutions, compare Zentner (2004: 27).
6.	cit. Osten, op.cit.: 22.
7.	Taking up on a distinction made by Stadler and Wagner, at the beginning of their collected papers entitled *Schaulust. Heimliche und verpönte Blicke in Literatur und Kunst* ("Curiosity. Secret and illicit looks at Literature and Art") (2005: 7).
8.	Compare to the general situation Ash & Geuter (1985), more specifically Geuter (1984), especially Graumann (1985), who succeeded Johannes Rudert as Professor of Psychology in Heidelberg.
9.	Nietzsche in the fourth section of his *Unzeitgemäßen Betrachtungen* ("Thoughts out of Season") (1876/1973a: 53).
10.	*Rudert* had a high personal opinion of *Vetter* as he did for those representing "structural anthropology."
11.	Among the other papers students were permitted to use were the so-called "cookery books"—or cheat-sheets—which offered hallmarks or lists of symptoms for use in individual test procedures.
12.	Quoted from a private record of the lecture *Ausdruck* ("Expression")—given by Rudert in the winter semester 1957/58.

13. An altered quotation from Szerb (2005: 246).
14. *Postures* bear impressive witness to the relation to space of central emotions, those that are significant for people—as, for instance, *Melancholy* in great paintings, which was the theme of an exhibition from Paris in Berlin's New National Gallery at the Kulturforum from February to May 2006. (*Melancholie. Genie und Wahnsinn in der Kunst*. "Melancholy, Genius and Madness in Art"). That as a continuation of a *World Panorama* with its pictures, (as Robert Burton, 1621, with a very lively piece of writing had already done) in which in the small pictures in the title, the gestures of the figures are shrunken and rigid.
15. A fundamental concept in Heidegger's philosophy, which was important for the direction taken by psychology in Heidelberg.
16. Quoted from a private record of the lecture *Ausdruck* ("Expression")—given by Rudert in the winter semester 1957/58.
17. Few psychologists in the German-speaking world were so important for the psychology represented in Heidelberg than Karl Bühler in his Vienna period—an appraisal which was shared in other places too. That is particularly the case in regard to his theory of expression, (1933) along with his monograph on language theory, and not forgetting his and Charlotte Bühler's work on development.
18. The changing of "names" for feelings, which Rudert speaks of at this point, is an especially strong incentive to further considerations. To return to the exhibition already referred to in note 14—what has been given the same "name" may historically change in meaning dramatically in its essential character, qualities, and the popular assessment of its worth, thus *melancholy* as the powerful "mother" of *depression*. It was, as Sennett shows in his cultural history of buildings and people, a spiritual pose or temperamental condition appropriate for religiously determined inwardness, something which encouraged a meditative condition, far removed from sadness and the agonizing standstill of time (cf. Sennett, 1994). Albrecht Dürer's famous etching of *Melancholy 1* depicts more an enigma of pensiveness than of mood (Böhme, 1989).
19. Quoted from a private record of the lecture *Ausdruck* ("Expression")—given by Rudert in the winter semester 1957/58
20. quoted from Peter von Matt in his monograph on *Intrigue* (von Matt, 2006: S. 26).
21. Von Matt (op.cit.: S.21)
22. There is a choice of several works in German, we cite here an especially well organized volume of selected writings from Mercier's 1049 chapters as an early example of literary reporting in the big city.
23. Szerb (1943/2005), in all this splendid piece of writing, especially p.169ff.
24. This conceptual clarification determined, for example, essential parts of the work on the human voice by this author, a work which also gathers the Heidelberg tradition as it arose in context (Görlitz, 1972), and the essential heretofore in Kirchhoff (1962).
25. Rudert quoted by Kirchhoff (op.cit.: 192).
26. Where not otherwise stated, all the quotations in this part of the text stem from Rudert's lecture on expression. (winter semester 1957/58).
27. Nietzsche (1876/1973a: S. 9).
28. Stendhal (real name Henri Beyle), a novelist of the soul from the French literary canon in the first half of the nineteenth century, placed a knowledge of then prevailing passion and the circumstances which stood in its way at the core of the protagonists in his novels and depicted their character and action from that basis.
29. C.f. Nietzsche (1876/1973a.: 27).

30. They are based on private and other unauthorized records of two lectures on educational psychology which Rudert held in the University of Heidelberg in the summer semester of 1958 and the winter semester of 1960/1.
31. on 28 June 1961 in the building of the new university.
32. Sebastian Haffner, who grew up in Wilhelmian, Berlin and later the Weimar Republic, wrote for the German reader as a close observer, chronicler, and captivator of the alarming atmosphere of the change to National Socialism in the 1930's. He emigrated in 1938 to England and worked there for major newspapers, returning to Germany after the war in 1954. When an epoch undergoes dramatic change, one which affected Haffner physically less harshly than it did the doctor in fascist Italy depicted by Carlo Levi in 1945, harsh illumination is called for. For representative writing of the disillusioning affect of such times of radical change, we have the reports of Curzio Malaparte, war correspondent and later liaison officer for the Americans at the end of the war—certainly an extreme and drastic example. A less dramatic parallel, as post war Germany was reunited which hardly anyone in West or East Germany had foreseen, is Günter de Bruyn's first-hand appraisal of this historical turning point (de Bruyn, 1996). Johannes Rudert, who lived in nearly all these historical periods, with Hitler's Germany in mind, warned of the powers of seduction exercised by the symbolical.
33. a then commonly used expression in both training and practice to denote practical, supportive lines of work which made use of psychology.
34. in Rudert's lecture from the summer semester of 1958.
35. in Rudert's lecture on educational psychology in the winter semester of 1960/61.
36. Epochs which stifle humanity manage it differently, as Haffner discovered in his national socialist education camp for attorney trainees in 1933 with its disdain for comradeship—and not just his experience there—as poison and a means to decivilize by which means the party of the Nazis had seduced the Germans (Haffner, op.cit.: 279).
37. as a concluding note to *Rudert's* winter lecture on educational psychology.
38. At that time new students were usefully told in the first semester in the institute that as part of their training they should learn to drive a car, use a typewriter, and most importantly learn shorthand at a time when the technical means of recording which we have today did not exist.
39. a characteristic which was cited in Ash & Geuter (1985: 221).
40. quoted from Haffner (2002: 204).
41. Friedrich Nietzsche in "Nietzsche contra Wagner—"Out of a Psychologist's Casebook" Aktenstücke eines Psychologen (1889), quoted here from the Reclam edition (1973b: 137).
42. Warnke (op.cit.: 36) is recalling here a saying by *Cicero*.
43. taken from the motto in the writing of Klüpfel und Graumann (1986) where it can be found on the front page without a source.

References

Ash, Mitchell G., und Geuter, Ulfried (Hrsg.). (1985). *Geschichte der deutschen Psychologie im 20. Jahrhundert. Ein Überblick*. Opladen: Westdeutscher Verlag.

Böhme, Hartmut. (1989). *Albrecht Dürer—Melencolia I*. Frankfurt am Main: Fischer.

Bolz, Norbert. (2005). *Blindflug mit Zuschauer*. München: Fink.

Bruyn, Günter de. (1992). *Zwischenbilanz. Eine Jugend in Berlin*. Frankfurt am Main: Fischer.

Bruyn, Günter de. (1996). *Vierzig Jahre. Ein Lebensbericht*. Frankfurt am Main: Fischer.

Burton, Robert. (1621). *The Anatomy of Melancholy.* Oxford. (After the sixth edition in German translation in 1651 as *Anatomie der Melancholie. Über die Allgegenwart der Schwermut, ihre Ursachen und Symptome sowie die Kunst, es mit ihr auszuhalten.* Zürich-München: Artemis, 1988).

Bühler, Karl. (1927). *Die Krise der Psychologie.* Jena: Fischer.

Bühler, Karl. (1933). *Ausdruckstheorie. Das System an der Geschichte aufgezeigt.* Jena: Fischer.

Engel, J.J. (1785/86). *Ideen zu einer Mimik.* Berlin: Mylius.

Frijda, Nico H. (1965). "Mimik und Pantomimik." In Robert Kirchhoff (Hrsg.), *Ausdruckspsychologie. Handbuch der Psychologie,* Bd.5 (S.351-421). Göttingen: Hogrefe.

Geuter, Ulfried. (1984). *Die Professionalisierung der deutschen Psychologie im Nationalsozialismus.* Frankfurt am Main: Suhrkamp.

Görlitz, Dietmar. (1960). "Zur Phänomenologie und Theorie des Sympathisierens." Unveröff. Zulassungsarbeit zur Diplom-Vorprüfung für Psychologen. Psychologisches Institut, Universität Heidelberg.

Görlitz, Dietmar. (1972). *Ergebnisse und Probleme der ausdruckspsychologischen Sprechstimmforschung.* Meisenheim am Glan: Hain.

Graumann, Carl-Friedrich (Hrsg.). (1985). *Psychologie im Nationalsozialismus.* Berlin-Heidelberg: Springer.

Greenblatt, Stephen. (2004). *Will in der Welt. Wie Shakespeare zu Shakespeare wurde.* Aus dem Amerikanischen. Berlin: Berlin Verlag. Original: *Will in the World. How Shakespeare became Shakespeare.* New York-London: Norton, 2004.

Haffner, Sebastian. (2002). *Geschichte eines Deutschen. Die Erinnerungen 1914-1933.* München: Deutscher Taschenbuch Verlag.

Hensen, Andreas, & Ludwig, Renate. (2005). *Straße ins Jenseits. Die römischen Gräberfelder von Heidelberg.* Remshalden: Greiner.

Kiener, Franz. (1956). *Kleidung, Mode und Mensch.* München-Basel: Schwab.

Kirchhoff, Robert. (1954). "Zur Problematik einer Ontologisierung der Psychologie." (Zugleichein Beitrag zur Diskussion des Strukturbegriffs). Psychologisches Institut der Uni-versität Heidelberg, 12. Mai, unveröff. Ms.

Kirchhoff, Robert. (1957). *Allgemeine Ausdruckslehre. Prinzipien und Probleme der allgemeinen Ausdruckstheorie. Ein Beitrag zur Grundlegung der Wissenschaft vom Ausdruck.* Göttingen: Hogrefe.

Kirchhoff, Robert. (1962). "Über pragmatische und semantische Handlungen." *Zeitschrift für Klinische Psychologie und Psychotherapie,*10: 104-118.

Kirchhoff, Robert (Hrsg.). (1965). *Ausdruckspsychologie. Handbuch der Psychologie,* Bd.5. Göttingen: Hogrefe.

Kirchhoff, Robert. (1975). "Ausdruck zwischen Empirie und Spekulation. Eine Auseinandersetzung in zwei Teilen." *Zeitschrift für Klinische Psychologie und Psychotherapie,* 23: 265-275, 343-358.

Klüpfel, Jürgen, & Graumann, Carl Friedrich (Hrsg.). (1986). "Ein Institut entsteht—Zur Geschichte der Institutionalisierung der Psychologie an der Universität Heidelberg—Bericht aus dem Archiv für Geschichte der Psychologie." *Historische Reihe* Nr.13, Diskussionspapier Nr.49. Psychologisches Institut der Universität Heidelberg.

Levi, Carlo. (1945). *Cristo si è fermato a Eboli.* (Deutsch: *Christus kam nur bis Eboli.* München: Deutscher Taschenbuch Verlag, 1982). Torino: Einaudi.

Lönker, Fred. (2002). *Poetische Anthropologie. Robert Musils Erzählungen* Vereinigungen. München: Fink.

Malaparte, Curtio. (1949). *La Pelle.* Roma-Milano: Aria d'Italia.

von Matt, Peter. (2006). *Die Intrige. Theorie und Praxis der Hinterlist.* München: Hanser.

Mercier, Louis Sébastian. (1781-88/1979). *Mein Bild von Paris.* Mit dreinundvierzig Wiedergaben nach zeitgenössischen Kupferstichen. Mit einem Nachwort von Jean Villain. (From the French.) Frankfurt am Main: Insel.

Mey, Günter (Hrsg.). (2005). *Handbuch Qualitative Entwicklungspsychologie.* Köln: Kölner Studien Verlag.

Mruck, Katja, & Mey, Günter. (2005). "Qualitative Forschung: Zur Einführung in einen prosperierenden Wissenschaftszweig." *Historische Sozialforschung/Historical Social Research, Sonderheft : Qualitative Sozialforschung,* 30, No.1: 5-27.

Musil, Robert (Anonym). (1912).*Vereinigungen.* Zwei Erzählungen. *Neueste Nachrichten* (früher ,*Heidelberger Nachrichten'*) Nr. 94, 22. April.

Nietzsche, Friedrich. (1876/1973a). *Unzeitgemäße Betrachtungen . Viertes Stück. Richard Wagner in Bayreuth.* Stuttgart: Reclam.

Nietzsche, Friedrich. (1889/1973b). *Nietzsche contra Wagner. Aktenstücke eines Psychologen.* Stuttgart: Reclam.

Osten, Manfred. (2004). *Das geraubte Gedächtnis. Digitale Systeme und die Zerstörung der Erinnerung.* Frankfurt am Main: Insel.

Personal. und Vorlesungsverzeichnis der Ruprecht-Karl Universität Heidelberg, vom Winter-Semester 1952/53 bis zum Sommer-Semester 1957 (in Ergänzung). Heidelberg: Verlag Dr.Hörning.

Rudert, Johannes. (1926). "Kasuistischer Beitrag zur Lehre von der funktionellen Asymmetrie der Großhirnhemisphären." *Neue Psychologische Studien,* 1: 613-692.

Rudert, Johannes. (1944). *Charakter und Schicksal.* Potsdamer Vorträge 5. Potsdam: Eduard Stichnote.

Rudert, Johannes. (1948/49). "Charakterologisches Tagebuch. Notizen aus dem Privatbesitz von Johannes Rudert."

Rudert, Johannes. (1956). *Erziehung wozu?* Stuttgart: Kröner.

Rudert, Johannes. (1957/58). "Psychologie der Ausdruckserscheinungen." Skriptum zur Vorlesung im Winter-Semester an der Universität Heidelberg.

Rudert, Johannes. (1958). "Pädagogische Psychologie." Skriptum zur Vorlesung im Sommer-Semester an der Universität Heidelberg.

Rudert, Johannes. (1959). "Psychologenkongreß in Heidelberg. Ruperto Carola." Mitteilungen der Freunde der Studentenschaft der Universität Heidelberg, XI.Jahrgang, Band 26: S.152-154.

Rudert, Johannes. (1960/61). "Pädagogische Psychologie." Skriptum zur Vorlesung im Winter Semester an der Universität Heidelberg.

Rudert, Johannes. (1965). "Vom Ausdruck der Sprechstimme." In Robert Kirchhoff (Hrsg.), *Ausdruckspsychologie.* Handbuch der Psychologie, Bd. 5 (S.422-464). Göttingen: Hogrefe.

Rudert, Johannes. (1966). "Der Weg, ein psychagogischer Leitbegriff." In Maria Hippius (Hrsg.),*Transzendenz als Erfahrung—Beitrag und Widerhall.* Festschrift zum 70. Geburtstag von Graf Dürckheim (S.428-439). Weilheim/Obb.: Wilhelm Barth.

Rudert, Johannes. (1968). "Versuch über den Anteil des Glaubens am menschlichen Handeln." In *Wirklichkeit der Mitte. Beiträge zu einer Strukturanthropologie. Festschrift für August Vetter* (S.138-147). Freiburg-München: Karl Alber.

Rudert, Ruth. (O.J.). "Forderung und Überforderung in der Erziehung." In Frieda Sopp (Hrsg.),*Elternhilfe in der Erziehungsunruhe unserer Zeit.* Schriften des Pestalozzi-Fröbel-Verbandes, (S.21-42). Heidelberg: Quelle & Meyer.

Rudert, Ruth, und Stein, Rudolf. (1959). "Erziehungsberatung." In Hildegard Hetzer (Hrsg.), *Pädagogische Psychologie. Handbuch der Psychologie,* Bd.10 (S. 503-522). 2.Aufl.Göttingen: Hogrefe.

Sennett, Richard. (1994). *Flesh and Stone.* New York: Norton, London: Faber & Faber.

Stadler, Ulrich, und Wagner, Karl (Hrsg.). (2005). *Schaulust. Heimliche und verpönte Blicke in Literatur und Kunst.* München: Fink.

Szerb, Antal. (1943/2005). *Das Halsband der Königin.* From the Hungarian. 2.Aufl. München: Deutscher Taschenbuch Verlag.

Valsiner, Jaan. (2004). "Glory and misery of fame in psychology: Hero-myths in the making of a social science." *History of Psychology and Psychology Studies,* 6: 23-28.

Warnke, Martin. (1984). *Cranachs Luther. Entwürfe für ein Image.* Frankfurt am Main: Fischer.

Zentner, Christian. (Hrsg.) (2004). *"Adolf Hitlers* Mein Kampf." *Eine kommentierte Auswahl.* 17. Auflage. München: List.

6

Jan Smuts and Personality Theory: The Problem of Holism in Psychology[1]

Christopher Shelley[2]

In the early twentieth century, psychology as discipline crystallised much of its epistemology and methods around positivism and the associated experimental method. For the developing scientific discipline, this modernist foundation seemed the most valid means with which to produce empirical facts that were reliable, verifiable, and which acceded towards the goal of establishing universal truth claims. At that time, very few schools of psychology in Anglophone contexts worked with the challenge of holism. Rather, experimental psychology's penchant for elemental reductionism was the mortar of fact building, consonant with a positivist approach. In contrast, those schools that did pursue holism in psychology were outside of the Anglo-American favoring of Humean[3] informed approaches (e.g., German psychology). The implicit rationale for a rejection of holism was that it chimed too closely with the introspectively based realm of philosophy, especially metaphysics, to which the new science of psychology had recently split from and wished to retain a demarcated distance. However, such a split was artificial; from its disciplinary inception in the late nineteenth century through to the present day, psychology has engaged underlying cross-fertilizations with philosophy—hence the Humean aspect (Danziger, 1990; Tolman, 1994).

This chapter explores the generally unthought-of, yet lasting contributions that the statesman and philosopher of holism, Jan Christiaan Smuts, has made to Anglo-American psychology. Whilst there are those in psychology who remain ambivalent towards holism, preferring knowledge claims based on elemental reductionism, the active adoption of holism via Smuts nevertheless transpired within certain threads of psychology and psychiatry. Over the course of the twentieth century, psychology continued to develop and entrench itself as a distinct discipline, containing a plethora of sub-disciplinary threads. From its disciplinary beginnings, psychology's variegation was seeded (such as through the work of William James) and multiplicity ensued. Hence, psychology also extended itself beyond its core attempts at enshrining elementalism, evolving into an umbrella discipline to which holistic schools such as Alfred Adler's Gestalt therapy theory and Adolf Meyer's psychobiology (the latter associated primarily with psychiatry) are contained. In terms of holism, Smuts played an inconspicuous yet instrumental role in this extension.

Jan Smuts lived an illustrious, prominent, and interdisciplinary life combining an erudite knowledge of biology and botany with contrasting and overlapping interests in philosophy, psychology, law, literature, and politics. He was born in 1870 to a Boer family in rural South Africa, near the Cape of Good Hope. As a young man he entered Victoria College in Stellenbosch, graduating in 1891 after studying science and literature. Subsequently Smuts earned a scholarship to Cambridge where he graduated with a law degree in 1894. Before returning to South Africa he completed a study at the British Library in London on the personality of Walt Whitman, a work that was published posthumously (Smuts, 1973). The Whitman study preceded Smuts' major scholarly contribution (written decades later in South Africa): his 1926 publication *Holism and Evolution*. Smuts, in retrospect, was an interdisciplinarian, and *Holism and Evolution* is a text of interest to multiple disciplines—a treatise positioned on "the borderland between science and philosophy" (p. v.). The earlier Whitman study foreshadows his later concentration on personality theory and its relation to the doctrine of holism. Indeed, a substantial portion of text is devoted to exploring the nature of personality in *Holism and Evolution*.

Upon his return to South Africa, Smuts entered politics and was eventually elected to hold several cabinet positions in the national government. He was subsequently elected prime minister, a position he held from 1919-1924, and again from 1933-1948. Two other key political accomplishments were as equally eminent; he was a founding member of the *League of Nations* and its successor the *United Nations*.

In addition to his political achievements, Smuts also garnered two notable academic accolades, a honorary Doctorate [D.Sc.] from London University in 1931 followed by a prestigious post of leadership at the helm of British science: President of the *British Association for the Advancement of Science*. These were remarkable achievements considering that Smuts was a political figure—a professional politician and statesman—and one who never claimed to be a professional scientist.[4] Nevertheless, Smuts retained a keen interest in science until his death in 1950. Ansbacher (1994) notes that, "Tragically, after his second political eclipse in 1948, a fast deterioration set in, so that his country is today far better [remembered] for *Apartheid* than for *holism*" (p. 488). It is an extraordinary case of irony that a philosopher and statesman concerned with the ideal of the "whole" should find his legacy trumped by those who radically partitioned—pulled apart—the peoples of South Africa. The subsequent developments in the contemporary South African polity, with the spectacular collapse of apartheid in the 1990s, constitute one of the greatest human rights advances in the twentieth century. The end of apartheid moves the South African state towards reconciliation, perhaps again in the direction of holism.

Holism and the Holistic Personality

Holism and Evolution is primarily a philosophical treatise relevant to science and, as this chapter argues, psychology especially. Through this book, which brought together ideas formulated in an earlier unpublished paper, Smuts argues that the concept of *holism* is grounded in evolution and is also an ideal that guides human development and one's level of personality actualization. As Smuts's biographer Hancock (1968) notes, holism, which he equated with the German term *Eenheid* (unity), "became his philosophic quest" (p. 177), it was his "*vera causa*" (p. 188).

Smuts coined the term "Holism" in the early twentieth century (Esfeld[5], 2001; Harper, 2001). He was acknowledged for the contribution by writing the first entry of the concept for the 1929 edition of the *Encyclopedia Britannica*. Contemporarily, the Oxford English Dictionary defines Holism as follows: "(1) the theory that certain wholes are to be regarded as greater than the sum of their parts (compare *reductionism*); (2) the treating of the whole person including mental and social factors rather than just the symptoms of a disease" (p. 673). For Smuts, holism elevates the synthetic over the analytic and the organic over the radically discrete element.

Smuts's Critical Thesis on Holism and Personality

Smuts considered the thesis of holism as an apt refutation of the predominant reductionist psychology of his day; he was philosophically opposed to positivism. He argued that a reductive, conceptual abstraction produces a view of the natural world that constitutes "a mere collection of *disjecta membra*, drained of all union or mutual relations, dead, barren, inactive, unintelligible" (as cited in Hancock, 1968: 180). Instead, Smuts argues for a general synthetic principle that is universal. He grounds this principle in the biological stratum, accepting Darwin's thesis yet disagreeing with the post-Darwinians and their penchant for reductive and causal mechanics. Smuts counters that, "Evolution is nothing but the gradual development and stratification of [a] progressive series of wholes, stretching back from the inorganic beginnings to the highest levels of spiritual creation" (Smuts, 1926: v.). Although grounded in biology, Smuts nevertheless envisages wholes as bearing relevance to problems of general philosophy, ethics, art, psychology, and "the higher spiritual interests of mankind" (ibid.: vi.). The first great pinnacle of wholes, having risen through evolution from a primordial, base level of matter (or lesser wholes), is to be ideally found in human personality: "Personality [is] the highest [potential] form of Holism" (ibid.: 292). Drawing from Immanuel Kant's *synthetic unity of apperception*,

Smuts argues that the idea of the self, which he describes as "the most elusive phantom in the whole range of knowledge" (p. 263), is the key to understanding the holistic foundation of personality.

In his analysis and summary of Smuts's philosophy, Linden (1995) ascertains that there are seven levels of holism:

> (1) Definite structures of synthesis with little internal activity, e.g. a chemical compound; (2) Functional structures in living bodies, the parts co-operating mutually for the maintenance of the whole, e.g., the plant; (3) Co-operative activity co-ordinated and regulated by a central, mainly implicit and unconscious control, e.g., the animal; (4) Centralizing control that becomes conscious and culminates in personality, e.g., human beings; (5) Central control interacting with its field forming composite holistic groups, e.g. society; (6) Superindividual associations of central control, e.g., the state and/or institutions; (7) Emergent ideal wholes or holistic ideals, e.g., truth, beauty, and goodness that lay the foundation for a new cultural order. These wholes are hierarchical and expansive. (pp. 254-255)

Smuts's life work was concerned with all seven levels of holism: His ebullience for science and nature (levels 1 through 3); a passion for understanding human personality (level 4), which as a middle category, intersects the lower levels with the higher; his concern for society as expressed in his pursuit of a law degree and political office (level 5); while his extra-political work as a statesman is apparent in levels 6 and 7. For example, Smuts's (1926) remarks on the ideals for the League of Nations express his holistic beliefs, arguing that the organization served as

> the chief constructive outcome of the Great War, [it] is but the expression of the deeply-felt aspiration towards a more stable holistic human society. And the faith has been strengthened in me that what has here been called Holism is at work even in the conflicts and confusions of men. (p. 344)

Implicitly, the United Nations, as successor to the League of Nations, is consonant with the same general aspiration that he espoused.

The last and highest pinnacle of wholes is expressed in metaphysical and teleological conceptions of perfectionist ideals, a supraordinate pull towards what he describes as the highest conceptions of "Truth, Beauty, and Goodness" (ibid.: 345). He summarizes this ideal pull, "The rise and self-perfection of wholes in the whole is the slow but unerring process and goal of this Holistic universe" (ibid.: 345). Moreover, an actualized personality potentially propels it from its mid level ranking to the "highest form" of holism, a matter to which attention now turns.

Smuts's Ideals of Personality and the Holistic Self

Smuts (1926) views "Personality"[6] as potentially the highest form of Holism, yet due to its general "infancy" in the diachronic scale of evolution, it is often fragile and can be subject to maladaptiveness,

Not seldom, of course, the personality finds it impossible to overcome the defeats it has sustained and goes under; for it is as yet weak and inchoate as a function of Holism, and in some cases it is weaker than in others. (p. 299)

Ascending towards greater wholeness is construed as a core teleological ideal of personality, one predicated on a governing *self* whose task is that of striving for unity. This premise is akin to William James's (1890) "I," which delegates the integrating task—a function of cohering the various "me-s" that populate the self over time. Personality refers to the uniqueness of the individual self. And, Personality, in whatever its evolutionary state, is viewed as a constituent feature of the holistically motivated self. Smuts's articulation of the self resonates strongly with James's original tripartite conceptualization of the self (material/social/spiritual) —a self that was also configured holistically and in ways that saw the necessity of the conception as integral for any human psychological inquiry. Danziger (1997) notes that after James's pre-disciplinary self was conceptualized at the disciplinary birth of Anglo-American psychology, the concept was subsequently disavowed by a nascent psychological establishment. Early academic psychologists were concerned with strict adherence to Humean inspired empiricism and methods to which the elusive self would not submit. The self carried too many Romantic features that were in defiance of the Zeitgeist shifting as it did from Romanticism into late modernity (Brinich and Shelley, 2002). The Anglo-American repudiation of Wundt, aside from hearty celebration and importation of his experimental method, was also a move away from a perceived and disdained introspectionism,[7] the psychologically stated flaw of philosophy. Moreover, the complete evasion of Wundt's *Völkerpsychologie* (which posited a social-developmentally relevant psychology, see Diriwächter, 2004) cemented an Anglo-American tradition of a psychology that was (and in many cases remains) either ambivalent or even hostile towards intangible concepts that defy disciplining. But without the self such a psychology became barren, irrelevant, and to many, meaningless. Hence, Danziger (1997) also notes that Gordon Allport long ago made a famous plea for the readmission of the self back into psychology. And it did return but operationalized so heavily that its parochial representation bore no resemblance to James's original outline.

Smuts argues that personality is holistically contained within physical embodiment, a conceptualization that challenges the longstanding problem of Cartesian dualism by replacing the polar doubling of mind/body with synthesis. The whole of personality is both above and beyond the natural world (metaphysics), yet simultaneously and irrevocably an aspect of it. This premise sets-up a seemingly irreconcilable contradiction in Smuts's holistic thought, human subjects are natural yet also simultaneously beyond the natural. The embodied person is posed as a product of evolution that is underpinned by an unknown creative force, one that ultimately synthesizes towards "universal Holism."

Within this conception, Smuts proposes four characteristics of personality: (1) Creativeness, (2) Freedom, (3) Purity, and (4) Teleology.

1. Creativeness

Smuts (1926) maintains that, "Our very conception of Personality is that it is a unique creative novelty in every human being" (p. 275). The uniqueness and originality of personality variance is grounded in the notion of a creativeness that is universal.

> Each human individual is a unique personality; not only is personality in general a unique phenomenon in the world, but each human personality is unique in itself, and the attempt at "averaging" and generalising and reaching the common type on the approved scientific lines eliminates what is the very essence of personality, namely, its unique individual character in each case. (p. 279)

Hence, Smuts adopted an early critical stance against psychology as empirical science, a project that he dismissed as "unintelligible" (p. 292). "The province of psychology is much too narrow and limited for the purpose of Personality; and both its method and procedure as a scientific discipline fail to do justice to the uniquely individual character of the Personality" (p. 280). This disavowal is the basis of his rejection of psychology's attempts to abstract and sort personality into measurable types. As an opponent of a science of Personality, he argued that Personality would fare better if taken-up by *personology*. Such a shift, he believed, would remedy the epistemological problems that subject personality to psychology's insufficiencies, such as an often-unthought-of retention of Cartesian dualism predicated on the enigma of the subject/object binary. A reductive and mechanistic psychology fails, according to Smuts, to capture the creative and synthetic foundation of enduring uniqueness. Objective measurements of disposition elide the possibilities of transcendence, the freedom to realize what is not yet apparent, that which defies measurement. Like the psychodynamic theorists, Smuts contends that there are limits to human agency. Recognizing and overcoming these limits increases the freedom of the personality.

2. Freedom

"Freedom means holistic self-determination, and as such it becomes one of the great ideals of personality, whose self-realization is dependent on its inner holistic freedom" (Smuts, 1926: 291). One of the ideal aims of Personality, freedom is achieved through the process of self-realization, through *conscious* acquisition so that the human subject is less swayed or menaced by *unconscious* forces.

It will be generally admitted that this province of the subconscious is most important, not only for mental science itself, but more especially for the knowledge of the Personality in any particular case. For most minds, perhaps for all minds, the conscious area is small compared with the subconscious area; and beyond the subconscious area is the probably still larger organic or physiological area of the nervous, digestive, endocrine and reproductive systems, which all concerned the personality most vitally and closely. (ibid.: 280)

For personality to reach towards its ideal, Smuts constitutes it as "an organ of self-realization" (p. 290), "the whole is the essence of Personality, so wholeness in self-realization and self-expression is its essential aim and object" (p. 295). He suggests that awareness through conscious control is the goal of the "Free Personality," "the fuller and more complete a personality is the greater its power of central self-control, or the fuller its Freedom. Weak characters have much less freedom than strong characters" (p. 310). The extent to which a Personality is free becomes "the measure of its development and self-realization" (p. 311). The two principles cited in the achievement of a self-realized and Free Personality are *Libertas* and *Imperium*. The ability to exercise these principles propels the holistic personality upwards: "To be a free personality represents the highest achievement of which any human being is capable" (Smuts, 1926: 312).

3. Purity

The function of freedom in the personality is to achieve what Smuts refers to as Purity (Gr. *Reinheit*). "A pure, free, homogenous spirit is the ideal of Personality" (p. 312). Purity is posed as a guiding principle for mental health, the resolution of all dissonance leading to dispositional harmony, or a pure state of unfettered mended-ness, the ideal of wholeness, healing (etymologically traced to "holiness").

If a person keeps out of his nature any warring or jarring elements or complications, keeps himself free of all moral or spiritual entanglements, and is nothing but himself—whole, simple, integral and sincere—he will also be pure in the vital holistic sense. (p. 303)

Assimilation of all fractures, the healing of all splits and final resolution of conflict are the overriding ideal aim. This idealist sense of purity suggests that direct access to the transcendent ideal of the "whole" is attainable, yet naively overlooks the realm of context and the concrete social facts of life; it glaringly lacks pragmatism as to who is better poised to access these ideals and how this might be achieved. However, Smuts is also positing a guiding ideal, directionality and aspirations that seem more than worthy of pursuit independent of such factors as material barriers. The pursuit itself may bear fruit regardless of any woolly-minded sense that this may necessarily be concretely achievable by everyone in all contexts and settings.

4. *Teleology*

The final premise of Personality overlaps with the previous points. Teleology points to the realm of ends in which the evolution of Personality carries with it a directional purpose with a conclusive aim. This purpose is completion, achieving a final life goal of unification, the striving for a state of perfection. Personality in Smuts's scheme is pulled towards universal Holism,

> The ideal personality is a whole; it is a whole in the sense that it should not have in it anything which is not of a piece with itself, which is alien or external to itself. Any such extraneous or adventitious element in it which does not really harmonize with it prevents it to that extent from being whole. Now as the personality as a self-realising holistic activity in us, it follows that its imminent end and ideal is to realise and develop itself as a whole, to establish and secure its wholeness. (p. 302)

The unique aspiration that Smuts points to is his contention that, "Personality transforms the material into the spiritual" (p. 304). The implication is that the evolutionarily 'weak' Personality is capable of healing itself given the proper conditions and facilitation. For Smuts such healing occurs if aligned in the correct direction of self-realization and the synthetic pull of Holism. His point of view is aligned with, but not explicitly credited to, Kierkegaard (who emphasised self-realisation) and, separately, German idealist philosophy and its varied discourses, which generally argue for the merits of holism (Bowie, 2003).

Smuts's writing on personality constitutes a narrative that is faithful to much of the Western/humanist discourses on the fulfillment of the individual self. However, this faithfulness is not intended to be solipsistic. He tempers his ideas with a curious and confounding threat to the individual self,[8] "earnest men will always find that to gain their life they must lose it; that not in the self but in the whole (including the self) lies the only upward road to the sunlit summits" (p. 316). Hence, he cautions against viewing the process of becoming self-realized as being self-indulgent or egoistic in aim. The goal of integrating self is akin to Jung's process of *individuation*, neither whimsical nor hedonistic but rather a process of acquiring wisdom and maturity, realizing one's self so that in the end it may ultimately be surrendered. In one of his more esoteric passages, Smuts proposes that self-realization is the implicit solution to the affects of pain, suffering, and sorrow:

> Learn to be yourself with perfect honesty, integrity and sincerity: let universal Holism realise its highest in you as a free whole of personality; and all the rest will be added unto you - peace, joy, blessedness, happiness, goodness and all the other prizes of life. (p. 315)

As an important early theorist on holism, what impact did Smuts's philosophy have on personality theory within psychology? A recent *PsychInfo* database search of hundreds of thousands of psychological abstracts yields no direct reference whatsoever to Jan Smuts. However, his term "Holism" does garner a substantial number of articles, though only a minutia of each abstract refers to Smuts directly. Was Smuts' doctrine irrelevant to the genesis of Anglo-American psychology? Indeed not, both his holistic thesis and holism more broadly have played, and continue to play, a crucial theoretical role in some threads of Anglo-American psychology.

Alfred Adler's *Individual Psychology*

Adler's (1956) school synthesized Smuts's holistic philosophy in a conscious and evocative way. For Adler, the adoption of Smuts's doctrine served the purpose of further distancing his school of depth psychology, known as *individual psychology*,[9] from a persistent historical association with Freud's drive psychology, which Adler notoriously departed from. Ansbacher (1994) notes,

> Among the first [of the psychodynamic thinkers] to appreciate the work of Smuts was Alfred Adler. He wrote to Smuts in January, 1931:
> *Reading your book Holism and Evolution, I felt very much moved by all your explanations. I could see very clearly what had been the key of our science. Besides the great value of your contributions in many other directions, I recognized the view in regard to what we have called "unity" and "coherence". I feel very glad to recommend your book to all my students and followers as the best preparation for Individual Psychology.* (Italics in original, p. 490)

Linden (1995) notes that Adler's adoption of Smuts's philosophy occurred long after his break with Freud in 1911. Adler synthesized his subscription to Smuts's doctrine with a similar endorsement of the neo-Kantian philosophy of Hans Vaihinger (1925). Vaihinger's philosophy of *as-if* emphasizes constructivism through the construct of perceptual fictions, hence, Adler speaks of the guiding influence of *fictions* in mental life. For example, Adler's concept of *fictional finalism*, the striving for an unconscious fictional goal (e.g., perfection), follows Kant, Nietzsche, and Vaihinger's thought. This is clear in his positing of the *private logic* or *biased apperception* of the subject who purportedly constructs fictions as a way of dealing with reality and to compensate for deep feelings (often unconscious) of inferiority. These constructs are part of the *style of life*[10] that loosely constitutes Adler's particular take on the idea of character or personality. One's style of life, constructed with deep and pervasive fictions, is generally unconscious. It functions to unify the person (although often in less than ideal ways) and is creative rather than solely libidinous in force. Adler's school is intrinsically and fundamentally an analysis of the self in the social and ideal context of a *feeling of community*[11] (Gr. *Gemeinschaftsgefühl*). The self/social dynamic is conceived of in a holistic way, yet with the hybrid incorporation of Vaihinger, holism is often reconfigured by Adlerians under the guise of being a useful fiction (Slavik, 2006). This reconceptualization of "holism" appeases those constructivist Adlerians who are less comfortable with the metaphysical and transcendent aspects of Smuts's more orthodox views.

Upon hearing of Adler's death in 1937, Smuts wrote to the British Adlerian Hertha Orgler, one of Adler's biographers:

> *Professor Adler was one of the first to write to me on the appearance of my book, Holism and Evolution, to express his agreement with my general standpoint, and to give the work his blessing. Indeed, he went so far as to say that he looked upon my theory of holism as supplying the scientific and philosophical basis for the great advance in psychology which had been made in recent years. ... There can be no doubt that Adler has laid his finger on some of the most important aspects of human personality... He has left behind him a solid and lasting contribution to the science of psychology.* (Italics in original, Smuts as cited in Ansbacher, 1994: 491)

Fritz and Laura Perls's *Gestalt Therapy* Theory

Gestalt Therapy Theory also actively endorsed the work of Smuts. When the Nazi threat was too great to endure, "Fritz" and Laura Perls fled from Germany to South Africa. It was here that they became acquainted with Smuts's *Holism and Evolution*. They subsequently imported and interwove Smuts's work as one of many philosophical influences underpinning Gestalt Therapy. They particularly approved of the ways in which Smuts's ideas complimented another central influence, that of the holistic work of Kurt Goldstein (1939). Gorten (1987) outlines the philosophical and psychological influences that aided the Perls in constructing Gestalt Therapy, and Smuts is prominently listed as a prime influence—a point also validated in a similar analysis by Wulf (1998). Smuts also indirectly affected the course of the Perls's lives. In an interview, Laura Perls describes why they fled from South Africa to the USA:

> Because Jan Smuts (then Prime Minister of South Africa) was retiring and a young man of about forty-three, a very brilliant guy, a Wunderkind, who was supposed to succeed him, suddenly died of a heart attack and there was no one who was in the Union party, which was the democratic party, to have a chance to be elected. We knew what would be coming because the nationalists had been working all along. They were pretty well organized and we wanted to leave before the 1948 elections. Fritz left in 1946 and I left in 1947. (Rosenfeld, 2004: 15)

The Perls were able to immigrate to America by recourse of an affidavit provided by Karen Horney—another figure who makes use of holism by reference to her brand of psychoanalysis which she termed *Holistic Psychoanalysis*. However, like Carl G. Jung who also championed the idea of holism, one is unable to find a reference to Smuts's work in their collective writings. Gestalt Therapy and, to a slightly lesser extent, Adler's Individual Psychology are network modalities under the umbrella term *Humanistic Psychology*. In his analysis of the general paradigm (content, method, approach) Aanstoos (2003) argues that the humanistic vision has historically been constituted on holism. The author further argues that holism is necessary to resolve crucial contemporary and future problems such as posed by the interrelationship between globalization, ecology, and health.

Adolf Meyer and Psychobiology

Logan (2003), Lidz (1985), and Neill (1980) point out the ways in which Meyer (1951) was concerned with either holism or the issue of unity in the human being (such as mind-body integration). In the U.S. and also Britain, Meyer was a monumental figure often described in an historical salutation as "the Dean of American Psychiatry" (Neill, 1980: 460).

Meyer[12] wrote to Smuts in 1945 supporting his goals for the United Nations, those of "Respect of Self-and-Others and Equity for Peace." The letter concluded with a disclosure of admiration:

> Long one of your admirers, and cheered with your declaration of a wonderful conception of the San Francisco [UN] conference goal, I beg to send you my words of admiration and gratitude…
> Deeply stirred by your gift to the cause, I send you these words,
> Sincerely, your humble fellow-*holist*. (Italics added)

Meyer's statement, "Long one of your admirers," demonstrates that he was familiar with Smuts's work. Moreover, the "fellow-holist" insignia further suggests a general concurrence with Smuts's holistic thesis. It seems no great leap to suggest that Smuts also influenced one of the great founding figures of American psychiatry. Lidz (1985), in explicating Meyer's doctrine of *psychobiology*, writes:

> Meyer had been primarily concerned with the mind-body unity and the integration of the individual. He had stopped with his important realization that human behaviour is integrated through mentation . . . Man has two heritages—a biological and a cultural—and it is necessary to understand their interrelationship and fusion to achieve a general "field" theory. (p. 49)

Meyer was clearly a holist as reflected in his psychobiological conception, however, as Lidz (ibid.) also notes, he failed to clarify cultural and social factors in such integration—tending to focus on illness patterns and psychiatric approaches. However, his field theory approach clearly left the question of etiology open to *include* covariant factors drawn from the contextual/social world (Neill, 1980).

Having outlined the general thesis of Smuts's holism and briefly traced its importation into at least three schools of psychology/psychiatry, a critical discussion of the potential limitations of holism more broadly is warranted.

Critique of Holism

Smuts was clearly a structuralist and sought to articulate a totalizing grand narrative that unites dualisms through positing a teleological conception summarized in the following formula: smaller wholes synthesizing with larger wholes, and so on, towards universal Holism. Wholes are not isolated, abstract, or frozen entities. Rather, they are dynamic structures that contain an intrinsic motility, striving for further and more comprehensive integration. Contemporary critics of structuralism and their modernist penchant for master theory as expressed in totalizing meta-narratives, disagree with universal theories such as that of Smuts. For example, postmodern and poststructural refutations of the "one and the whole" point in contrast to the ubiquity of multifarious incongruencies, splits, fractures, and disjointed points. These discourses implicitly counter Smuts's hybrid thesis of a Romantic/modernist claim to the panoptic singular. In deconstruction, critics draw attention to glaring fissures and absences that render holistic grand narratives as merely a novel representation of the impossible, an erroneous postulate, and if remotely "true" then certainly beyond the actual telling (Gergen, 1991). These discursive discourses challenge the thesis of a logical progression towards (original/lost) wholeness as another manifestation of modernity's grand narrative of progress. Postmodernists perceive the contemporary desire to "be whole" as an outcome of the decline of certainty or a yearning for a return to Romantic idealism based on the nostalgia for a lost (original) home—to which holism tries to remedy (for example, as expressed in the yearning for such things as belonging, union, or reconciliation).

Yet a detailed reading of Smuts's thesis reveals a paradox; he does not preclude the fractures of difference to which grand theories of unity tend to mask. Nor does he deny the implicit multiplicity that could be revealed through the critical task of deconstruction. For example, plurality and multiplicity are clearly acknowledged in Smuts's (1926) discourse on the self and personality expressed in his phrase, "self of our very selves" (p. 263). He further elaborates,

> The individual self is not singular, springing from one root, so to say. It combines an infinity of elements growing out of the individual endowment and experience on the one hand and the social tradition and experience on the other. (p. 246)

Smuts also proposes that the human personality is often distorted, mystified, obscured, and conflicted by an unconscious[13] dimension. In psychoanalytic thought, the unconscious is claimed to be a realm of conflict that undermines a false (defensive) sense of unity to which the ego maintains its perceptual task of a rational ordering and mediating between internal and external demands. Psychoanalytic theorists such as Lacan (1977) argue for the impossibility of an ego that is whole or unified insisting on the fragmented constitution of the human subject (Rose, 1986). However, Smuts's acceptance of the unconscious concurs more strongly with Adler's (1956) and Jung's (1957) view of the phenomenon rather than psychoanalytic accounts. In exploring consciousness as an act of legislative agency, Smuts writes of the influence of the unconscious on human subjectivity,

> Much of this control and direction is conscious will, but far more is unconscious and operates in the subconscious field of the personal life, and it is only on great occasions or crises that light comes suddenly to be thrown on this inner leading in the personal life, and the individual becomes conscious that he has been guided or led along paths which were apparently not of his choosing. (Smuts, 1926: 296)

There are postmodernist-influenced psychologists who retain a problematized holism. For example, Andrew Samuels (1989) writes from a post-Jungian paradigm, preserving the influence of the personal and collective unconscious stratums yet abandoning Jung's more problematic holistic metaphysics. Others, like the personality and developmental psychologist Dan McAdams (1997), explore possibilities of integrated selfhood by acknowledging the postmodern insistence on multiplicity, plurality, and the striving for congruence and consistency with/in the apparent absence of the singular whole.

> The developing self seeks a temporal coherence. If the me keeps changing over the long journey of life, then it may be incumbent upon the I to find or construct some form of life coherence and continuity in order for change to make sense. (p. 62)

Hence, McAdams refers to the process of "selfing." Selfing constitutes the phenomenal self as having the purpose of lending a constructed sense of unity and coherence to the ontology of multiplicity in an increasingly fractured and contradictory (postmodern) world (Gergen, 1991). Such a world at least threatens the annihilation of self and certainly challenges its classical understanding.

The observation of contradiction and splits as articulated in *cognitive dissonance theory*, such as those demonstrated by the famous work of Festinger (1957), are anticipated and rationalized in Smuts's thesis by recourse to the evolutionary state of the human Personality; "Personality is still a growing factor in the universe, and is merely in its infancy. Its history is marked by thousands of years, whereas that of organic nature is marked by millions" (Smuts, 1926, p. 297). He concludes that Personality, "is still indefinite and undetermined" (p. 297); it is in a dynamic state of evolution, evolving towards the whole and therefore should not be confused with the ideal: Personality as a finished whole. Yet, resolution of splits, contradictions, dissonance, and so on are nevertheless envisaged in his thesis, which is posed as the tension between lesser wholes that are striving to integrate into larger ones. Smuts's paradigm views resolution/integration as both natural and desirable: people are to strive to be whole. Critics may very well take issue with this presumption, arguing that disunity has, in some circumstances, merit of its own that does not require unification or resolution. Holistic theses tend to deny the prevalence and utility of fracture in human subjectivity; such as the Lacanian insistence on the fundamental split of subjectivity, the infant's gradual realization of being separate from (m)other and the painful quest for individuality (beginning with the mirror phase where subjects come to recognize their reflection in ways that divide them—one is two, not one). In Lacanian and poststructural theory, the subject is fundamentally a split subject. Melanie Klein's psychodynamic theory also articulates a similar insistence on splitting. As O'Connor and Ryan (1993) note, "Klein stresses the impossibility in every psyche of ever achieving complete and permanent integration: there are always residues of paranoid and schizoid feelings and mechanisms" (p. 82). These fractures may be the source of tremendous creative output to which the subject requires rather than to have them extinguished through resolution.

A final problem in Smuts's discourse is a general failure to adequately *foreground* his own prejudices in the construction of his grand narrative. Donna Haraway (2004) refers to the imposition of an all-encompassing master narrative as a "god-trick" (p. 87) —one that does not account for the complex construction of history or the impact of culture. For example, Hau (2000) traces the social construction of a holistic approach to medicine that predominated in early twentieth-century Germany, a "masculinist . . . synthetic gaze" based loosely on "the art connoisseur who appreciated works of art as a coherent whole" (pp. 499-500). This cultural configuration,

> was reminiscent of the aesthetic gaze of the male educated bourgeois (*Bildungsbürger*), and only a physician who shared the aesthetic sensibilities of the *Bildungsbürgertum* could truly judge whether a person was normal, healthy, and beautiful.   (p. 495)

Smuts does not acknowledge his holistic philosophy as being culturally embedded. This is a politics of visioning a quasi-utopia that fails to contextualize the concrete social dynamics of *who* can become self-realized, of who is or is better poised to become whole. Nor does he say *how* one can become a "Free" and "Pure" Personality. In this sense, he elides the second definition of Holism as represented earlier in the Oxford Dictionary[14] which refers to social factors. The paradox is that on the social/political level, holism has been used to both subjugate groups (a utopia of the master's) and to promise an ideal of liberation (such as the Marxist ideal of solidarity and a unified worker's utopia). In what ways has holism been justified as a social force that curtails or subjugates others? For example, in early twentieth-century German medicine, Hau (ibid.) notes that holism was used to exclude women from medical practice because,

> women and the uncultivated were neither capable of creating great and timeless works of art nor capable of practicing the art of medicine. In German medicine, empathy, the ability to build a bridge from soul to soul and intuition, the ability to grasp the essence of a human being in its wholeness as a piece of art, represented the values and aesthetic ideals of the male educated bourgeois. (p. 524)

Smuts's "partial and situated knowledge," to borrow a phrase introduced by Haraway (2004), was from the center standpoint of being a white statesman in South Africa—one who carried on with the imperial project of Euro-centric colonization that he and his historical compatriots were an inextricable part of. Smuts did not see the world from the peripheries or the margins, but from the center, above from the platforms of power. Smuts cannot escape his historicity nor his role as an imperial leader. For example, he held only a cursory sympathy and an undemocratic regard for the South African Black majority of his day denying them the right to vote. He also did not discuss the situation of women, who, in the early twentieth century, were still largely denied basic rights (such as voting, to own private property, or accessing the academy); and in most jurisdictions women did not have the full legal status as persons, they ostensibly lacked complete selves (de Beauvoir, 1989/1952). "Lacking selves," women, non-whites, and the "uncultivated" were delegated as "Other" (alterity), deemed a "foreigner," and the "foreigner has no self," they are not whole in a "civilized" or masculine sense, but "constantly Other" (Kristeva, 1997: 270). This theme was also taken up in regard to women by Luce Irigaray (1985) in her book *This Sex which is not One*. As Others, women have been historically represented in contradistinction to and deviation from the universal "Man," he who has apparently always had a whole self replete with "superior morality" and greater "rational capacities," one not bedeviled by irrationality or associated with being the source of original sin.

Foucault (1988) denied such a thing as the *a priori* self altogether. In his discursive and genealogical formulation, the *technology of the self*, he articulates the self as a socially constructed entity disciplined to serve the interests of ruling institutions (e.g., the church). Selves exist in the West, says Foucault, merely to confess to the authorities, such as the previous universal order of the Roman Church or in modern "confessional" settings such as the psychiatrist's office or the courtroom. Such surveillance, what Foucault terms *panopticism*, resolutely establishes the constructed self as subject to institutional cultivation, regulation, and complex networks of power (Dreyfus and Rabinow, 1982). This "self" too is divided and not whole; its function is to reflexively evaluate one's inner transgressions (Sin/Law) and account for these interiorized infractions upon demand and external decree.

Having considered some of the criticisms levied against grand doctrines of the whole, I nevertheless contend that Smuts's ideas and contributions ought not be wholly discredited. His legacy of helping to found the United Nations and his influence in the eventual structural development of interdisciplinary study in the academy (which Julie Thompson Klein [1996] partly credits Smuts for) perchance redeems him. Indeed, the concept of interdisciplinarity has, after all, aided "the studies" such as women's studies, black studies, post-colonial theory, etc.—many of which focus on social justice and emancipation projects. As a social-justice minded psychologist, I remain enriched, edified, and stimulated by Smuts's holistic account regardless of his historical impediments and transgressions which cannot be overlooked. In this sense, I agree with Hans-Georg Gadamer's (1960) assertion that "the concept of the whole is itself to be understood only relatively. The whole of meaning that has to be understood in history or tradition is never the meaning of the whole of history" (p. xxxv). Smuts's holism was poised with prospective emancipatory aims such as the ideal of universal human rights to which organizations such as the United Nations still pursue.

Conclusion: Holistic Parallels with *Ganzheitspsychologie*

It is noteworthy to consider some rather obvious, if not striking, parallels between Smuts's doctrine and the second school of Leipzig: the *Ganzheitspsychologie*. Diriwächter (2003a; 2003b) points out that this school developed by attempting to resolve some arguable problems in German Gestalt Psychology (such as disputing objectivist representations of *form*) and Wundt's *Völkerpsychologie* (psychology of a people or folk). Wundt argued for the starting point of analysis as the totality of the person, their synthesis. However, Wundt's students, in bringing forward the second Leipzig school, took issue with his assertion of a creative synthesis, arguing that his position was, "another form of aggregation based on . . . elements" (Diriwächter, 2004: 100). The second Leipzig School alternatively perceives *all* planes as consolidated wholes and, hence, more closely approximates a school of pure holistic psychology. Also, the *Ganzheitspsychologie* attempted to coalesce ideas gleaned from the philosophical tradition of German idealism (e.g., Fichte, Schelling, Hegel, and so on) into a concrete psychology.

The main holistic parallels between the *Ganzheitspsychologie* and Smuts' work cluster around the premise that a person's psychological development does not proceed from scattered elements but rather, "progresses from one totality/whole to another" (Diriwächter, 2003b: 5). The *Ganzheits*-psychologists were more adept, however, at integrating psychology with the social context and provided a more socially relevant account. In this sense, the *Ganzheits*-psychologists held an immediate scholarly base to draw upon, the richness of the historical and social developmental *Völker* discourses stretching back to Humbolt, Lazarus and Steinthal, and culminating in Wundt's work (Diriwächter, 2004).

Ganzheitspsychologie fundamentally means "holistic psychology" and similar to Smuts's work represents a form of epistemological *structuralism* that was common in early to mid-twentieth-century psychological theorizing (as this present volume on holism demonstrates, the topic of holism remains a prevalent theoretical force). Moreover, the school of *Ganzheitspsychologie* proposed a similar argument to what Smuts declared, the idea that lesser wholes strive to synthesize into more developed ones and so on. Occasionally, however, Smuts lapses by invoking the term "element" in his argumentation in ways that confound and beg for clarification, for example:

When, however, we go on to analyse an organic whole into its elements, we notice at once that there must be something more besides those elements, something commonly called life which holds all those elements together in a living unity. This "something more" we have identified as Holism, and we have explained it as not something additional quantitatively, but as a more refined and intimate structural relation of the elements themselves. (pp. 272-273)

The *Ganzheitspsychologists* cautioned against any analytic digression into elements, asserting a notion of *Komplexqualitäten* (complex quality) that negates elemental existence (Diriwächter, 2003b).

Diriwächter (2003a) suggests that the *Ganzheitspsychologie* is an approach that has largely been forgotten or "lost in time." And whereas this school is peculiar to the genesis of German psychology, its ideas are not limited to Germanic spheres. Jan Smuts may have arrived at some similar conclusions to the first Leipzig school (Wundt) but stronger parallels are evident with the second school (the *Ganzheitspsychologie*). Smuts impacted threads of Anglo-American psychology through the humanistic and psychodynamic works of Alfred Adler (an Austrian émigré to the U.S.) and Fritz and Laura Perls's Gestalt therapy school (German/South African émigrés to the U.S.). Moreover, Smuts probably influenced Adolf Meyer (a Swiss émigré to the U.S.) and his school of psychobiology. Finally, Smuts's philosophy and the second school of Leipzig arose at similar points of time in history, arriving in culturally and linguistically distant contexts. I have uncovered no evidence to suggest that Smuts was familiar with the original *Ganzheits*-psychologists or vice-versa. However, Smuts was aware of the Nazi's enigmatic and dangerous distortion of holism, an appropriation which did not follow the second Leipzig School's original formulations. Hancock (1968) cites Adolf Meyer's suggestion (to Smuts) of opening an Institute of Holism in Germany:

Smuts told him the idea was premature. Yet he soon found out that Germans could do worse things to his ideas than bury them in an Institute. "Ganzheit-Theorie", as some Nazi writers were expounding it, shocked him. He thought it a monstrous parody of everything he believed in—"a queer compound of Holism, romanticism, racialism, ethics and religion . . . a ruthless scrapping of ideas and methods which we consider part of the moral and political heritage of the human race." (pp. 300-301)

Brush (1984) notes that the term holism was challenged by critics as being both "totalitarian" and "imperialist." Hitler, however, despised Smuts's version of holism (he banned the German translation of *Holism and Evolution*) and his Nazi government forbade Adolph Meyer, who was in allegiance with Smuts, from opening a proposed *Institute of Holism* in Hamburg (Hancock, 1968).

Karl Popper (1961), who misunderstood Smuts's holism and conflated it with the tendency towards totalitarianism, warned his readers against the dangers of *all* holistic doctrines. The totalitarian inclination (the whole equals the Total) that the Nazi's picked up in their political version of holism is a case in point that Popper seized upon. Indeed, holism as political doctrine (such as expressed in fascism) points to a potential problem with the concept, the misuse of the organic metaphor of "blood and soil" for heinous political purposes. This metaphor has been consistently distorted by fascist ideologues that seek, for example, to "cleanse" a land/"race" by rhetorical recourse to the abhorrence of the dark "Other," which led to campaigns of racialized exclusion, pogroms, and genocide. Popper was not entirely wrong in pointing out potential misuses, indeed, holism is an idea that requires political and scholarly care; it can succumb to totalitarianism, new age dogma, religious fundamentalism, and other unsavory manifestations.

For Smuts and the second Leipzig School, however, their mutual yet unknowingly similar conclusions suggest that they were on to something significant. Their simultaneous emergence strikes one as an aspect of the same *Zeitgeist*, developing in parallel. A revival of their collective ideas and (re)engagement with current philosophical problems in psychology and the social world (e.g., globalization and ecological degeneration) will generate further interest, scholarly criticism, and innovations. Such engagement could produce cross-fertilization and problem posing for those of us who believe that these conversations generate new questions and contribute in meaningful ways to the whole.

Notes

1. An earlier version of this chapter appeared in: *From Past to Future: Clark Papers in the History of Psychology*, 5(1): 40-53, under the title: "Holism, Personality Theory, and the Self: The Contribution of Jan Christiaan Smuts (1870 – 1950) to Anglo-American Psychology." The present edition is an elaborated version of a paper presented to the 11th Biennial Conference of the International Society for Theoretical Psychology, University of Cape Town, Cape Town, South Africa, June 2005.
2. The author expresses gratitude for permission to cite from the *Adolf Meyer Papers*, which was granted by *The Alan Mason Chesney Medical Archives* of the John Hopkins Medical Institutions.
3. David Hume (1711-1776), Scottish philosopher.
4. The BAAS appointment probably carried some political overtones considering Smuts's faithfulness and service to the British Empire during World War I.
5. The Swiss/German scholar Michael Esfeld (2001) (University of Konstanz, Germany) also acknowledges Smuts as the originator of the term *Holism* (Gr. *Holismus*; e.g., *die holistiche welt*). In German and English there are obvious and similar conceptions that predate Smuts's usage (e.g., whole/unity/completion or *Ganzheit*/Einheit/Vollständigkeit respectively). German philosophical discourse holds a long history of contemplating the idea of the whole (Bowie, 2003). Smuts was undoubtedly influenced by these discourses through secondary means, such as ideas that filtered through English translations of the German idealists, philosophers with which he had some intellectual acquaintance.
6. In *Holism and Evolution*, Smuts generally spells Personality with an upper case P (as he also does with Holism and the Self).
7. The perception of Wundt as an introspectionist (such as along the lines of J.S. Mill) requires clarification. Diriwächter (2004) writes: "Wundt was opposed to

the form of introspection (*Selbstbeobachtung*) that J. S. Mill or Edward Titchener would much later advocate. For Wundt, as for many other psychologists of those days, introspection was closer to retrospection, or the observation of an unreliable memory image" (p. 96).

8. This premise was, incidentally, also echoed in a rather provocative paper by Harry Stack Sullivan (1950), another uncommon interdisciplinarian in the history of psychology.

9. Adler's social and psychodynamic school of "individual" psychology uses the term "individual" in a very specific sense, drawn from the Latin root *individuus* meaning indivisible.

10. Adler sometimes referred to the German: *Lebens-Schablone/Apperzeptionsschema*, however, the translated English term "style of life" is intended to be much broader in meaning.

11. Also referred to, especially in North America, as *social interest*.

12. Adolf Meyer to J. Smuts, 4 May 1945, folder I/22/I, Adolf Meyer Papers, The Alan Mason Chesney Medical Archives of the John Hopkins Medical Institutions, Baltimore, MD.

13. Whilst Smuts speaks of the unconscious in *Holism and Evolution*, he strangely elides Freud, Adler, and Jung in the process.

14. "[2.]: The treating of the whole person including mental and social factors rather than just the symptoms of a disease."

References

Adler, A. (1956). *The individual psychology of Alfred Adler.* H. L. Ansbacher and R. Ansbacher (Eds./Trans.). New York: Harper Torchbooks.

Ansbacher, H. L. (1994). "On the origin of holism." *Individual psychology, 50(4)*: 486-492.

Aanstoos, C. M. (2003). "The relevance of humanistic psychology." *Journal of humanistic psychology, 43(3)*: 121-132.

Bowie, A. (2003). *Introduction to German philosophy: From Kant to Habermas.* Cambridge, UK: Polity.

Brinich, P. and Shelley, C. (2002). *The self and personality structure.* Buckingham, UK: Open University Press.

Brush, F. W. (1984). "Jan Christian Smuts and his doctrine of holism." *Ultimate reality and meaning: Interdisciplinary studies in the philosophy of understanding, 7(4)*: 288-297.

Danziger, K. (1990). *Constructing the subject: Historical origins of psychological research.* Cambridge, UK: Cambridge University Press.

Danziger, K. (1997). "The historical formation of selves." In: R. D. Ashmore and L. Jussim (Eds.). *Self and identity: Fundamental issues.* (pp. 137-159). Oxford (UK): Oxford University Press.

de Beauvoir, S. (1989). *The second sex.* New York: Vintage. (Originally published 1952).

Diriwächter, R. (2003a). Ganzheitspsychologie: A holistic approach lost in time. Paper presented at the Clark University Multidisciplinary Conference, Worcester, MA. March 2003.

Diriwächter, R. (2003b). What really matters: Keeping the whole. Paper presented to the 10th Biennial Conference of the International Society for Theoretical Psychology, Istanbul, Turkey. 24 June 2003.

Diriwächter, R. (2004). "Völkerpsychologie: The synthesis that never was." *Culture and psychology, 10(1)*: 85-109.

Dreyfus, H. L. and Rabinow, P. (1982). *Michel Foucault: Beyond structuralism and hermeneutics*. London: Harvester Wheatsheaf.

Esfeld, M. (2001). *Holism in philosophy of mind and philosophy of physics*. Dordrecht, NL: Kluwer Academic Publishers.

Festinger, L. (1957). *A theory of cognitive dissonance*. Evanston, IL: Row, Peterson.

Foucault, M. (1988). *The care of the self: The history of sexuality, volume three*. London: Allen Lane.

Gadamer, H. G. (1960). *Truth and method*. Second revised edition. J. Weinsheimer and D. G. Marshall (Trans.). New York: Continuum.

Gergen, K. J. (1991) *The saturated self: Dilemmas of identity in contemporary life*. New York: Basic Books.

Goldstein, K. (1939). *The organism: A holistic approach to biology derived from pathological data in man*. New York: American Book Company.

Gorten, D. (1987). "Gestalt therapy: The historical influences on F. S. Perls." *Gestalt theory, 9(1)*: 28-39.

Hancock, W. K. (1968). *Smuts: The fields of force*. Vol. II. Cambridge University Press.

Haraway, D. (2004). "Situated knowledges: The science question in feminism and the privilege of partial perspective." In: S. Harding (Ed.). *The feminist standpoint theory reader: Intellectual and political controversies*. (pp. 81-101). London: Routledge.

Harper, D. (2001). Holism. *Online etymology dictionary*. Retrieved 31 May 2004 from http://www.etymonline.com/

Hau, M. (2000). "The holistic gaze in German medicine, 1890-1930." *Bulletin of the history of medicine, 74(3)*: 495-524.

Irigaray, L. (1985). *This sex which is not one*. C. Porter (Trans.). Ithaca, NY: Cornell University Press.

James. W. (1890). *The principles of psychology*. London: Harvard University Press.

Jung, C. G. (1957). *The undiscovered self*. Collected Works, 10. Bollingen Series XX. New York: Pantheon Books.

Klein, J. T. (1996). *Crossing boundaries: Knowledge, disciplinarities, and interdisciplinarities*. Charlottesville, VA: University Press of Virginia.

Kristeva, J. (1997). *The portable Kristeva*. K. Oliver (Ed.). New York: New York University Press.

Lacan, J. (1977). *Écrits: A selection*. A. Sheridan (Trans.). London: Tavistock.

Linden, G. W. (1995). "Holism: classical, cautious, chaotic, and cosmic." *Individual psychology, 51(3)*: 253-265.

Lidz, T. (1985). "Adolf Meyer and the development of American psychiatry." *Occupational therapy in mental health, 5(3)*: 33-53.

Logan, C. A. (2003). "The legacy of Adolf Meyer's comparative approach: Worcester rats and the strange birth of the animal model." *From past to future: Clark papers on the history of psychology, 4(1)*: 25-38.

McAdams, D. (1997). "The case for unity in the (post)modern self." In: R. D. Ashmore and L. C. Jussim (Eds.). *Self and identity: Fundamental issues*. (pp. 46-78). Oxford (UK): Oxford University Press.

Meyer, A. (1951). *The collected papers of Adolf Meyer: Volume III medical teaching*. E. E. Winters (Ed.). Baltimore, MD: The John Hopkins Press.

Neill, J. R. (1980). "Adolf Meyer and American psychiatry today." *American journal of psychiatry, 137(4)*: 460-464.

O'Connor, N. and Ryan, J. (1993). *Wild desires and mistaken identities: Lesbianism and psychoanalysis*. London: Virago.

Popper, K. (1961). *The poverty of historicism.* Second edition. London: Routledge and Kegan Paul.

Rose, J. (1986). *Sexuality in the field of vision.* London: Verso.

Rosenfeld, E. (2004). "An oral history of Gestalt therapy: Part one, a conversation with Laura Perls." Retrieved 30 March 2004 from http://www.gestalt.org/perlsint.htm

Samuels, A. (1989). *The plural psyche.* London: Routledge.

Slavik, S. (2006). "Therapeutic strategy in a holistic psychology." In: P. Prina, K. John, A. Millar and C. Shelley (Eds.). *Adlerian yearbook 2006.* (pp. 137-153). London: Adlerian Society (UK) and Institute for Individual Psychology.

Smuts, J. C. (1926). *Holism and evolution.* London: Macmillan Company.

Smuts, J. C. (1973). *Walt Whitman: A study in the evolution of personality.* Detroit: Wayne State University Press.

Sullivan, H. S. (1950). "The illusion of personal individuality." *Psychiatry, 13(3):* 317-332.

Tolman, C. W. (1994). *Psychology, society, and subjectivity: An introduction to German critical psychology.* London: Routledge.

Vaihinger, H. (1925). *The philosophy of as-if: A system of the theoretical, practical and religious fictions of mankind.* New York: Harcourt, Brace and Co. (Originally published 1911).

Wulf, R. (1998). The historical roots of Gestalt therapy theory. *Gestalt Journal, 21(1):* 81-92.

7

Janet's Emotions in the Whole of Human Conduct

Tania Zittoun[1]
University of Neuchâtel[2]

As William James said, one sees what one is
prepared to see, so too, one cannot study the
psychology of man without guiding ideas, without
philosophical or even religious interests.
—*Pierre Janet*, Autobiography.

There are some everyday situations that are very difficult to account for from a psychological point of view. Imagine Paul working on his laptop in a local coffee house. He writes, but also listens to Bach through his headphones, watches the customers, and takes sips of his coffee; every couple of paragraphs, he switches his screen from his text to a chessboard, where he tries a few moves, hoping to win over a friend with whom he plays on-line. Or imagine Virginia, who goes to the cinema: she knows she soon will be traveling to meet a friend in a remote country, and feels that her life is changing; she knows that the romantic exotic story she will see on the screen will bring her somewhere else, calm her, and also help her to imagine her uncertain future.

These situations are difficult to account, for they are at the junction of phenomenon that psychologists have come to examine as distinct and independent. From a first viewpoint, one might say that these vignettes convoke dynamics and entities that belong to the sociocultural sphere: internet-chess games or movies are the products of a place and a time in history; they carry shared meanings, are public, and reflect widespread networks of representations. These two situations present us with specific social frames that have their own rules (coffee house, cinemas) or with interpersonal relationships (distant friends, close consumers). They finally illustrate intrapsychical, subjective, and partly non- or un-conscious dynamics: Paul's taste for coffee and Bach, and Virginia's personal version

111

of the movie she will see, at specific moments of their lives. Hence, these vi-gnettes allow us to see experiences that—thanks to the mediation of symbolic objects—are at the junction of the cultural, social, public, and shared and the individual, private, internal, and unique. From a second viewpoint, these two vignettes can be said to illustrate conduct that intermesh dynamics of feeling, perceiving, doing, and thinking.

In other words, to understand everyday interactions within our symbolic worlds, we need a psychological theory that can account for the embeddedness of the sociocultural and the subjective, as well as the cognitive and emotional aspects, of human experience. We need a form of holistic understanding of human conduct.

The French psychologist Pierre Janet (1859-1947) constructed a complex model of human conduct seen as a whole, where emotions play a central role. I will argue that Janet's holistic model can illuminate current issues in psychology.

In what follows, I will thus try to present this model, which has been largely ignored in non-clinical psychology until recently (see Meyerson, 1947; Sjövall, 1967; Ellenberger 1967; Valsiner & Van der Veer, 2000 for various accounts). I will first locate Janet's work, and highlight its proximity and differences with other *Ganzheit* approaches (Diriwächter, 2003b). I will then give the main lines of his theory: first, the hierarchy of conduct and the principle of tension and, second, the question of the regulation of emotions, and their semiotic compo-nent.[3] On this basis, I will finally apply this model to a modern, everyday cultural experience—Lily goes to the cinema. This will, I hope, show the relevance of such a holistic model for contemporary analysis.

An Informed Ambition

At the turn of the twentieth century, European scientists were observing with some perplexity the abundant, but extremely parcellized psychology just emerging in new American laboratories (Schelgel, 1904; Herbert, 1904; Dela-barre, 1894). On their side, scientists from France, Germany, and Austria were trying to offer integrative views of human behavior in its situated complexity (Diriwächter, 2003; 2003c; 2004).

Pierre Janet had a double ambition in that context. First, he wanted to offer a unifying vocabulary for the endless observations accumulated by psychologists. Second, he aimed at proposing an integrative understanding of human conduct as a whole (for example 1926: 204).

His enterprise can be seen as based on three pillars. First, Pierre Janet's double training as a philosopher and a medical doctor brought him to define the exact scope of a psychological enterprise: it should avoid, on one side, the danger of becoming a physiology, and, on the other side, that of being a phi-losophy. Second, Janet's professional positions gave him a privileged access to the ongoing scientific production. Chair of experimental psychology at the

College de France, researcher at *La Salpêtrière* in Paris, he participated to major international meetings, and was invited for lectures all around the world.[4] As co-creator and director of the *Journal de Psychologie Normale et Pathologique*, which was abundantly reviewing French, Austrian, German, American, and British psychology, he translated original foreign contributions, which kept him informed of the ongoing researches. Additionally, Janet was an attentive reader of the works in progress of Piaget,[5] Durkheim, and Levy-Brühl. The third pillar of Janet's work was his clinical work at *la Salpêtrière*, where he took care of hysterics, neurasthenics, and psychotics. He collected numerous case studies, did experiments with patients, and followed a few of them over the years, thus creating longitudinal data.[6] Janet's writings are based on his own observations in the hospitals and in everyday situations, with adults and children, and on existing ethological and anthropological studies. He published extensively and systematically on most aspects of human psychology, including the unconscious (in parallel to Freud) and the development of children's thinking (before Piaget).

Janet's project of unifying psychology is not meant to be a top-down process; a unified theory will, on the contrary, grow through a bottom-up movement: accumulated data is grouped and common categories eventually emerge. Formulations are at times close to common sense, probably as a consequence of Janet's attempt to simplify and unify the descriptive vocabulary; his theoretical notions also evolve through time. I will thus have to translate some of Janet's propositions and limit my reading to one state of the evolution of his changing model.[7]

French Holism

In France, psychology was closely linked to psychiatry and psychopathology. These sciences were strongly anti-idealist in a tradition going from Maine de Biran to Taine. They identified the volitional and embodied components of thoughts, as well as their automatic, elaborated, or creative aspects (Skövall, 1967). At the same time, German Gestalt and *Ganzheit* psychologists developed their approaches against "elementists" schools. In the line opened by Wundt, they were attentive to preserve the totality of an experience (*Erlebnisganzheit*, Diriwächter, 2003; 2003c; 2004).

As a French scientist, Janet started identifying subparts of human conduct. Yet his unifying project brought him to fix the *conduct* as unity of analysis for his psychological inquiry. A *conduct* can be seen as an ever-changing composite of embodied emotions, thoughts, and actions. This unity of analysis reassembles phenomenon ranging from perception and automatic behavior, to moral and religious ones. A *conduct,* thus, seems to approach the more holistic notions searched by the Germanic traditions.

Janet's studies on conduct and the work of the *Ganzheit*-psychologists, as presented by Diriwächter (2003; 2003b; 2003c; 2004), appear to overlap on many points: the notion of *act of synthesis,* the centrality of *emotions,* and a *developmental* orientation. They diverge on the place given to *sociocultural* dimensions and to *meanings* in the psychological enquiry.

The *act of creative synthesis* notion, developed by Wundt and redefined by his followers, plays a central role in Janet's theory. Wundt gave two meanings to the *creative synthesis.* It first designates the reverse operation to that of *analysis,* as psychologists practice it. It also means the emergence of a unitary experience out of a constellation of lower processes. Applied to empirical cases, the notion can show how a myriad of partial impressions can melt into the perception of a spatial form (Diriwächter, 2003b; 2004). *Ganzheit*-psychologists, such as Volkelt, refused the summative quality of this approach where the whole seems to be an aggregation of parts. They preferred to see synthesis as a transformation of relationships, or of totalities in other totalities. They also showed that Wundt's *creative synthesis* did not explain the move from elementary processes to higher human conducts (Diriwächter, 2004).

Without explicit reference to these authors and issues, Janet defined *acts of synthesis* in a non-summative way, which accounts for the linking of process of various complexities. Janet proposed a major division between two types of conducts. *Actions* are reactions to things as they appear within one's interaction with the world; *intelligence* (thought) is made out of representations of these conducts. *Acts of synthesis* belong to the latter and make these superior to the former, for what

> often allows one to recognize that a state is superior to another one is what one could call, the "grasp of consciousness" of the psychological operation. (1926: 209)

In effect, an *act of synthesis* contains, groups, and systematizes other acts; it enables the emergence of a new unified conduct, which "cannot necessarily be analyzed in its parts."[8]

Act of synthesis is a key concept for a complex, hierarchical theory of human conducts. Higher-level conducts emerge through the "coup de force" of an *act of synthesis.* Conducts themselves can be structured composites of various levels of complexity. Consistently with this model, Janet's empirical observations are descriptions of conducts that include embodied actions, perceptions, thoughts, and emotions constantly moving and merging from one state to another and from one degree of complexity to another one.

Similarly to the centrality of *Gemüt* in experience defined by Krueger (Diriwächter, 2003b), Janet saw emotional qualities at the core of conducts. *Ganzheit*-psychologists retain, after Wundt, that emotions can be distinguished according to their depth: love or religious faith are "deep" emotions. For Janet, love and faith are also to be separated from other emotions. Yet, it is not because of their "depth," it is on the basis of their place in the hierarchy of conducts. Love and faith are extremely social in nature (faith depends on institutions, shared meanings, social regulations, etc.) (Janet, 1935: 98). As they are completed by higher-level regulatory principles (e.g., "becoming a better person"), they can have an orientation power for people (e.g., a person would thus avoid committing "bad" conducts). They can be constitutive of people's identity and confer unity to their conducts. Thus, as some *Ganzheit*-psychologists would agree, emotions might be experienced as qualities of the world (e.g., poor people appear as "charity inspiring") and confer orientation to a person's development.

In effect, like Wundt in his *Völkerpsychologie*, Janet wanted to offer a developmental psychology. On the one hand, drawing on historical comparisons, he worked with the hypothesis of a similarity between human phylogenesis and ontogenesis. On the other hand, when looking at individual cases, Janet always took the developmental story of a person into account, within his or her historical and societal location, as *Ganzheit*-psychologists promoted (Diriwächter, 2003b).

Contrary to Wundt, Janet never tried to account for social or historical processes, or to analyze the development of communities. He always kept the person's human conduct as unit of analysis. The social, the cultural, and the symbolic became relevant for him only because they are part of the genesis of a person's conduct. It is, thus, through a person's social and located conduct that the community as a whole operates and has to be studied.

Finally, Janet was adamant about keeping psychological processes, such as meaning-constructions, at the heart of his enquiry; it is on this ground that he distanced himself from the *Gestalt*-psychologists. Indeed, their emphasis on the parallelism between the organization of perception and the brain was, for Janet, missing the object of psychology—meaning in the whole of conducts (Janet, 1935: 232-256).

In sum, Janet addresses most of the issues raised by the promoters of a *Genetic Ganzheitspsychologie* as described by Wellek (1950, in Diriwächter 2003b)[9]: holism, as an attempt to take in account all the aspects of human experience in a psychic totality; the structured nature of conduct; the centrality of emotions in these totalities; and their developmental nature. Yet, in Janet's holistic project, emphasis is put on the person's conduct as constrained, constituted, and mediated by social and historical forces; social forces are not examined by themselves.

A Hierarchy of Conducts

Janet's psychology is a dynamic hierarchy of conducts; thanks to *acts of synthesis*, consciousness emerges "like a flame burning out of these regulations growing out of action" (Janet, 1926/2003: 116).[10]

In his attempt to offer a systematic and genetic model of human action, Janet proposed a tripartite hierarchical organization.[11] The thresholds between three levels of conducts are synthetic acts of various degrees of complexity.

Inferior conducts are the most "animal" of human's actions. They are directly caused by or linked to external stimulations: reflex answers, perceptive acts, and elementary social acts, but also basic operation of thought.

Among such basic elementary operations of thought, Janet identified *relational acts* (1936). Janet's paradigmatic example is the conduct of the "apples in the basket": to comprehend apples in a basket, a composite of the perception of the apples *and* a perception of the basket are required. That is, there is "the act of synthesis of two perceptive conducts" (1926: 217), hence, the conduct includes a *relation*. These first relational conducts always suppose an interaction with the world: these are seen *in* the world, not in one's mind. Janet described examples of what we might call relations of countenance ("this in that") and of transformation ("if I pull the drawer, it will be open") and the first conducts implying signs, that is, mediated actions ("this stands for that").

Relational acts enable the emergence of language, seen as relations between conducts and words. Words can affect the world, contain, and transform. At this level, relational acts also enable memory—an action can be done in relation to another absent conduct. Hence, a sentinel is doing an inferior conduct—keeping watch—yet it requires the relational act of memory of linking his present watching with the memory of a past attack. For Janet, the emergence of language and memory was what distinguished human from animal conduct. Memory and language will enable the next levels of conducts: operations of thoughts.

Middle conducts are independent from the external world. Their objects are not the world or others, but previous thoughts, beliefs, or words. Here, relational acts occur between representations. For Janet, inner thoughts result from the interiorization of social conducts. In human genesis, there is a progression that goes from talking aloud to oneself, to talking in a low tone, to internal speech—out of which emerges thought (this idea has later been developed by Vygotsky).

Relations between thinking and external reality take the form of *beliefs* and *will*. Will is a thought that is immediately translated into conduct; belief is a thought that sees its realization indefinitely postponed. At this level emerge also conducts of *reflection*. These require the suspension of action that is doubt and a delaying of satisfaction. Reflection can thus take the form of a *decision*, an internal deliberation between various tendencies. These can lead to relations between thoughts and actions, such as beliefs or will, or to new synthetic acts between thoughts.

Higher conducts include reflective acts about thoughts. Reflective conducts can take the form of an evaluation of the consequences of tendencies or of the origins of these. They imply the mobilization of memories and the explorations of possible futures.

Regulative acts belong to this level of higher conducts. Regulative acts can sustain people's commitment into unpleasant or non-gratifying conducts and orient, and canalize their action. Morality, responsibility, long-standing commitment, goals, and expectations are regulative acts. They appear as inherently social. When people adopt them to regulate their conducts, those in turn change them . People's various conducts can become oriented towards one goal, their identity acquires unity, and the world appears to them as consistent and filled with truth.

Janet's hierarchical organization of conducts is not strictly a stage theory.[12] The three types of conducts coexist in various proportions in everyone. The hierarchical model, rather, offers a tool to analyze most everyday behaviors as well as cases of psychopathology observed by Janet.

Everyday irrationalities and psychopathology can be seen as anomalies of relational acts made between perceptions of the world (inferior conducts) and thoughts (beliefs or will, which are middle conducts) or a lack of acts of synthesis. Hence, an alcoholic who makes the decision not to drink anymore and is at the bar next hour, is a man who has had a reflection (internal deliberation) that has not been followed by the related action; it can be seen as a belief, but mostly it lacks long-term tendencies and regulating functions.

Additionally, in his attempt to account for everyday and clinical conducts, Janet developed a *model of tension* within the hierarchical model. Every action needs a certain strength to be achieved; the "ability to concentrate and the number of phenomena that one can hold in consciousness define the psychological tension one is capable of at that moment" (Valsiner & Van der Veer, 2000, p.106).

The higher in the hierarchy of conduct an action is, the stronger the psychological tension has to be, and the more important will be the person's expense of energy. Due to a lack of tension, neurasthenic, or epileptic persons often accomplish acts that seem normal but that lack goal directedness.

Tension and strength vary according to people's particular life events, to their fatigue, or to strong emotions; they also vary from person to person. However, external means can sustain, reinforce, or guide a tension. On one side, interpersonal relationships can support tension: a hypnotist guides his patient's tension and enables her to effectuate a psychological synthesis; the encouraging director of a factory can "drain" his workers' engagement into work and support their tension. On the other side, higher forms of conducts do precisely support such tension. As we have seen, one's commitment to moral, religious, or professional ideals has unifying virtues and can sustain long-term efforts. It appears that semiotic means, such as socially shared principles, sustain and guide the tension required for a person to engage into various middle- and low-level conducts beyond fatigue or emotional variation.

Composites of Emotions

Janet was interested in everyday anomalies, which he saw as results of inadequate relational acts. But how can such inadequate relations occur? This is where feelings, *les sentiments* in French, enter the hierarchy of conducts: strong feelings are indeed responsible for unrealistic or misleading relations or the absence of required acts of synthesis. The role of emotions in the hierarchical model thus has to be understood.

Emotions are difficult to observe as conducts. Janet defined the problem following Ribot, who was reading Wundt, Külpe, and Stumpf. Emotions are not actions directed toward the world or the others. They rather seem to be a tonality or a quality that does not change action (1928: 11). Contrary to representations of things or objects that can be discussed in reference to the world, they seem to be part of people's inner life, and are idiosyncratic and difficult to share. Hence, it is impossible for two persons to agree on what the feeling of a shared supper has been when one felt it as a joyful meal and the other, a sad one. How then do we to define emotions within a psychology of conducts? Janet defined two criteria for theorizing emotions.

First, a good theory of emotions needs to account for what is specifically psychological, that is, the complexity of a human conduct.

> The psychological fact is neither spiritual, nor corporal; it occurs in the human being as a whole, since it is nothing but the conduct of that human being, taken as a whole. (1928: 36)

Janet rejected mentalistic approaches to feelings—emotions are ideas—as well as "peripheric" theories, which (in the legacy of James, 1884) saw emotions as the result of organic affection. Both consider feelings as consequences and overlook their complexity. Janet felt closer to what he calls the "American pragmatists" (he quoted among others G. Stanley Hall, John Dewey, David Irons, and HN Gardiner) and German intellectuals (after Arthur Schopenhauer and Baruch Spinoza).[13] The first ones reintroduce the course of actions as components of emotions; the second, the course of representations and their mutual relations as part of emotions. The two approaches, hence, locate emotions at two of the levels of Janet's hierarchy of conducts.

Second, a theory of emotions needs to account for empirical cases: usual emotions, as well as the inexplicable clinical cases of emptiness or absence of feelings.

Janet reported a patient's description of a case of emptiness:

> It is a state where one does not feel, does not think, does not represent what one does or what one says. One does whatever with a total indifference, as if one wouldn't be concerned. . . . I am in the emptiness, I am a body without soul, when I am somewhere it is as if I wouldn't be there, if I speak about something, as if I would never have seen it . . . I see without seeing, I am a blind who sees. (1928: 69)

Creating a theory of emotions that can be integrated in his hierarchy of conducts and that satisfies this double constraint, Janet distinguished emotions linked to *primary actions* from emotions linked to *secondary actions*.

Primary actions are all the conducts that are produced as reactions to the world—automatic actions, obedience, routines, verbal answers, or memories. These include bodily actions as well as forms of language or thoughts; they can also be reflective, as long as they are directly stimulated by an encounter with a person or an event located in the world.

Secondary actions are of the same type as primary ones (thoughts, expressions, behavior), but they follow, or are *caused by primary actions* (1928: 122). These are thoughts about thoughts, inner attitudes towards primary actions, tensions toward the past or the future, spontaneous conducts, productions of new sentences, actions, grasps of consciousness, etc. In terms of emotional conduct, a person "does not contemplate his or her perception like one contemplates a spectacle," but adds to that numerous secondary actions:

> Sentimental regulation seems to be essentially made out of the addition of secondary actions which, by their presence, modify primary actions, increase or diminish them, or orient them in various ways. (Janet, 1935: 103-104)

The distinction between primary and secondary actions does not strictly overlap the previous hierarchical division. Any given action can be either primary or secondary according to where its impulse is located. It does not correspond to the division between automatic versus synthetic acts; a person in a emptiness state can be asked to recall his or her last trip to Oxford, and this can be told with the right details, clarity, and humor even if it is for the first time. As a story told the first time, it is not an automatic act; yet the person would not have initiated a memorization by himself; it occurs, because another person stimulates it; it is thus a primary conduct.

The distinction between primary and secondary conducts is enough to account for states of emptiness that were resisting to previous theories of emotions. A mother sees her son climbing a chair and being in disequilibria; and she does not react to prevent his fall. She would react if ordered by Janet—and her act would be a primary action. Her lack of spontaneous action is not necessarily due to a lack of fear or love, but due to her lack of secondary thoughts (what she knows about falling, what might happen, what would be the consequences, what the child means to her, etc.). States of emptiness can be thus explained as states in which the secondary actions are absent.

If the distinction between primary and secondary emotional conduct can account for difficult clinical cases, it can *a fortiori* account for normal emotions:

> If the feeling of emptiness and the state of emptiness depend on the suppression of thousands of secondary actions, of thousands of echoes and harmonics that normally go along with normal actions, it is quite likely that the opposite phenomenon, the development of secondary actions, must play a role in normal feelings. (Janet 1928: 126)

Janet explained most emotional behavior in terms of combinations of primary and secondary actions in the hierarchy of conducts.

Basic feelings are primary conducts, provoked by external or internal conditions that constrain or facilitate physical and mental conducts. Effort, tiredness, sadness, and happiness are such basic feelings. They can involve specific and shared patterns of conducts that are easy to identify and can be reflectively known as *feelings*. Emotions "choc" are less clearly definable; they come from brutal modification within one's environment and can disorganize thought (Sjövall, 1967: 56).

As primary conducts, emotional phenomena are provoked by conditions affecting one's possibility of actions; these might be soon objects of reflections, or awake secondary conducts that modify the initial conduct. Sadness in memory is less sad than real sadness; emotions that are expressed and are about unrealities have a more remote, less precise impact; or the reflective awareness that one's fantasy is not real and reduces the strength of its feelings.

In fact, the relations created around emotional conducts quickly expand, and emotional conducts appear as complex ones. The complexity of emotions comes from their location in time and in the social world, as well as from the fact that they are composites of inferior, middle, and high level conducts. An emotion occurs to a person in a time and place. At this point, the person is engaged in conducts linked to his or her perception of the situation, which include physiological states, thoughts, and emotions. These can immediately trigger secondary thoughts, such as memories of similar situations, thoughts about its cause, or memories of situations involving similar emotions. These thoughts and memories might provoke other physiological reactions and actions. The person will have to interpret them as they appear at this time and place, given his or her current future orientation and their emotional correlates. The emotional state emerges out of this complex set of relations. Hence, on a happy day, a woman might see the scarf of a dear friend and feel her heart beat—which would remind her of the intense moment of the gift of the scarf and its related love feelings; that would be reinterpreted in the present moment, that includes the knowledge that this friend will not come back. A form of regret finally emerges out of this present sadness and past happiness.

A felt emotion appears to emerge as a result (not necessarily a reflective synthesis) of a vast composite of modified basic feelings, perceptions, mental conducts, memories, internalized social regulation, that have personal and shared meanings and prolongations in the social and symbolic world.

Semiotic Regulations of Emotions

Janet was not so much interested in categories of emotions than in the processes in which these are involved—*regulation* processes (Janet, 1928; 1935). The regulations are bi-directional; on the one hand, emotions modify one's conducts at various levels, perceptions, actions, and thoughts. Basic emotions, such as fatigue or sadness, regulate conducts as well as complex emotions that result from internalized pattern of behavior. On the other hand, generalizations of conducts, reflective thoughts, and secondary emotions regulate emotional experiences and, thus, the whole conduct.

A closer look to these complex and looping emotional regulations will highlight their social, cultural, and symbolic nature and thus, the social and cultural nature of conducts.

First of all, life-preserving instincts such as self-love and love for others can be seen as having a social origin. Hence, some feelings are to actions what a person's warnings are to a child's action (1935: 101). A trace of this external origin of regulation can be observed in Janet's patient who mumbles to herself, with a particular voice: "you are thirsty, so drink a bit"—and thus takes care of herself as another would do. On the contrary, the sudden absence of a person assuring such an external regulation can bring the abandoned person to self-hatred (Janet, 1926).

Then, a person's emotional regulations can be expressed so as to be readable by others and shared with them. Janet, thus, identified various semiotic forms that mediate relationships and that enable someone to awake in someone else a similar thought, intention, or action (Janet, 1936).

Language is one semiotic way of sharing feelings. Conscious feelings can be the objects of deliberate expressions to others, with the aim of touching or moving them. Yet, language is imprecise; it is more efficient to formulate actions that are already shared than to catch internal regulations. It is also often socially marked in a way that renders personal uses difficult. But this difficulty should not be overlooked. Janet described how his patients develop complex metaphors when trying to express their feelings. These attempts have their function: numerous attempts of expressing a feeling through various metaphors might contribute to specifying a feeling and to transform it (Janet, 1926).

Hence, the manipulation of semiotic means—even in a clumsy "trial-and-error" manner—is part of the person's work of grasping his or her emotions and contributes to their reflective regulation. This point is particularly clear in Janet's (1935) presentation of play as a way through which a person can transform his or her emotional state. Against cathartic models of play, he observes how a child, exhausted after a school day, might recover all her energy after half an hour of play (1928, 1935).[14]

On a social level, art offers other semiotic mediations of emotions. Discussing the work of artists and the reception of art, Janet (1936) saw symbols as enabling relational acts between emotions. The poet's symbolic work allows the reader to establish new relations between memories, images, and emotions and to construct a new composite that enables him to feel the emotion intended by the artist. Thus, semiotic means in general, and not only language, participates to personal and social regulations of emotions.

Through semiotic mediations, the social and the personal become deeply intermeshed and mutually constitutive—as Janet showed in his analysis of the role of beliefs in the regulation of emotions. Janet defined *beliefs* as forms of representations, without necessary link to the real, which can be socially shared. Beliefs triggered as secondary conducts modify people's primary actions and thus their perception. It thus transforms emotions themselves:

> Objects, people, situations become interesting or insignificant, real or unreal, sacrilege, dangerous, ugly, amoral, catastrophic or flattering, advantageous, superb, etc. This coloration that the feelings confers to things becomes one of the most important component of beliefs. (Janet, 1927/2001: 111-112)

Emotions coupled with beliefs that have a necessary interpersonal, social, or symbolic dimension modify a person and his or her world. In effect, on the one hand, feelings can become objectified and perceived as being characteristics of the world—as when one says: "everything in this house is ignoble, ugly and dirty; everything is sad and lugubrious" (Janet, 1928b: 297). On the other hand, feelings that are not attributed to external objects become parts of the intimacy of the person.

Finally, the social domain enters in the regulation of emotions at a higher level of generalization. Beliefs can themselves be objects of reflection. This is where they become general regulating ideas, such as the idea of the difficulty of work, success, or luxury. These higher-level socially shared semiotic means regulate both beliefs and emotions.

At the higher levels, "rational" and "experimental" beliefs—that is, regulations that come from the socially produced science—finally replace and suppress strong personal feelings. In effect, explains Janet, rational and experimental conducts have to be undertaken by all human beings in the same way, and a scientist has to make abstraction of his feelings. Hence, laws such as rules of religion, moral, or logic can finally replace emotions as regulatory principles (Janet, 1928: 158).

The dynamic and hierarchical nature of emotional conducts leads logically to an interactive developmental understanding of conducts. Janet indicated microgenetic as well as ontogenetic development.

Firstly, emotional composites can be generalized within a person, either applying to a wide range of situations, or as automatic answers. Secondly, as a given person regulates some situations in a certain way, others with whom he or she interacts might react in a constant way; she or he would then adjust her or himself to the others' reactions. Social emotional regulations, thus, are part of the construction of one's personality. Third, conducts change with age: older persons are, for Janet, involved in more generalized conducts and spend less time in the torments of primary feelings.

To summarize, Janet saw emotions as including modifications of the perceptual systems and of the inner organic state, but also behavioral reactions, related memories and thoughts, and situational and personal constraints. In Janet's definition of emotions in the whole of conducts, dynamics of emotions can occur at four levels: one primary layer of basic feelings (positive or negative, with or without activation) can be seen as the embodied consequences of modifications of the conditions of the conduct; second, these can be apprehended mentally; third, these first modifications evoke secondary conducts, memories, echoes of other situations, and their social and cultural prolongations and their emotional tonalities; fourth, these composites can be reflectively identified and synthesized—as a complex emotion, as part of one's regulation or reorientation of actions, thoughts, and emotions. Each of these levels can be regulated by semiotic mediations, as well as modify the whole of the conduct.

With this centrality of emotions in conducts and its developmental orientation, Janet's theory of emotions corresponds to the *Ganzheits* agenda. However, in contrast, Pierre Janet refuses to see the social and the cultural as abstract entities. He rather examines these as constitutive of conducts from *within*, through internalized patterns of conducts and semiotic regulations. These characteristics—developmental and semiotic orientation, centrality of emotions, complex conducts—are what might turn Janet's model into a resource to address current problems in psychology.

Whole Conducts Today

Pierre Janet had a double agenda—reunifying the diversity of psychological research and giving a model of human conduct as a whole. His model has not been retained by psychology as a unifying frame, not even in the limits of researches on emotions. That field has indeed been for a long time concentrated on the division and the relation between emotion and cognition (Piaget, 1954; 1964; Oatley, 2001; Kahneman, 2003; Schnall & Laird, 2003; Laird, 2007); mainstream psychologists are currently trying to define ways to unify their field and empirical data. Although they come to propose hierarchies of conducts (Izard, 1993) and distinctions between primary and secondary emotions (Lambie & Marcel, 2002; Russell, 2003), they do not mention Janet and mostly ignore that these issues have been addressed by him and others in the past.[15]

Nevertheless, cultural psychology and theories of action are currently engaged in a work of defining ways of accounting for complex phenomena, hence, rejoining Janet's second objective. In that respect, I want to examine how Janet's hierarchical model, his theory of emotions, and his developmental and semiotic orientation can contribute to our understanding of everyday cultural experiences.

As mentioned in my introduction, one of the challenges of psychological inquiry today is to account for people's everyday interactions with cultural objects in their symbolically saturated environments. Developing children do not only interact with elders and peers; they spend increasing time interacting with virtual worlds, through complicated machines, religious participations, and various cultural experiences ranging from listening to downloaded music, to visiting interactive museums, reading novels, and seeing 3-D movies. These cultural experiences trigger complex dynamics of perceiving, feeling, understanding, and interpreting.[16]

Given their importance in everyday life, cultural experiences necessarily participate to the development of the person and the making of individual and shared meanings. We thus need a more holistic understanding of cultural experiences. Can Janet's model help us to frame these phenomena?

As Janet proposed, one criterion to evaluate a theory is to test its power to account for empirical facts. I will thus apply Janet's model of complex conducts and emotions to an empirical vignette.[17]

* * *

At the time she was <u>interviewed</u>, Lily was in a period of uncertainty during which she had to decide what to do the following year—whether to study or not, whether to work, in which country to live, etc. Asked whether she had seen any noticeable movie during that period, she answered[18]:

> Something is a movie I watched, about—and it is recent, it must have been the first days of September, I thing it was called *After-life*—it is a Japanese movie . . . they end up.. it is like an immigration office, and they have to pick up a memory. . . and it is all about the selection process . . . So you have young people, you have old people, and all kind of people. And it is all about this process, you know, about going, choosing, and being able or not able to choose, and these people who are unable to choose, xx so they are stuck there, for centuries. I always think of that—I think about that often for a reason or another. I've thought about it the other day, just a couple of days ago—but I can't remember xxx. It is interesting, because when I watched that movie, I didn't think automatically what would I choose. But the people I was watching the movie with, just asked me xxxx—what would I choose, I really don't know—it would be sort of logical, but I didn't ask myself xxx . . . I think about [this example] because—when death comes in memory . . . xx I think about it when I think about sorts of life . . . about relative happiness, and the difference between being content, and not, or having lots of energy, or not much energy. I mean all these things I have been thinking for a long time, it is a schedule for life. So every time these things come out, and because I am thinking about the future quite a lot right now, and about people, whether they are staying my life or not staying in my life. xxx Because how people choose their memories, has a lot to do with how people choose their lives.

Applying Janet's hierarchical model, let me identify some involved dynamics of emotional regulation and of semiotic mediation. This movie belongs to "independent cinema"; for Lily to see it with her friends is a social conduct, guided by symbolic rules, and expressing some personal choices. It is seen with friends—and is, thus, part of the regulation of these relationships. It had a "strong" effect on Lily during watching. It was, for one part, an emotion "choc"—but created in a non-real space, that is, with the gratuity offered by play. In that space, Lily engaged in a perceptual suite of conducts, which have their emotional impact, and which might awaken secondary conducts.

In effect, the story of *After-life* is located in a strange school; characters wear brown uniforms, furniture is metallic and anonymous, and the ambiance is dusty and faded. We see offices in which young and old people sit in front of what appears to be civil servants, trying to answer their difficult questions—they have to choose something. Slowly, through the strangeness of the dialogues, thinking about the title, we understand what it is about, and why these persons seem to have such difficulty answering. These people are dead and have been asked to choose their best memories. The civil servants will recreate it for them, and people will be sent to stay within that memory for all eternity.

We can reasonably think that Lily, perceiving such images and experiencing various bodily and physiological changes by having memories triggered by various cues, was experiencing a specific emotional state (inferior conducts). The semiotic organization of the movie—in which the viewer perceives changing colors, décor, childhood, and dream-like qualities—implies various relational acts. These might awake memories as secondary emotions with their own qualities.

After having seen the movie, Lily's friends pushed her to reflect upon her own experiences; this offered a social "drain," an external regulation sustaining the tension to operate synthetic acts on her experience. This lead her to try to express what the movie had been for her; that is, she used language and its approximations, both to articulate and modify her own emotions and thoughts (inferior and higher conducts), and to offer them in social exchange (middle conducts). During these attempts, she might have reflected upon these relations themselves and realized that the embarrassment, confusion, incertitude of the characters might have captured and reflected quite precisely her own apprehensions—having to choose where and what to study.

But the movie adds something more to her questions. It frames issues of choices in terms of "afterlife." They are formulated not only as "what do I want," but elevated in terms of "what is a good life," that is, at the level of values and commitments (higher conducts). Thanks to the relation Lily creates between the film and her life through "choosing one's memories is choosing one's life," Lily can consider her fears, thoughts, and future projects in terms of these higher-level values. Now, Lily adopts a canalized, unified reading of her thoughts and fears: questions of choices of studies (middle conducts) are solved within the boundaries fixed by higher principles, and they become oriented towards an aim—to have a good life. Primary emotional states are apprehended through synthetic acts; these are named "contentment" and "low energy." Then, thanks to higher regulatory principles, Lily's life gets a unity and a goal orientation: the past memories—those of sadness—are turned into a future where one can be content and have energy. Finally, often recalling that movie, Lily appeared to have internalized its high-level regulatory support.

For a while, then, Lily uses that movie as a complex symbolic resource (Zittoun et al., 2003; Zittoun, 2006; 2007) that allows her to confer some unity and orientation to the diversity of her changing experience, and thus, to change her world.

* * *

Through this brief analysis, I have sketched one way to use Janet's theoretical tools to analyze the complexity and mutability of contemporary cultural experiences.

A Future for Conducts as a Whole?

As it was the case a century ago, psychology is specialized in investigating infinities of sub-aspects of human behavior. As a consequence, it becomes very difficult to unify this knowledge in order to understand everyday situations; these then appear redoubtably complex.

To account for persons' thinking, feeling, and doing in changing, multiple, real, and virtual symbolic networks, holistic theoretical models are required. The model proposed by Janet enables one to analyze the complexity of human conduct without reducing it to either of its aspects—mental or social, abstract or embodied—while also showing its constant evolution. The semiotic orientation of the model confers to it a surprising modernity; and Janet's exploration of a wide range of themes—fiction, pathology, or everyday life—have shown the flexibility of a model open to evolution through the confrontation with new case studies. Thus, Janet's hierarchy of conducts might help us to a more sounded understanding of the complexities of everyday situations.

Notes

1.   This chapter has been enabled by a research grant from the Swiss National Research Fund, a Corpus Christi Research Fellowship (Cambridge), and the kind hospitality of the Frances Hiatt School of Psychology and the Goddard Library at Clark University (Worcester, MA). My special thanks go to Rainer Diriwächter and Jaan Valsiner for their invitation to explore Janet's work and their guidance. Lastly, I would also like to thank Rosemarie Sokol, Sarah Strout, and the participants of the Evolution & Culture Seminar for their feedback.
2.   Contact address: Institut de psychologie et éducation, FLSH, Université de Neuchâtel, Louis Agassiz, CH-2000 Neuchâtel, Switzerland. Email: Tania.zittoun@unine.ch
3.   I will ignore other aspects of his work—his theory of the unconscious in link with Freud, as well as his therapeutic propositions. About their relevance for modern therapeutic of trauma, see van der Kolk & van der Hart, 1989.
4.   He seems to have been the guest of two series of lectures at Clark University in 1904 and 1906, before Freud (Koelsch, 1984; unconfirmed information).
5.   Examining the genesis of symbolic thinking and language, Janet (1934a, 1934b) mentions the promising work of the young Piaget. He also never fails to add that it would be better if the observed children would talk less!
6.   He indicates in his autobiographical notes that his clinical observations constitute his most important work (1930). Here, I cannot do justice to this work.
7.   See Valsiner and van der Veer (2000) for a presentation following the historical evolution of the work.
8.   "Not necessarily be analyzed" is Janet's formulation; it, thus, prudently refuses to decide between Wundt's and Volkelt's propositions.

9. This parallelism cannot be strictly explained. It is not clear how much Janet had first-hand access to German literature. Of course, Janet knew German authors (such as Külpe, Stumpf, or Wundt) through Ribot's writing (Janet, 1928). He had access to the papers of authors that have been translated for the *Journal de Psychologie* and other French and English journals (for instance, Külpe, 1910), and he met some German authors at international symposiums, such as the Wittenberg symposiums on emotions (Reymert, 1928). He included German works in his 1929 review of theories of emotions and devoted a chapter to discuss Gestalt theory (1935: 232-256). Janet pointed out the fact that German psychologists did not sufficiently distinguish between a *Gestalt* "in the world" and a *Gestalt* as perceived by an observer. Janet also considered that the definition of *form* was too loose. It applied to a too-wide range of situations (class of objects, concepts) and was therefore imprecise, hiding, for example, that the motive-ground relation examined by Gestalt authors is just a sub-case of container-content relationships. To show the weakness of the notion of form, Janet gave an example: the "form" of a plum needs also the "matter" of a plum to be recognized as a plum; matter and form are part of the "scheme of the plum." The "conduct of the plum" includes the apprehension of matter, form, and notion that must have been mentally put in relation. One would not try eating a plum in paper (form, not matter); and one knows that plum marmalade is not a plum (matter, not form). Therefore, *Gestalts* are not enough to account for conduct. For a discussion of Janet's reading of Gestalt theory, see Sjövall 1967: 68-69. Janet's explicit theoretical affiliations go, rather, to Henri Bergson (Janet, 1935, 1936), William James (with whom he has kept a correspondence over the years), John Dewey, and James Baldwin. It is probably more on the basis of American pragmatism that Janet develops his dynamic theory of emotions as central and in constant evolution and rearrangement. Hence, if Janet's work can be seen as a French holistic approach to psychology and as sharing many properties with the second Leipzig laboratory, it is not certain that this proximity is intentional.

10. All references: my translation from French—except Janet, 1928b.

11. The model was reworked through most of Janet's lectures and writings. I choose to present the tripartite models presented in the two volumes of *De l'angoisse à l'extase* (1926 and 1928) and in a later summary of the hierarchical model in *Les débuts de l'intelligence* (1935).

12. Janet's propositions will be largely developed by Piaget (1954, 1964)—especially the ones regarding the thresholds between types of conducts. Piaget retains them as an ontogenetic succession, whereas Janet seemed to have a more broader project (and more speculative).

13. First convinced by the James-Lange Theory of Emotions, Janet will progressively move away from it, addressing all the objections it raised (Janet, 1928 for an account).

14. As Freud (1908), Janet emphasized the continuity of play and some of adult's experiences—especially his relationship to art. For Janet, playing is pleasurable before anything else; it is "gratuitous," does not have any aim within the real and allows one to explore possibilities and to live experiences and emotions that have no place in the reality—all while being highly economical. All the negative sides and consequences of such actions in real life are avoided. This economy is part of the overall positive (mood enhancer and re-energizing) effect of playing conducts. This view lead Janet to argue fiercely against any pedagogic canalization of children's play (1935).

15. These approaches do not avoid the two dangers that Janet had indicated: they are philosophical, or mostly physiological (looking for emotions in neurons), or they

ignore the fundamental symbolic nature of human conduct. There are, however, a few important integrative theoretical elaborations of emotions that keep a holistic character. See in particular Valsiner, 2004; Magai & Haviland-Jones, 2002; and De Rivera, 1983.

16. Promoters of these artifacts often have their consumers' emotions as their target. Correspondingly, psychologists have mostly examined the effect of these cultural experiences on people's behavior, and, in particular, on socially condemnable behavior; violence is thus understood as a consequence of the emotional load of cultural experiences, and cognitive responses are often seen as a way to overcome these emotional dangers.

17. This extract is part of a research project on young people's symbolic resources in transitions, enabled by a European Marie Curie Research Fellowship and a Corpus Christi (Cambridge, UK) Research Fellowship (Zittoun, 2006).

18. "xxx" indicates unclear word.

References

Delabarre, E.-B. (1894). "Les laboratoires de psychologie en Amérique." *L'année psychologique*, I, 14: 209-255.

De Rivera, J. (1983). "Biological necessity, emotional transformation and personal Value." In S. Koch & D. E. Leary, *A Century of Psychology as Science* (pp. 364-389). New York: McGraw-Hill Book Company.

Diriwächter, R. (2003). "What really matters: keeping the whole." Paper presented at the 10th Biennale conference for the International Society for theoretical psychology, Istanbul. June 24, 2003.

Diriwächter, R. (2003b). "The forgotten connection: Völkerpsychologie and Ganzheitspychologie." Draft paper. Worcester: Clark University.

Diriwächter, R. (2003c). "Ganzheit & Feelings: A series of investigations into the processes of psychological synthesis." PhD Dissertation proposal. Worcester: Clark University.

Diriwächter, R. (2004). "Völkerpsychologie: The synthesis that never was." *Culture & Psychology*, 10 (1): 85-109.

Freud, S. (1908/1985). "Creative writers and day-dreaming." In *The Pelican Freud Library,* vol. 14 (pp. 131-141). New York: Penguin Books. (S. E., 9, 141-153).

Izard, C. E. (1993). "Four systems for emotion activation. Cognitive and noncognitive processes." *Psychological review*, 100, (1): 68-90.

James, W. (1884). "What is an emotion?" *Mind,* 9, 34: 188-205.

Janet, P. (1926/2001). *De l'angoisse à l'extase*. Tome I. Paris : Librairie Félix Alcan. Republished: http://www.uqac.uquebec.ca/zone30/Classiques_des_sciences_sociales/index.html

Janet, P. (1928/2001) *De l'angoisse à l'extase*. Tome II. Paris : Librairie Félix Alcan. Republished: http://www.uqac.uquebec.ca/zone30/Classiques_des_sciences_sociales/index.html

Janet, P. (1928b). "Fear of action as an essential element in the sentiment of melancholia." In M. L. Reymert (Ed). (1928). *Feelings and emotions. The Wittenberg Symposium* (pp. 297-309). Worcester (MA): Clark University Press.

Janet, P. (1930/2000). "Autobiography of Pierre Janet." In C. Murchison (Ed). *History of Psychology in Autobiography,* Vol. 1 (pp. 123-133). Worcester: Clark University Press. Republished: http://psychlassics.yorku.ca/Janet/murchison.htm

Janet, P. (1934/1935). *Les débuts de l'intelligence*. Paris: Flammarion.

Janet, P. (1934b/1936/2003). *L'intelligence avant le langage*. Paris: Flammarion. Republished: http://www.uqac.uquebec.ca/zone30/Classiques_des_sciences_sociales/index.html

Kahneman, D. (2003). "A perspective on judgment and choice: Mapping bounded rationality." *American Psychologist*, 58, (9): 697-720.

Koelsch, W. A. (1984). *"Incredible Day-Dream": Freud and Jung at Clark, 1909*. Worcester: Clark University, The Friends of the Goddard Library.

Külpe, O. (1910). "Pour la psychologie des sentiments." *Journal de Psychologie Normale et Pathologique*, 7: 1-13.

Laird, J. D. (2007). *Feelings: The perception of self*. New York: Oxford University Press.

Lambie, J. O., Marcel, A. J. (2002). "Consciousness an the varieties of emotional experiences: A theoretical framework." *Psychological review*, 109, 2: 219-259.

Magai, C. & Haviland-Jones, J. (2002). *The hidden genius of emotion. Lifespan transformations of personality*. Cambridge: Cambridge University Press.

Meyerson, I. (1947). "Pierre Janet et la théorie des tensions." *Journal de psychologie normale et pathologique*, 40: 5-19.

Oatley, K. (2001). "Emotions in cognition." In *International Encyclopedia for Social and Behaviorial sciences*, (pp. 4440-4444). Elsevier.

Piaget, J. (1954/1981). *Intelligence and affectivity: Their relationship during Child Development*. Palo Alto: Annual Review Inc.

Piaget, J. (1964 /1966). *Six études de psychologie*. Paris: Denoël/Gonthier.

Reymert, M. L. (Ed). (1928). *Feelings and emotions. The Wittenberg Symposium*. Worcester, MA: Clark University Press.

Russell, J. A. (2003). "Core affect and the psychological construction of emotion." *Psychological review*, 110, 1: 145-172.

Schnall, S. & Laird, J. D. (2003). "Keep smiling: Enduring effects of facial expressions and postures in emotional experiences and memory." *Cognition and emotion*, 17: 787-797.

Sjövall, B. (1967). *Psychology of tension. An analysis of Pierre Janet's concept of "tension psychologique" together with an historical aspect*. Nortedts: Svenska Bokförlaget.

Valsiner, J. & van der Veer, R. (2000). "Pierre Janet's world of tensions." In: *The social mind: construction of an idea* (pp.61-137). Cambridge/New York: Cambridge University Press.

Valsiner, J. (2005). "Soziale une emotionale Entwicklungsaufgaben im Kulturellen Kontext." In J. Asendorpf & H. Rauh. (Eds). *Soziale, emotionale une Persönlichketisentwicklung*. (Bd. 3 Entwicklungspychologie—Enzyklopädie der Psychologie). Göttingen : Hogrefe, 677-728.

Van der Kolk, B. A. & van der Hart, O. (1989). "Pierre Janet and the breakdown of adaptation in psychological trauma." *American Journal of Psychiatry*, 146, (12): 1530-1540.

Zittoun, T., Duveen, G., Gillespie, A., Ivinson, G. & Psaltis, C. (2003). "The uses of symbolic resources in transitions." *Culture & Psychology,* 9 (4): 415-448.

Zittoun, T. (2006). *Transitions. Development through symbolic resources.* Coll. Advances in Cultural Psychology: Constructing Development. Greenwich, CT: InfoAge.

Zittoun, T. (2007). "The role of symbolic resources in human lives." In J. Valsiner & A. Rosa, (Eds). *Cambridge handbook of Socio-Cultural Psychology* (pp. 343-361). Cambridge: Cambridge University Press.

8

Ernst E. Boesch's Holistic Cultural Psychology

Lívia Mathias Simão
University of São Paulo, Brazil

My aim in this chapter is to put in dialogue two fields of ideas in psychological knowledge, the *Ganzheits*-psychological thought and the cultural psychology of Ernst E. Boesch. Concerning to the first field, I will take advantage of Diriwächter's systematization and discussion (2004; see also Chapter 3). Concerning to the second, I will be basing my analysis mainly on Boesch's Symbolic Action Theory (Boesch, 1991).[1]

What follows should be understood as an integrative effort to highlight some holistic aspects of Boesch's cultural psychology, aiming to collaborate to the constructive return to *Ganzheitspsychologie*, as proposed by Valsiner (2004).

The Four Theses of *Ganzheitspsychologie*

The *first thesis* of *Ganzheitpsychologie* advocated by the second school of Leipzig proposes that the definition of a whole should be done "through the lack of obvious parts, that is through the non reducibility of the whole" (see Diriwächter, Chapter 3). This is so because the parts of a whole "are not independent of one another and do not merely relate to each other, rather *they are interwoven in to each other*" (Diriwächter, 2004; see also Diriwächter, Chapter 3), leading to the nature of the whole as simultaneously functional (processual) and structural.

The *second thesis* states that feelings are the central experiential qualities of human beings and not secondary at all. As social beings, we have an inherent disposition for feeling states that address us as a whole and affects our consciousness, which by its turn, impacts on our human character (cf. Diriwächter, Chapter 3).

The *third thesis* touches on the issue of life as continuous development through the process of transformations of synthesis. There is an overarching "drivenness" of the totality into a certain direction, whose changes can be understood genetically. Changes are dynamically linked and integrated in a uniform whole, where the interacting components are quantitatively different (cf. Diriwächter, Chapter 3).

The *fourth thesis* touches to the notion of structure, stating that it is hierarchical organized according to holistically related forces, giving to the structure its frame. Each actual hierarchical organization encompasses a transformative synthesis of the previous states of the structure (cf. Diriwächter, Chapter 3).

Boesch's Theory Revisited[2] from the Perspective of *Ganzheitspsychologie*

For Boesch, cultural psychology is necessarily a holistic enterprise; it should concentrate itself in "human action within its systemic anchoring," where the function and impact of each action changes according to its place in the whole field. Additionally, he emphasizes the belongingness of his cultural psychology to the field of "molar studies"; from this perspective, the psychological knowledge construction only based upon "observable behavior" is not enough. It is necessary to take into account the subject-actor's[3] "experienced meaning" assessed by introspection (cf. Boesch, 1991: 17-18).

Boesch's notion of *culture* is central in his ideas. According to him,

Culture is a field of action, whose contents range from objects made and used by human beings to institutions, ideas and myths. Being an action field, culture offers possibilities of, but by the same token stipulates conditions for, action; it circumscribes goals, which can be reached by certain means, but establishes limits, too, for correct, possible and also deviant action. The relationship between the different material as well as ideational contents of the cultural field of action is a *systemic one; i e., transformations in one part of the system can have an impact in any other part. As an action field, culture not only induces and controls action, but is also continuously transformed by it; therefore, culture is as much as a process as a structure.*" (Boesch, 1991: 29; my emphasis)

Summarizing his theory, Boesch has stated the three basic assumptions on which his cultural psychology rests:

Culture psychology rests on three basic assumptions. First, culture is a system of reference, meaning that every item or event in a *cultural* field relates to other items or events. . . . The second assumption is that the *individual* acts in a cultural field and doing so progressively constructs a personal history. . . . Finally, action, in as far as it is taken in pursuit of a goal, aims at *future states* of the individual and his or her situation. . . . These three "systems" of reference—cultural, biographical and anticipatory—constitute the pool from which action derives its symbolic qualities (as to my use of the word "symbol", see, Boesch, 1991). (Boesch, 2001)

Boesch's main formulation of the notion of culture and the three basic assumptions above summarized show us the possibility of trying to establish a dialogue between Boesch's *Symbolic Action Theory* and *Ganzheitspsychologie*.

Boesch addresses us to the systemic and processual nature of culture as a system of reference. The same holist relation can be seen concerning tó the relationship between culture and subject's action. In both cases, the non-reducibility of the whole is at stake. Transformations happen in a bi-directional systemic way through symbolic action (culture ↔ action), having impact in the whole structure. Besides, symbolic action is oriented to the anticipation of desired future states, bringing in the prime and regulatory character of feelings. In such an extent, the subject-actor continuously constructs his/her biography through symbolically acting according to the possibilities and limits of the cultural field system while also transforming it in the systemic relation to other subject-actors.

In what follows, I will detail some aspects of Boesch's theoretical construction trying to illustrate its just mentioned holist belongingness.

The Culture-Individual-Culture[4] Holistic Cycle

Boesch's Symbolic Action Theory has the interrelated concepts of *culture*, *action* (implying a *subject-actor*), and *object* as its tripod.

Departing from a critic view of Kroeber and Kluckhohn anthropological formulation of culture, Boesch goes to a more Lewinian conception where culture is conceived as a bi-directional regulating field for the subject-actor's action.

In his conception, culture acts as a constraining field for action. Culture suggests possible goals, gives opportunities, but also puts barriers, points to limits and dangers for actions, and establishes taboo zones for them. Culture is then a field of dynamic zones of symbolic grounding for action, which allows for their enhancement or interdiction, also encompassing limits of tolerance for them.

Through his/her symbolic culturally grounded actions, each subject acts meaningfully in the cultural field. His/her actions—in the dynamic of meanings constructed by other subject-actors, in present and past times, here and there—can become part of the cultural field at some moment.

Nevertheless, subject-actors are not always conscious of the opportunities and limits offered by their cultural field at some moment and "part of the individual's growing up in his culture consists precisely in *discovering* such unknown action possibilities—probably without ever discovering all of them" (Boesch, 1991: 32).[5]

These dynamic features of the culture-individual-culture cycle can be illustrated taking a piece of a popular narrative of the Brazilian myth of *Curupira* for a brief analysis.[6]

It is an indigenous myth, already known in the times of the Portuguese arrival to Brazil in 1500. The myth story refers an enchanted being (the *Curupira*) who, according to believers, lives in the forests. Curupira protects the forests and animals from ravagers and hunters who kill the animals only for the fun of chasing. His is pictured as boy with a furry figure and red hair, with green teeth. His main feature is his reversed feet. The usual punishment inflicted by *Curupira* is getting people lost in the forest. Because of his reversed feet, he succeeds in disorienting the hunters with his false *rasto*.

A researcher who invited a participant to talk about the enchanted beings dwelling in the regional folk imaginarium collected the following piece of narrative:

> *Interviewer:* Well, have you already heard, you know, about *Curupira*? Here in Belém, we have always heard about it, isn't that so? People also talk about those... those enchanted beings, isn't that right?
> *Narrator:* Ya, ya ! *Curupira* also enchants. *Curupira* also enchants people; don't you see what she does? We are in the forest; we know all the ways we have to take, right? Then all of a sudden, things fade away. We do not know . . . Moving around without knowing how to come back. It is she who is doing that to us. I . . . I was eleven years old. I had gone to catch crabs. My, my father always likes to be careful about us, little children. We went along with him. When we got there, we knew that our father was on that side. Then we got lost; my sister and I were lost. But it was so easy just to get there! Can you imagine?! In that small piece of land we were . . . Walking there, wrong way. Walking here, wrong way. It was she who was joking about us.
> (In Simões and Golder, 1995; my translation from Portuguese)

According to the perspective here in focus, human subjectivity is constructed based on the personal cognitive-affective elaborations of cultural suggestions. From this perspective, we can say that the collective culture (Valsiner, 1998) is actualized, in our illustration, through the enchanted beings of the Brazilian folk mythology. The folk mythology of the enchanted beings is then a semiotic organizer of the narrator's personal experience, who found herself *unwonted*[7] lost in a place where "*it should be easy to be situated.*"

In this kind of process, referred as the *knowledge cycle* of culture-individual-culture by Boesch (1992), there is interplay among selective perception, transformation, and integration of messages. In such a way the cultural suggestions can fit, to some extent, the individual cognitive-affective and "actional" structures. Thus, the mythical stories are always changing over the time in order to account for the particular aspects of the different and successive personal experiences. For instance, taking our illustration, the story told by the narrator's grandmother or mother would probably have some different details from the story she is now telling to the interviewer.

On the other hand and simultaneously, some aspects of the personal experience are more or less noted, emphasized, explained, and, above all, *felt and assessed* in the sight of the mythical story. In such a way, some aspects attain a more prominent meaning if compared to others, sometimes even excluding others: getting lost in a well-known place would not be the same experience—in its subjective existential sense—in the light of another myth.

To give meaning is closely related to make distinctions, which are demanded by experiences that are disquieting in face of the semantic field the person has developed. We are referring here to the distinction between *what something is as it appears to us* and *what something should be in our thinking, liking, desiring* as I discussed elsewhere (Simão, 2003). In our illustration, to be situated in a well-known place is something given for granted and it is put against the disquieting feeling of not being situated. By comparison, the latter feeling acquires a reality that should be signified in the organization of the actor's personal experience.

The myth of the enchanted *Curupira* offers itself as a possibility for the personal elaboration, suggesting a way for reorganizing the experience in face of the new element, since it allows the emergence of a relational meaning. The unexpected difference between *what the experience should be* and *what it was*, in Boeschian terms, is explained by the fact that *Curupira* is used to joke about people. In this extent, the socio-cultural suggestion is actually experienced. At the same time, the myth is transformatively internalized in the personal culture.

Last but not least, the folk myth, when becoming part of the personal culture in the form of a mythical story, has its veracity strengthened and its versions updated and contemporarily tuned. By this process, its permanence is kept throughout the times. Myths are narrated in a polyphonic dialogue (Bakhtin, 1986; Holquist, 1990) by the voices of the otherness. There is someone who keeps the group wisdom and comes from the past to talk in the present situation to the other who still needs to know something more. That someone from the past, through the mythical narrative, designs possibilities and limits about the I-world relationships to the other. This latter, on his/her side, actively listens—i. e., transformatively appropriates the narrated content.

A dialogue between past and present is then established, channeling future experiences. Here we have one of the roles of the imagined other in the narrative construction of the world by the self, as pointed out by Hermans (1996). Retracing the myth with the help of her ancestors, the narrator could give an understandable organization to her disquieting experience—at the same time keeping the images of her father, sister, and herself as owning a tacit knowledge (locating themselves in the forest).

In short, Boesch's theory brings in a subject-actor whose development happens by discovering opportunities and limits for acting in his/her cultural field. These actions—in the dynamic field of others' actions—can create newness in the dynamic cultural field.

In such an extent, Boesch does not conceive culture as some "independent macro-variable" directly determining the individual's behavior; nor does he conceive the individual-culture bi-directional transformations as if they were unlimited.

On the one side, the subject-actor is selective concerning the perception, transformation, and integration of cultural information, seeking to fit them in to his/her already existing structure of symbolic action. This selective movement happens according to the mechanisms of assimilation and accommodation, as postulated by Jean Piaget. However, the relevance of action in this structural-genetic process of individual development is greater than in Piaget's account. According to Boesch (1991),

> should we want to look at individually or culturally different results of construction processes, we cannot divorce them from the experiences on which they are based. Action thus becomes a concept of much greater importance than Piaget ever ascribed to it. (p. 10)

Differences in attribution to the importance of the action concept—between Piaget and Boesch, as pointed by the latter—can be understood as a consequence of their different approaches to the role of individuality and culture in the processes of knowledge construction. This difference, in turn, addresses to another: their differences respect to the role of affectivity and emotion in the genesis of what is peculiar to each of us, that is, in the genesis of our individuality.[8]

On the other side, the cultural field also produces a mechanism of self-preservation, filtering the innovations created and proposed by the individual's symbolic action, balancing stability and change, and so avoiding its shredding (Boesch, 1992).

In such an extent, Boesch proposes "culture" as a construct aiming to focus structure and process, stability and transformation. This structural process encompasses the behaviors for "feeling good, feeling at home," which are more tacitly experienced than consciously realized. Boesch's option implies the *emic* perspective of understanding cultural processes, where the researcher tries to understand the process from the subject-actor's perspective. This perspective is emphasized by Boesch and counter-posed by him to a more reflected experience with culture (cf. Boesch. 1991: 38), implying the *etic* perspective of understanding cultural process, where the researcher looks for universal aspects that can only be grasped from an outside observer's view.[9]

The Action-Object Holistic Relationship in the Cultural Field

The concept of "object" has a twofold centrality in Boesch's theory: objects, either concrete or imaginary, not only form culture but are also demanded for action. According to Boesch, "action and object cannot be separated but: every action has an object (which is but an imaginary one) and every object is defined by its actional value" (Boesch, 1980: 23-24, my translation from French).[10]

Almost paradoxically, although they cannot be strictly separated, action and object can be experienced as two separated instances. This happens thanks to our perception of distinctiveness of internal world as we realize that our actions are originated from us as active agents from external world (we realize that the objects on which we act upon have their existence independent of us).

This twofold way of experiencing reality leads to two kinds of developmental structuring of the reality (Boesch, 1980: 24). On the one hand, there is the "objective" structuring that happens according to the factual, instrumental, and spatial-temporal qualities we experience as "real" and outside of us, allowing to communicative sharing and social coordination (for instance, we can think of a CD on a shelf which subject-actor A asks a subject-actor B to bring to him/her, and B brings it). On the other hand, there is the subjective structuring that comes into being through actions and situations that are meaningful to our "I–world" relationship (Boesch, 1997: 426). For instance, we can think about the meanings that specific CD has for A, because he/she has listened to it in some pleasant situation, and now he/she wants to symbolically bring in again that situation for sharing it with B. Hence, the subject-actor A can experience all objects as having a double quality: their objective-rational aspect, which is socially shared, and their subjective-functional aspect that is loaded with personal meaning and that sometimes can be shared but sometimes cannot—this happens at different "levels" with the other B (for instance, while bringing the CD, B can say "that's nice," "I know," "I'm glad," or "why that? Let's listen to another."

This symbolic I–world relationship allows to the subject-actor to act upon the object in ways of structuring it according to personal meanings. In this symbolic actional process, however, the meaning of the structured object will also be dependent on the possibilities of its symbolically anchoring in the whole cultural field.[11]

Hence, action and object are practically inseparable: every action is directed to an object and each object acquires meaning due to the action directed to it (see Boesch, 1980: 23-24). As every action implies a subject-actor, and action and object are inseparable, so subject and object are also inseparable. In such an extent the subject-actor and the object compose a dyad in which each one defines the other, however, without a fusion that would render them indistinguishable—as they are in the epistemological model of subject/object inseparability. On the contrary, inclusive separation, as postulated by Valsiner (1998), is implied here; subject-actor and object are simultaneously active parts of the system delimiting one another; that is, the relationship between them is itself one of the parts of the system and is essential to the understanding of its constitution (cf. Valsiner, 1998: 15-16).

This kind of subject-object relationship has some remarkable features. As far as the subject-actor is continuously acting upon objects—and there are multiple social actors constantly and simultaneously doing that—each subject-actor's action is a new action upon an object that already has its cultural history. From this perspective, we can say that the object is also active for it will never offer itself as a *tabula rasa* to the subject-actor's action. At each action, the subject-actor will then be in a new action of re-signifying that object, which can resist or shelter the subject-actor's action.

Each object has a history of multiple meanings. As the actions themselves are in constant organization and re-organization, according to systemic complexes of meanings, and given the symbolically inseparability between objects and actions, the objects will also be submitted to that dynamic organizational constellation of meanings.[12]

The Subject-Object Holistic Relationship in the Structuring of Identity

One of the more extensive proposals of Boesch's theory (Boesch, 1991) refers to the role of subject-object relationship in the process of identity construction. It touches on the representational mediation of the object in the subject's self-structuring as a person.

The concern is a threefold process. For explaining it, Boesch (1991) makes use of a beautiful and clearing illustration of the travel *souvenir* as a symbolic object.[13] According to his illustration, when a subject-actor experiences an object (for instance, during travel, he/she sees an object that is displayed as in a souvenir shop), the subject-actor not only gives meaning to that object (for instance, *beautiful, nice for my sister, reminds me my childhood*, and so on), but also experiences his/her personal potentialities for action (for instance, *that's incredible I am buying that here! I will take it with me!* Or *I will buy it for my sister, because she couldn't come too*). In short, the travel *souvenir* can represent the subject-actor's possibility of having been in a place—his possibility or potential of enjoying it.

Besides, in the structuring of identity, the objects are important in two other additional aspects; they mediate the link between past and present, as well as between subject-actor and others. When a person keeps a travel *souvenir*, he or she is keeping in the present the past of what had been in that place. When a person gives a travel souvenir to another person, he or she is trying to share—in the present—a meaningful past experience with the other.

Insofar, the link made by the object establishes continuity and consistency between past and present; the subject-actor, through his/her symbolic action upon the object is, in last resort, doing an integrative activity. Using the object symbolically, he/she gives continuity and consistency to his/her temporal experience, thereby increasing the unity of his/her self-experience, giving it a historical dimension. At the same time, the souvenir that is given to someone represents a meaningful link: someone brings his or her enjoyable past and offers it to the other. The symbolic object, therefore, also modulates social relations.

In such an extent, the objects give opportunity for the subject-actor to experience his/her action potential[14] and also collaborate for structuring of his/her psychological world; both are fundamental for the identity process:

> Objects give us a regulating frame for our identity feelings, by many ways: they give permanency to past, inserting meanings in the material environment, instrumentally facilitating our actions, suggesting positive forms of action and—remarkable—mark-

ing our social roles and positions. The reality of the object is a reality of action; following James and Janet, this was demonstrated by Piaget and his school; action and its support, on the other hand, are selected and created through the objects; and both jointly—action and object—that allow us for forming and keeping the I identity. (Boesch, 1980: 31; my translation from French)[15]

The "I experience with objects" implies the awareness of being a subject-actor. It also implies the construction of consistency in action, as it is based on the possibility of the subject's constant behavior related to an object or person (cf. Boesch, 1991: 300-304). Finally, it implies the awareness about the action potential through the evaluation of the action results facing the aimed objectives.

In sum, the "I experience with objects" implies the subject's awareness as actor; his /her identity as someone who is a co-constructor of his/her memories and who has the possibility of reconstructive appealing for them in different moments of his/her I-World, I-self/selves, I-Other relationships (Gillespie, 2006; Simão, 2004b; Zittoun, Duveen, Gillespie, Ivinson, & Psaltis, 2004; Zittoun, 2006).

The Action-Future Holistic Relationship

The concern of reconstructive action, either from memories or other symbolic material, addresses us to the issue of the subject-actor's orientation to the future.[16] This issue is very present in Boesch's formulations about the central concept of *action*:

> It is a goal-directed activity, carried out within a specific environment, and utilizing a certain number of instrumental techniques which allow to the actor to bridge the gap between the initial intention and the concrete realization of the goal. (Boesch, 1991: 43)

Action is then temporarily organized according to three phases: the initial phase (e.g., the time necessary for initiating it); the process phase (e.g., the time needed for performing it); and the terminal or consumption phase, which is the time needed for evaluating its effects (cf. Boesch, 1991: 49).

The temporal perspective is very coherent to Boesch's developmental conception about human action. Besides, and like culture, action is as much a process as a structure. In order to highlight the holistic aspects here involved – touching specially to the third and fourth thesis of *Ganzheitspsychologie* (Diriwächter, Chapter 3 of this book) —I will discuss each phase in more detail.

The Initial Phase of Action

The initial phase is when *the action goal is formed*; it has a very special place in Boesch's theory: "At a first glance, the essential of an action is its goal, that is, the anticipation of results of a complex psychological meaning" (Boesch, 1995: 25, my translation from French).[17]

In the initial phase of action, the subject-actor seeks, selects, and combines the needed environmental conditions—or tries to create them—in order to act according to some planned way. However, not only external conditions are needed for the subject's action. It is also necessary that the subject-actor appeal to internal conditions, like skills and past experiences. It is only when he/she establishes some relationship between these two kinds of conditions that he/she will be able to construct an intention. Goal formation is, therefore, a process. That is, it has a historicity and is settled in both individual external and internal conditions (cf. Boesch, 1991: 49-50).

Moreover, by joining and organizing those conditions, the subject-actor is not only structuring a situation, which allows him/her a specific action at that moment; but he/she is also structuring a field for his/her future actions, channeling them in some direction in the future (cf. Boesch, 1991: 50).

Finally, forming a goal representation demands—besides those external and internal conditions—the subject's motivation for action. Otherwise, the goal will remain at the level of confusing and poorly elaborated ideas. Therefore, intention also implies motivation in the sense of excitement for action.

According to Boesch, this motivation comes from the symbolic qualities of the goal itself. They are the goal images that are loaded by personal values, motivating the subject-actor to act in the direction of its attainment. Therefore, the motivational potential of a goal lies less in its objective content rather than in its personal attributed value (cf. Boesch, 1991: 51).

Here we have one of the aspects in Boesch's theory where the role of subjectivity is more prominent, as subjectivity (symbolization) structures action from its very beginning. As a consequence, Boesch emphasizes more the examination of the goal formation and action anticipation than the examination of the causal antecedents of actions, as in the linear causal model of behavioral explanation. As for Boesch, the subjective process of goal formation is the real antecedent of action; he brings back the action antecedent to the subjective domain. In such a way, the process of goal formation is more related to the syncretism in the evaluation of global situations, which is mainly based on the subject-actor's "good nose" and "intuition" than "conscious verifications" (cf. Boesch, 1995: 81).

The Affective-Cognitive Whole in the Systemic Process of Goal Formation

According to Boesch's theory, human beings are constantly forming images of multiple joint goals that they seek to reach. These goals are chained in hierarchical structures and the subject-actor tries to attain them through equilibration, coordination, and adjustment among them (cf. Boesch, 1991: 52).

There are three basic processes for goal formation: *imitation, construction,* and *centration.* They do not exclude one-another, but are usually "melted."

Boesch (1991) points out that in all cases, there are four important questions for understanding the process: "First, how does the individual chose the goal

(goal-selection)? Second, how does she or he structure it (goal-formation)? Third, how does he integrate it within his actual situation (goal-assimilation)? Fourth how does he/she invest it with an "appeal" sufficient to induce concrete action (goal-arousal)?" (p. 52).

In the process of goal formation through *imitation*, the subject-actor chooses a model to be followed as a goal. The presence of a model to be observed and followed can mislead to the idea of an easy process. However, Boesch (1991) points to many interrelated steps to get there: first, the subject-actor should make a selection among possible models; second, the models are usually polyvalent, including simultaneously positive and negative aspects to be managed by the subject-actor; third, not all aspects of the selected model are usually accessible to observation, requiring the subject-actor to fill the gaps. In this whole process the subjectivity and emotionality of the subject-actor are very active.[18]

However, Boesch (1991) points out that a goal is not always strong enough for starting an action, as in the case of imitation. Hence, to establish a goal can itself be a process of goal *construction*. In this case, the subject-actor assesses the potential value of the goal, its possible functions in his/her field of action, as well as the foreseen "psychological distances" or "costs" for its attainment. Like in imitation, here the affective regulations and evaluations also play a more important role than the rational actions that justify those choices.

The primacy of affective-emotional aspects in the process of goal formation becomes more evident in the process of *centration*. In the process of goal formation through centration, there is a sudden appeal from the object to the subject-actor:

> . . . here there is no need to choose the goal. Rather, it somehow imposes itself; we feel its "call". At the maximum we feel compelled to search for the means to reach or obtain it. As examples I mentioned the doll the girl suddenly craves for, or the painting from which I cannot detach my thoughts; love at first sight or other spontaneous likings are sufficiently known to most of us, but there are also the spontaneous "unexplainable" aversions, as examples of "anti-goals". In such cases we do not "build up" or structure valences, they are immediately felt; we may start processes of rationalizing, of justifying them for ourselves or for others. (Boesch, 1991: 55)

Still, according to Boesch (1991), the process of goal formation through centration encompasses a feeling that the object-goal fills a gap, replacing something that is lacking. "The experience is somehow as if aspirations related to the valuation of one's ego would 'crystallize' in an object or person" (Boesch, 1991: 56).

In short, each subject-actor's decision about a goal implies his/her evaluation in respect to the potential value of that goal, its possible functions in his/her field of action and, finally, the "psychological distance" or "costs" of the anticipated required action for the goal attainment. Sometimes this evaluation can be increased by the meaning of some required renounce of a goal in favor of the other. According to Boesch, throughout this process affective regulations and evaluations play a more important role than the rational ones. Feelings of gladness, stress, anxiety, happiness, longing, and awkwardness are examples of forms through which we get conscious about those evaluations. At the same time, they illustrate that those action regulations are "a priori" of subjective-affective order (cost, style, morality, beautifulness, elegancy) before being objective-rational judgments that justify them (Boesch, 1991: 55-57).

Finally, and perhaps the most important aspect of this process, is the "goal appeal" concerning to the personal I-world consistency. It is through the extent in which some goal fits or complements gaps in the subject-actor's developing I-World view that its motivational potential emerges.

The Processual Phase of Action

It is during the processual phase of action that the regulation between means and ends takes place. Through the goal anticipation, the subject-actor constructs an imaginary standard—an image about what should be the result of his/her action (the *should-value* or *soll-Wert*). However, that result usually does not correspond exactly to what was imagined, but is something nearer or farther to that (an *is-value* or *ist-Wert*).

During this process, at each step, the subject-actor realizes deviations between the should-value and the is-value, trying to decrease that difference by changing the course of action and/or the representation and value of the goal. The first case can be illustrated by the fact that many times we need to change strategies to reach something, and that need is realized only while we are performing, not at the beginning. The second case can be illustrated by the fact that sometimes, as far as we perform, we can feel our goal less attractive than at the beginning of our action, because it seems too easy to get there or because something happens in between and the former goal seems less important in face of the present situation. The subject-actor's satisfaction or dissatisfaction express in what extent—according to his/her subjective evaluation—he/she could approximate the is-value to the should value (or how much he/she felt him/herself able to diminish the gap between them).[19]

Moreover, the regulation between changes in action and/or goals, on the one hand, and their maintenance, on the other hand, will depend on the personal, interactive, and cultural contexts. They "show marked individual as well as cultural differences. . . . Actions are never isolated occurrences, but are always located in a broader field of obligations, interests and interactions" (Boesch, 1991: 59 and 60).

The Terminal Phase of Action

According to Boesch, we can consider an action as finished when one of the following situations has happened: the subject-actor *believes* that he or she has attained the goal, the subject-actor *believes* that he or she is not able to attain the goal, or he or she *is not eager* or *willing* to pursue the goal any more. The criterion is, therefore and again, the subject-actor's subjectivity—which is based on the proximity-divergence imbalance between the goal image and the concrete result of an action.

In this process, there are personal and group limits of tolerance for the gap between what is felt as reached and what was expected. Besides, both experienced success and failure will regulate the action flux, decreasing or increasing the subjective potential for future actions. "Thus, here too, emotion functions both as a regulator of action in the sense of Janet, *and* as a quality of consciousness indicating the individual's action potential in relation to given situations" (Boesch, 1991: 61).

The Holistic Web of Action Relationships

Our usual experience as subject-actors is that our and others' actions are meaningfully linked to one another. Taking into account this experiential fact, Boesch proposes a model that could be called a holistic web of action.

According to it, subject-actors coordinate their actions in many functional ways, trying to have a momentary arrangement among their actions in order that they could support (or at least not to disrupt) one another in the quest for a goal. In situations of anxiety or fatigue, for instance, we begin to whistle, in a kind of *side-action* supporting the main one. During interactions—as the concept itself points out—the subject-actors need to deal with the coordination among their actions, even if they are conflicting. Subject-actors also face the situation of coordinating the relationship between their actions and the environment—even when they are not committed to "ecological consciousness." Moreover, the subject-actor should deal with objective-subjective coordination for acting, in the interplay between objective aspects of the situation and emotional aspects of him/herself as subject-actor.

Coordination is a dynamic process. In *I-Other* coordination, for instance, as far as the involved persons are acting, they can change their self-evaluations, their evaluations about the other, and even their *should-values*. According to Boesch, this happens mainly because of changes in the perceptual-emotional structures of the involved actors (cf. Boesch, 1991: 66-67). Here we have one of the multiple ways in which Boesch approaches the human development in its character of subjective transformation and emergency of novelty.

In short, Boesch highlights that each action is embedded in a web and should be planned and regulated according to the actor's perception of that. The most important aspect of being successful in coordinating actions is that successfulness is usually identified at the symbolical level with I-world consistency, touching on the construction of identity. The criterion for considering that consistency was reached varies according to the actor's subjective situation, moment, and culture. Nevertheless, consistency is an objective always searched and it can over-coordinate a great number of interrelated actions. Boesch calls this an *overarching goal* (cf. Boesch, 1991: 66).

Identity, Consistency, Conflict:
The Holist Structuring by Myths and Fantasms

Boesch begins his article *Action et Object—Deux Sources de l'identité du moi* (Boesch, 1980) counter-posing physical identity to experienced identity:

> Physical identity is evident; although transformations imposed to us by the lifespan, a permanent background structure allowing us to recognize ourselves still remains. Experienced identity, that one of subjective experience, on the contrary, seems less easy to explain. Undoubtedly we realize ourselves as an identical being throughout the time, but this subjective experience of our "self" is mingled with that of constant changes. (Boesch, 1980: 23; my translation from French)[20]

For Boesch, the subjective experience on identity is not a matter of perceptual illusion, but of biological-cultural nature, as the self is the effect of biological as well as cultural personal structuring from immediate action experience (cf. Boesch, 1980: 23).

From this constructivist perspective, identity is a process that bridges the self-consistency and the personal experience in the world, which experience presents obstacles to that consistency. The key word for understanding this point is "assimilation," in the Piagetian sense. This does not mean fixity without conflict nor the reification of a transcendental subject beyond the experience. On the contrary, self-perception encompasses a continuous dynamic process of association, elimination, and transformation in order to progressively integrating successive personal experiences in the quest for a "better personal equilibrium," which is nevertheless only temporary. "Better personal equilibrium" means the subjective self-surpassing as an overarching goal that increases the subject's action potential. It is, for instance, the case of the violinist in his intimate relationship with the violin (see Boesch, 1993). Moreover, conflict leads to the revaluation and reconstruction of the personal symbolic field and is linked to the permanent and simultaneous tendencies of stabilization and innovation in action.

As synthesized by Valsiner and Van de Veer (2000), in Boesch's conception, self- experience happens mainly through personal generalized symbols (called by Boesch "fantasms") which, in turn, are formed through the selective personal elaboration of socially available myths (cf. p. 415). According to Boesch (1991), myths are "unreflected frameworks of judgments which somehow appear to constitute our commonsense" (p. 255). They intimately interact with subjective and personal standards of aspirations, like peace, love, happiness—which are called fantasms by Boesch (1991).

Needs to be edited !
Whole book does ! Aaargh

Boesch's Holism: A Whole New Cultural Holism?

I will dedicate the last part of this chapter to stressing some important aspects of the previous dialogue I have stated between Boesch's Symbolic Action Theory in Cultural Psychology and *Ganzheitspsychologie*. These aspects can merit future development in the constructive return to *Ganzheitspsychologie*, as proposed by Valsiner (2004). In what follows, the aspects in focus are organized according to their relationship with each of the four main thesis of *Ganzheitspsychologie* (Diriwächter, Chapter 3 of this book).

The relationship between culture and action is one of the nuclear points of Boesch's Symbolic Action Theory. Culture is a systemic, organized whole that channels the emergence of symbolic actions, allowing some of them while preventing others. By the same token, culture can be transformed by symbolic action.

The dynamics of those transformations are dependent on the whole cycle of culture-individual-culture. This cycle itself is as much a process as a structure, allowing simultaneously for cultural transformation and conservation.

Objects are part of the cultural field of action and are also related to one another as a whole. Objects and actions compose a dyad in which each one defines the other, however, without being fused. They are active parts of the cultural system delimiting one another. In such an extent the relationship between action and object are paradigmatic of I-world relationships, where an active subject-actor and a cultural object form a system. Therefore, if we would like to understand a specific cultural system, the action-object relationship itself should be taken into account as part of that cultural system. Here we can see the aspects as encompassed by the *first thesis* of *Ganzheitspsychologie*.

Nevertheless, perhaps the most holist aspect of Boesch's thinking is his emphasis on understanding the constant quest of human kind for consistency in I-World relationship. This would be a kind of meta-holism; it could explain even the creative emergence of the *Ganzheitspsychologie* itself as a human construction.

According to Boesch, one important feature of action-object relationship is the subject-actor's selectivity concerning the consistency in I-World relationship. The subject-actor's symbolic action addressed to the objects allows him not only to construct a cultural world of meaningful objects, institutions, ideas, and myths, but also to experience his/her personal potentialities for action, continuously (re)constructing his/her I-World relationship.

Besides—perception, transformation, and integration of objects in the cultural field depend on their integration in to an already existing symbolic structure, that is, integration to the subject-actor's biography as a whole.

Affectivity and emotion play a special role in this process of continuous biographical construction, as we have seen, for instance, in goal formation. In this process, future desired states are the motive of symbolic actions; for acting, the subject should be affected by feelings concerning to the goal. These summarized aspects touch upon the *second thesis* of *Ganzheitspsychologie*.

Future desired states mean transformation in I-World relationships, here included I-Other relationships. Consistency in them is at the core of the process of identity construction as continuous self-transformation. During his/her life span, the subject-actor is continuously trying to integrate, in a coherent way, transformations in him/herself with those that he/she realizes in the world, arriving to a new synthetic I-world relationship. This new I-World relationship— which is not necessarily "better," "more developed," or "more complex" than the previous one—will, by its turn, allow for new demands and aims for the subject-actor, who will try to integrate it, and so on. Here we are now in the ambit of the *third thesis* of *Ganzheitspsychologie*: the drivenness of the subject-actor as a totality in a certain direction and whose changes are of genetic nature.

The quest of the subject-actor for consistency in his/her I-World relationship can be understood as a quest for keeping his/her self-structure as whole of related forces that, at the same time, allow for the transformation inherent to the life course. In such an extent, seeking for consistency means a constant challenge of the subject-actor for keeping the structural character of his/her self-structure while acting in the cultural field (the *fourth thesis* of *Ganzheitspsychologie*).

In a recent interview, Boesch (2007) has pointed out that the question "In what kind of universe am I living?" is "the basic human question." He gave us an illustrative situation:

> People who sit at the beer table in the pub and heatedly discuss globalization or politics in far-away countries, why are they interested in it? Because of this kind of global intuition. Of course, theirs is not a scientific idea of the universe, and yet they express a kind of total belongingness. It is this question, too, which also induces the human experience of the *numinous*. "Numinous" means the intuition of an all-pervading mysterious force in the universe" . . . But you can't describe it, it is, as I said, an intuition, rather more like a feeling. (Boesch, 2007)

Still, according to Boesch (2007), the intuition of numinous is not necessarily religious, but it could be. The numinous implies a feeling of a force beyond our rational understanding, an all-encompassing power that brings in disquieting feelings:

> We try to relate them to reasons which may make them understandable. . . . Now, you are a psychologist, you might try to understand them psychologically. But people who do not reason rationally might relate the numinous to some kind of superior power. And they would try to understand the nature of this superior power, relate it to some religious revelation, which then gives raise to further elaboration of religious ideas. Which includes ideas about what this superior power requires from you. If you don't fulfil these requirements, then this power may turn against you. Here seems to lay the origin of the numinous side of religion, because, should you not respond to the demands of the superior power, you would loose all Grace, risk punishment in all

eternity. And therefore you are called to fight those others, the disbelievers who live contrary to God's wishes, in order to prove your faith and loyalty. (Boesch, 2007)

We could understand "numinous" as a kind of holist "overarching drivenness" of the subject-actor as totality in the direction of the holist understanding of his/her being in the world; a feeling that requires an integrative intuition—the numinous—that happens at the pre-reflexive level of the psychological subjectivity.

Feelings are in the center of the human experience.

Notes

1. In face of the density of Boesch's *oeuvre*, and although trying to do justice to his work, my clipping in the present text will be forcefully very selective.
2. Part of the ideas presented in this topic was already developed in other texts for other purposes (Simão, 1998, 2001, 2002, 2005).
3. I am using the term subject-actor—instead of subject or actor only—to emphasize that in the epistemological perspective here adopted subjectivity is constituted through the actor's symbolic action, be it conscious or not for the subject. In such an extent, subject-action-object is an indissoluble tripod, as I will discuss in the next pages.
4. This sub-title was borrowed from Boesch (1992).
5. According to Boesch himself, here lies one important difference between Kurt Lewin's and his own conception about the subject-action field relationship. For Lewin, what the subject does not know, does not exist in his action field; while for Boesch, it exists and can be or not discovered by the subject (cf. Boesch, 1991: 31).
6. For a more through analysis of this mythical narrative according to the present perspective, see Simão (2004a).
7. "Unwonted" is an archaic English adjective whose meaning is "between unusual and surprising."
8. Here remains a side-question, that of Piaget's and Boesch's different readings of Pierre Janet's and perhaps William James' more intense influence on Boesch leading to different approaches by Piaget and Boesch.
9. For a discussion about the meanings of *emic* and *etic*, see, for instance, Helfrich (1999).
10. *"Il va de soi que les deux domains, action et objet, ne peuvent être séparés qu'artificiellement : tout action a un objet (ne serait-il qu'imaginaire), et tout objet se définit par sa valeur actionelle"* (Boesch, 1980: 23-24).
11. This conception has similarities but is not identical with those of collective culture and personal culture as proposed by Valsiner (1989, 1999).
12. For a more thorough discussion of this aspect, see Boesch (1983).
13. It is worth noting that this illustration has already been used by Janet in his 1928 book, entitled *L'Évolution de la Mémoire et la Notion du Temps*, as highlited by Kozulin (1990/1994: 38), when referring to Janet's influence on Vygotsky.
14. Action potential "might be defined as the extent to which one feels confident of meeting one's personal standards in any kind of situation" (Boesch, 1991: 108). It is defined by the "capacity that an individual attributes to him/herself of doing actions with a positive valence and of avoiding those with a negative one," where the valences "refer to attractions, hopes and beliefs according to which we try to

guide our actions," with the action potential based mainly on anticipations and prospective, although also depending on previous experiences (Boesch, 1980: 24).

15. "... *les objects nous fournissent un cadre régulant notre sentiment d'identité de diverses façons : en donnant de la permanence au passé, en insérent des significations dans l'entourage matériel, en facilitant instrumentalement nos actions, en suggérant des formes positives dáction—et enfin, à ne pas oublier, en marquant nos rôles et notre position sociales. La réalité de l'objet est une réalité d'action, ce qui, à la suite de James et de Janet, a été démontré par Piaget et son école ; l'action, par contre, se choisit e se crée ses supports par les objets, et ce ne son que le deux conjointements, action et objet, qui nous permettent de former et de maintenir une identité du moi*" (Boesch, 1980: 31).

16. This prominent role of "intentionality" in Boesch's approach dates back to William James (see, for instance, Simão, 1998, 2002).

17. "*L'essentiel d'une action, à première vue, est son but,c'est-à-dire l'antecipation de résultats à signification psychologique complexe*" (Boesch, 1995: 25).

18. This aspect is very near to James-Mark Baldwin's concept of *persistent imitation* which is nuclear for human development—as discussed, for instance, by Valsiner (2000: 29-31).

19. About the influence of Pierre Janet and Jean Piaget in these formulations by Boesch, see, for instance, *Culture&Psychology*, 3(3), 1997; Simão, 2004b. Furthermore, the strong influence of Janet on Boesch's thinking can be a bridge between Zittoun's chapter (See Chapter 7 of this book) and the present one.

20. "*L'identité physique de l'individu est évidente; malgré les transformations que nous impose le cours de la vie, il reste une structure de fond permanente qui permetra de nous identifier et de nous reconnaître. L'identité vécue par contre, celle de l'experiénce subjective, paraît moins aisée à expliquer. Indubitablement, nous nous percevons comme un être identique à travers le temps, mais cette expérience subjective de notre 'soi' se melle à celle de changements constants*" (Boesch,1980: 23).

References

Bakhtin, M. M. (1986). *Speech Genres and Other Later Essays*. C. Emerson and M. Holquist (Eds.). Austin: University of Texas Press.

Boesch, E.E. (1980). "Action et objet: Deux sources de l'identité du moi." In P. Tap (Ed.), *Identité individuelle et personalization* (Vol. 2, pp. 23–37), Toulouse: Privat.

Boesch, E. E. (1983). "The Personal Object." *Education*, vol 27. Tübingen: Institut für Wissenchaftliche Zusammenarbeit: 99-113.

Boesch, E. E. (1991) *Symbolic Action Theory and Cultural Psychology*. Berlin: Springer.

Boesch, E.E. (1992). "Culture-individual-culture: The cycle of knowledge." In M. von Cranach, W. Doise, & P. Mugny (Eds.), *Social representations and the social bases of knowledge* (Swiss Monographs in Psychology, Vol. I, pp. 89–95). Lewiston, NY: Hogrefe & Huber.

Boesch, E. E. (1993). "The Sound of the Violin." *Revue Suisse de Psychologie*, 52(2): 70-81.

Boesch, E. E. (1995). "Action, champs d'action et culture." In B. Werlen e S. Wälty (Eds.), *Kulturen und Raum*. Zürich: Verlag Rüegger: 23-44.

Boesch, E.E. (1997). "Reasons for a *symbolic* concept of action." *Culture & Psychology*, *3*(3): 423-431.

Boesch, E. E. (2001). "Symbolic Action Theory in Cultural Psychology." *Culture & Psychology*, 7(4): 479-483.

Boesch, E. E. (2007). "Transparency in the Meaning Making: Interview to Ernst Boesch." In L. M. Simão and J. Valsiner (Eds.), *Otherness in Question: Labyrinths of the Self.* Greenwich: Info Age Pub.

Culture & Psychology, 3(3), 1997. London: Sage.

Diriwächter, R. (2004). "*Ganzheitspsychologie*: The Doctrine." *From Past to Future*, vol. 5(1): 3-16.

Diriwächter, R. (2007). "Genetic *Ganzheitspsychologie*." In: Diriwächter, R. & Valsiner, J. (Eds.) *Striving for the Whole: Creating Theoretical Syntheses.* New Brunswick, NJ: Transaction Publishers.

Gillespie, A. (2006). *Becoming Other: From Social Interaction to Self-Reflection.* Greenwich, Connecticut: Information Age Publishing.

Helfrich, H. (1999). "Beyond the Dilemma of Cross-Cultural Psychology: Resolving the Tension between Etic and Emic Approaches." *Culture & Psychology*, 5(2): 131-153.

Hermans, H.J.M. (1996). "Opposites in a dialogical self: constructs as characters." *Journal of Constructivist Psychology*, 9(1): 1-26.

Holquist, M. (1990). *Dialogism—Bakhtin and his world.* London and New York: Routledge.

Kozulin, A. (1990/1994). *La Psicología de Vigotsky.* Madrid: Alianza Editorial.

Simão, L. M. (1998). Cultura como campo de ação: uma introdução à Teoria da Ação Simbólica de Ernst Boesch [Culture as action field: an introduction to Ernst Boesch' s Symbolic Action Theory]. *Cadernos de Psicologia*, 4(1): 57-66.

Simão, L. M. (2001). Boesch's Symbolic Action Theory in Interaction, *Culture & Psychology*, 7(4), 485-493.

Simão, L. M. (2002). "A Noção de Objeto e a Concepção de Sujeito em Boesch" [The notion of object and the conception of subject in Boesch]. In: L. M. Simão, M. T. C. C. de Souza and N. E. Coelho Jr., *Noção de Objeto, Concepção de Sujeito: Freud, Piaget e Boesch* [Object Notion, Subject Conception: Freud, Piaget and Boesch]. São Paulo: Casa do Psicólogo: 87-116.

Simão, L. M. (2004a). "Semiose e Diálogo: para onde aponta o construtivismo semiótico-cultural?" [Semiosis and Dialogue: to where the semiotic-cultural constructivism is pointing to?] In: M. T. C. C. de Souza (Ed.) *Os sentidos de Construção: o si mesmo e o mundo* [The Meanings of Construction: the self and the world]. São Paulo: Casa do Psicólogo: 13-24. (a first version of this text was presented at the 18th Biennial ISSBD-Meeting, Ghent, Belgium, July 2004).

Simão, L. M. (2004b). "Beside rupture—disquiet; beyond the other—alterity." *Culture & Psychology,* 9(4): 449-459.

Simão, L. M. (2005). "*Bildung*, Culture and Self: A possible dialogue with Gadamer, Valsiner and Boesch?" *Theory & Psychology*, 15(4): 549-574.

Simões, M. do S. e Golder, C. (Eds.) (1995). *Belém conta...* [Belém tells...]. Belém: UFPA/Cejub.

Valsiner, J. (1989). *Human Development and Culture—The Social Nature of Personality and Its Study.* Lexington: Lexington Books, cap. 3: 43-73.

Valsiner, J. (1998). *The Guided Mind—A sociogenetic approach to personality.* Cambridge: Harvard University Press.

Valsiner, J. (1999). "La Cultura Dentro de los Procesos Psicológicos: semiosis construtiva." *Revista Psicologia Y Ciencia Social*, 3 (1): 75-83.

Valsiner, J. (2000). *Culture and Human Development.* London: SAGE.

Valsiner, J. (2004). "What to Do With the Whole? Implications from Taking *Ganzheit-spsychologie* Seriously." *From Past to Future*, vol. 5(1): 85-87.

Valsiner, J. and Van der Veer, R. (2000). *The Social Mind—Construction of the Idea.* Cambridge: Cambridge University Press.

- Zittoun, T., Duveen, G., Gillespie, A., Ivinson, G., & Psaltis, C. (2003). "The use of symbolic resources in developmental transitions." *Culture & Psychology, 9*(4): 415-448.
- Zittoun, T. (2006). *Transitions: Development through symbolic resources.* Greenwich, Connecticut: Information Age Publishing.

9

Comparative Methodology as the Human Condition: Conwy Lloyd Morgan and the Use of Animal Models in Science

Jaan Valsiner
Clark University

> *. . . we have direct and immediate acquaintance with*
> *no other psychical processes than those which we*
> *can study by the introspective method in ourselves.*
> *Hence introspective study must inevitably be the*
> *basis and foundation of all comparative psychology.*
> —C. L. *Morgan,* An Introduction to
> Comparative Psychology, *1894 (p. 37)*

It may be quite a surprise to find that the person who has been hailed in psychology's rewriting of its history as the paragon of focusing on behavior and who co-founded the theory of organic evolution has made statements like this. Supposedly, C. Lloyd Morgan was at the forefront of the fight for an objective, behavioral turn in the psychology of his time. He is known for his call for the principle of parsimony—labeled conventionally as "Morgan's Canon"—which threatens behavioral scientists with expulsion from the objectivity of science if inappropriate explanations are offered. Yet, here we have in front of us an unashamed endorsement of all of the softness on non-science that psychology has supposedly expunged. How can a serious behavioral scientist put introspection into the center of the sacred temple of science?

Furthermore, this statement endorsing the centrality of introspection is made in the very same chapter in his classic *An introduction to comparative psychology* (Morgan, 1894)—where the famous "Morgan's Canon" has been formulated (ibid, p. 53—see Chapter 10 of this volume). But why is that canon famous while the rest of Morgan's work is barely remembered? Obviously, the story about his work—and of the role of comparative methodologies in science—is different from what we habitually believe to have happened in the 1890s.

Functions of Forgetting and Displacement

The history of psychology as a discourse belongs to the present. It is not surprising that most reconstructions in our contemporary history of psychology are selectively wrong. The rewriting of the history of a discipline is a kind of rhetorical device for reaching some goals among the interlocutors of the present time. It often selectively presents the directions that the discipline has taken in the past—in an apparent defense of them. Yet, why the need of constant defending of what has happened? Or, likewise, why the critique of it?

"Morgan's Canon" has been used as such a rhetorical tool in order to create a glory story of how behaviorist perspectives advanced psychology as a science—in contrast to the fuzzy softness of philosophy or subjectivist psychology. The relocation of the locus of social dominance in psychology from Europe to North America after 1933 has something to do with such appropriations of psychology's history. Both the attacks on—and defense of—the ill-defined idea complex called "behaviorism" were North American phenomenon. In Europe—including Britain where Morgan worked—it had no wide proliferation. It was nothing but an obscure ideology of the New World (after 1913)—something to be recognized, but not to be considered in serious scientific argumentation. More important questions were at stake—how to make sense of reported evidence about different animals' supposedly advanced mental capacities, the role of the researcher in the creation of knowledge, and how evolutionary processes work. These basic issues were puzzling Morgan all through his life and these continue unanswered in our present time.

In stark contrast to these open questions—Morgan's and ours—"Morgan's Canon" has been taken out of its context in most North American teachings of psychology in recent decades and made into a core weapon for the compulsory adoption of the behaviorist reduction of complexity to simplicity. It has been made into a dogma of objectivity—a rule to which myriads of empirical behavioral scientists are expected to follow. "Morgan's Canon" is not the only glorified orthodoxy that psychology has invented. Other examples abound. Vygotsky's "zone of proximal development" (Valsiner & van der Veer, 1993; van der Veer & Valsiner, 1991, Chapter 13) has been presented in defense of the social primacy of the developing person. Without doubt, Vygotsky adhered to Janet's law of primacy, yet the notion of "zone of proximal development" was an idea complex that highlighted individual processes of development—taking the social for granted as a basis. Similarly, the work of George H. Mead has been cast as that of a "sophisticated behaviorist" (Valsiner & van der Veer, 2000, Chapters 5 and 6) by sympathetic presenters of his ideas. "Sophisticated" probably has meant that his ideas did not fit well with the primary credo of behaviorism as an ideological credo. No doubt, any scientist who studies organisms or societies takes the behavior of organisms seriously—yet without the necessity of glorifying it as *the only* aspect one needs to look at.

Mechanisms of Mythologizing

Making reconstituted stories of psychology's history is mythologizing science through replacing fresh inquiry by way of adhering to social rules. How are such social rules produced? What has become usual in the era of fragmented knowledge of today is the use of *pars pro toto* excerption as a righteous vehicle of discursive creation or support of contemporary rhetorical positions. A key idea—perhaps a quote—from a classic thinker of the past is taken and presented in a new context of today to support a different perspective. The quote need not be wrong—its mere displacement from the original context to a new one creates a historical halo effect for the latter. The repeated use of the quote from Morgan is one of such displacements—it is usually provided as a moral imperative for serious scientists. Yet for Morgan himself it was a tool for clearer thinking and not an end of inquiry.

The case of how "Morgan's Canon" has been made into a selective mystification of history has been proven elsewhere (Costall, 1993; Robinson, 1977; Wozniak, 1993). We decided to reprint Chapter 3 of the Introduction here in order to give the serious reader of this issue a glimpse of the central concern of Morgan's long intellectual quest—the question of how any person can make sense of the minds of other persons—similar or dissimilar—and of other species, from amoebae to higher primates. This question has been and remains the center for any comparative approach in psychology. Since most researchers have been busily doing empirical work on different species—from rats to humans—the question of human psychology in this knowledge construction process has remained without attention. Or, more precisely, that question has been appropriated by philosophers of science, rather than be allowed to remain on the forefront of the psychology of scientific inquiry.

The Other Mind and His Context: Morgan's Life

Conwy Lloyd Morgan's life (1852-1936) was a trajectory of systematic efforts to find answers to basic questions in science. His background is that of a child who was eager to read poetry and the philosophy of Berkeley but who was sent to the Royal School of Mines in London (in 1869) to get a practically useful profession in mining and metallurgy. He was an excellent student—yet one of no intrinsic motivation to become a successful professional. Instead, he commented in his retrospect:

> . . . the scientific method, rather than its prospective application in a professional career, was what intrigued me. The practical vein was still there. To do something with it—yes. But the top men in science used it for the advance of knowledge for its own sake. (Morgan, 1961: 240)

This, of course, was still the time (1870s) where the focus on basic knowledge was not questioned as to its value, and the perils of pragmatist ideology had not yet captured the active efforts of many behaviorist minds (Valsiner, 2000). Instead, the major area of scholarly inquiry was the wide discussion of evolution, and Thomas Huxley was its active promoter. A chance encounter with Huxley led Morgan to a year working as his assistant and another to part-time teaching in a private school. Thus, instead of a career as an engineer, Morgan's mind abandoned the idea of mines for the sake of the pleasures and pains of lecture halls. The life of an educator needed some economic base—and Morgan moved to South Africa (Rondebosch, near Cape Town) to teach in a college (1878-1884). Such teaching included physical science, English literature, and constitutional history—a combination quite unusual in our time of intense talk about the value of "interdisciplinarity." Neither was it commonplace in his—but the well-roundedness of college education needed teachers who could provide such an environment. Morgan certainly did.

Following the years in South Africa, he returned to England and was appointed to the Chair of Geology and Zoology at University College Bristol. He remained in Bristol for the rest of his life, transferring his chair in a direction that fitted his preferred topic—psychology and ethics—and retiring after many years of leadership roles in the new Bristol University in 1919. Towards the end of his life he—somewhat in parallel to Henri Bergson's and George H. Mead's life courses—became overwhelmingly concerned with philosophical issues. Wisdom takes time to develop (Staudinger & Werner, 2002).

Ultimately, all areas of human inquiry—philosophy, science, literature—come together in one general quest: understanding the world we inhabit. There are no social rules for such inquiry as it takes place in the mind of a thinker and through that mind. The people around the thinker may have no idea of what is going on. Or if they do, they may have ready-made explanatory schemes to classify the thinker into anything between the weird, the crazy, and the genius. Morgan wanted to find out how one makes sense of anything different from oneself—animal or human.

The Human Condition: Understanding Minds Other than Our Own

How can we know anything about others? In science, it is usual to create mechanical models to explain complex processes. New technology usually provides the tools for inventing new terminologies. The use of the notions of chronometers as technical devices was widespread at the end of the nineteenth century as an analogy for making sense of the psychological functioning of the mind. Today, we use computers in making similar analogies. Of course, it was clear that the analogy was mechanical; no chronometer could reflect upon its own functioning, nor upon the functioning of others. Even our contemporary computers cannot (yet) be programmed to do that. But human beings can think about others and about themselves. And they have, over centuries, done much of that as the history of literature, art, and philosophy amply demonstrates.

What is the process of inquiry like? Morgan suggested a thought experiment built upon the clock analogy. His play with the idea of self-reflexive chronometers (Morgan, this volume, Chapter 10) illustrates the direction of movement of his inquisitive mind. He was eager to reveal the organized complexity of the human *psyche*—in continuity with that of other species, but not in ways reduced to the lower level organizational principles. Different levels of organization have different principles—hence, assigning a higher principle to a lower level is as inadequate as the interpretation of a higher level by principles at the lower ones. Yet both of these misattributions were rampant in psychology—hence the need for clarification of how knowledge is being made.

The Researching Chronometer

Morgan imbued a hypothetical chronometer with the power of investigation—the capability to observe the external appearances of other timepieces, as well as that of introspecting about one's internal clockwork. Such a hypothetical chronometer would move from oneself "outwards"—to other similar specimens—while creating an understanding about clocks at large. One's construction of knowledge is strictly based upon experiencing the behavior of others—but understood in terms of one's own introspection. As long as the others are similar, there is little problem in transposing the Researcher Chronometer's introspective account of one's functioning to others. If the others behave similarly to me, and I have an accurate model of how I function, I can carry my model of my own functioning over to that of all others of my kind. But, what if Figure 9.1 (a) encounters Figure 9.1 (b)?

The chronometer (a) above (as it looked around 1890s) will have to "make sense" of the kitchen clock (b) below. Here the Researcher Chronometer encounters a partially dissimilar "distant relative"—which performs the same function but need not operate through the same internal structure (see Morgan, this volume, Chapter 10). As long as the observation of the others did not reach a threshold of detecting a difference, the application of the model based on one's own immediately available understanding is easily projected onto the (similar) others. Yet, in that ease is a potential difficulty—a sufficiently "workable" construction of the model of the mechanism may remain satisfactory. The posited model may turn out to be wrong, or at least in need of modification *in lieu* of the newly obtained experiential evidence.

Thus, the adequacy of scientific knowledge is created by testing existing models on materials that are different from what is easily known on the basis of similarity. It is here that the value of comparisons appears while encountering clearly dissimilar, yet similarly functioning, other systems (the chronometer encounters a kitchen clock, or a naturalist encounters an animal of another species, or an ethnographer a person from another society). The observed dissimilarity

Figure 9.1

(a)

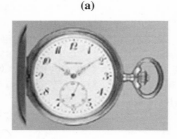

(b)

of form and similarity of function leads to the need to revamp the explanatory
model based on the introspection of the scientist.

Morgan's model of two inductions—the first internal, the second external
(see Chapter 10 of this volume, Figure 10.1)—is a blueprint for making sense
of the ways in which scientific knowledge is created. It is always necessarily
based on the first induction—the researcher needs to develop personal, only
introspectively available, intuitive understandings of the phenomenon in question. But it does not end with such introspective understanding—on its basis,
the researcher becomes involved in extrospection (second induction), letting the
external experience feed forward into the intuitive model (for our contemporary
version, see Branco & Valsiner, 1997). The key to scientific knowledge is not
in the use of the first or second induction, but the coordination of the two in the
knowledge construction process. It is through that coordination that the fit between appropriate levels of the observable phenomena (e.g., a dog performing a
complex problem-solving task) and the kinds of explanatory models appropriate
for explaining it, are worked out. In the case of the complex behavior of a dog,
both a higher-level explanation ("the dog thinks how to solve the problem") and
lower-level explanation ("the dog is trained to perform in this complex way")
are equally inadequate. A different explanatory system is necessary.

The Basis of All Understanding: Educated Self-Observation

Any question about comparisons in psychology—be they comparisons of species, societies, or individuals—is about the knowledge construction efforts of the comparer. No doubt differences exist between whatever phenomena are being made into the object of comparison—in fact such differences make the act of comparing possible. If the world were fully homogeneous, the very notion of comparison would be useless—and in fact could not emerge.

So making distinctions is a basis for comparison, yet how the comparative knowledge construction proceeds further on the basis of distinctions is not well worked out in psychology's epistemology. In our contemporary psychology, the making of distinctions is automatized by statistical procedures (e.g., statements like "differences between X and Y were found to be statistically significant at level Z"), without concomitant elaboration of how to think further on the basis of such established distinctions. Oftentimes the researchers merely consider the distinctions to be facts by themselves ("contributions to the literature"—see Valsiner, 2001: 209-212 on "democracy of the literature"). Morgan cautioned researchers against thoughtless reliance on merely finding such distinctions (through "second induction"—see Morgan, this issue). Instead, he called for the development of the capacities of "first induction":

> I would strongly urge upon my readers the advisability of testing, by careful intro-spection, all my statements concerning the mental processes of man. Only thus can a valid basis either of appreciation or of criticism be obtained. It must not be forgotten that introspective psychology is an essential preliminary to comparative psychology, and that, if it is to produce results of scientific value, it must be based upon exact and oft-repeated observation. Such observation, however, requires special training, not less than objective observation in physics or in biology. *It would be an inestimable boon to comparative psychology, if all those who venture to discuss the problems with which this science deals would submit to some preparatory discipline in the methods and results of introspective observation.* (Morgan, 1903, p. xii, added emphasis)

This didactic suggestion remains true a hundred years later. Psychology's conceptual confusions are not due to the lack of data, but to the limits of thought. Or perhaps they are due to not letting the flight of theoretical thinking move freely over the landscape of phenomena. Morgan's canon is not about the behavior of the others, but about the education of the introspection-based construction of knowledge by our own minds—albeit *through* careful observation of the others.

Morgan's Developmental Core: Evolution and Emergence

From Morgan's general viewpoint, it should look rather obscure that psy-chology in North America moved on in the twentieth century to use very few animal species in comparison with, or as models of, humans. The emergence of the gray (Worcester variety) or white rat as the model species for psychology (see Logan, 2003), later to be joined by pigeons, would be a rather artificial choice for the researchers moving out of their introspection towards extrospection of others' behavior. Of course, the selection of those few species fitted the disappearance of comparative methodology from psychology. It was retained in developmental biology from where it reappears in contemporary developmental science (see Gottlieb, 2003). Thus, more than a hundred years after C. Lloyd Morgan formulated his principles for comparative psychology, the discipline has not advanced its comparative thinking. When made empirically, comparisons return to common-sense questions (e.g., "do apes *have* language?" "do infants *have* a theory of mind?" "do people from developing countries *have* a gene for preferring Coca Cola to beer?"). These ontological ("do X have Y?") questions are elementaristic, rather than systemic, and do not differ —other than in permissibility of terminology—from other similar common sense questions ("do I *have* identity?" or "do animals *have* souls?").

For Morgan, such questions were moot. He solved the problem of separating common sense talk about psychological functions from scientific terminology through an axiomatic separation of the ontological descriptors—left to rage in the common language use—from scientific terminology. In his conviction,

> psychology as science has no concern with Mind as an agency, with Consciousness as a principle of activity, with Will as producing cause. Of course I am aware that I advocate a psychology without a Soul. What then? Psychology is not co-extensive with the whole field of human enquiry. It is, or should be, a branch of science which is aware of its limitations. It deals with *processes* instinctive, perceptual and ideational or volitional, not with *acts* of an agency. *They* are dealt with in mental philosophy. (Morgan, 1909: 18)

Morgan thus bypassed the problem of attribution of causality by leaving it in the hands of philosophers and laypersons, while keeping to science the focus on process mechanisms that underlie outcomes. Certainly this distinction itself is merely analytic—each moment in a process of some kind is an outcome of some conditions that unfold over time and feeds into future processes. This feed-forward cycle entails causality of a different kind than the mere attribution of it to some invented entity. Furthermore, natural history provides us with a set of hierarchically organized and mutually linked qualitatively distinct levels of organization.

But where do these levels come from? Morgan's perspective entailed the focus on emergence of new levels of the processes in the course of continuous experiencing. Experiencing is the process of adaptation to ever-new conditions *by way of adapting such conditions to one's own survival* as the organism. Hence, the possibility of emergence of new levels of psychological functioning in phylogenesis and the narrowing down of the role of natural selection. Morgan's careful consideration of the processes of development as consisting of emergent phenomena led him to specify the role of natural selection:

Every advancing step in the development of mental symbolism and of control it rendered possible must have been *presented to* natural selection, was not in any sense *evoked by* natural selection. (Morgan, 1892: 82)

The tasks of experiencing lead to the emergence of new process mechanisms—of previous or higher (or lower) levels—as an inevitable part of surviving. As those emerge, they become *presented to* the natural selection (at the level of phylogenesis of the species)—and thus become materials for that selection *after* they have emerged. Psychogenesis is an evolutionary adaptation that itself becomes the vehicle for presenting newly emerged adaptational tools to natural selection. This idea led Morgan a few years later to become one of the three (with James Mark Baldwin and Henry Osborn) co-founders of the theory of emergent evolution (Baldwin, 1897; Morgan, 1896; Osborn, 1896). The central aspect of experiencing is its guide to acting—*experience generates anticipation* (Morgan, 1897: 7). And anticipation can be the locus for emergence of new ways of acting. These new ways include construction of representations—abstracted tools for further acting based on past experience—which become bases for *apperceptive assimilation* in further experiencing (Morgan, 1909: 13-14). New encounters with humans or animals who are different from us, and from our emerged representations, guide development.

Others' Behavior—and Our Minds: The Use of Animal Models

Starting off this discussion on the history and role of animal models in psychology with a glimpse into the thinking of C. Lloyd Morgan can perhaps lead to wider gains. Instead of retrospectively evaluating and re-mythologizing stories of animals in the minds of psychologists, we could direct our inquiry to a basic issue—what can psychology learn from the study of species of varied closeness to *Homo sapiens*? That history of psychology has had only a meager success from the use of animal species and animal models in its history seems clear. Psychology's core knowledge is not comparative in the full richness of the possibilities the natural and cultural sciences can afford. Aside from learning a few selected fragments of knowledge through rats, mice, pigeons, rhesus monkeys, and a few higher primates, the core of general psychology remains unappreciative of the rich variety of biological species and their ever-fluctuating innovative adaptations. Similarly, psychology has been cross-culturally under-appreciative. Other than a few selected contrasts, usually between occidental and oriental societies or "developed" and "developing" ones, psychology has not appreciated the possibilities to create general knowledge of human *psyche* through systematic investigation of the *unity made available* by the experienced difference between societies or species. It is hoped that the future use of animal models, by our minds and our experience with others, leads towards a basic science in contrast with our all too fragmented discipline.

Acknowledgments

Frequent lunchtime discussions with Gilbert Gottlieb are to be blamed for the emergence of this discussion—in the author's mind and in the present volume of *Striving for the Whole*. Continuous discussions about the basic nature of novels in science and of issues of comparative psychology with Nick Thompson provided further impetus. Nick's comments on an earlier version of this paper are gratefully recognized.

References

Baldwin, J. M. (1897). "Organic selection." *Science, 5* (No. 121): 634-636.

Branco, A. U., & Valsiner, J. (1997). "Changing methodologies: A co-constructivist study of goal orientations in social interactions." *Psychology and Developing Societies, 9,* 1: 35-64.

Costall, A. (1993). "How Lloyd Morgan's canon backfired?" *Journal for the History of the Behavioural Science, 29*: 113-122.

Gottlieb, G. (2003). "Animal models of human development." *From Past to Future, 4*(1): 39-52.

Logan, C. A. (2003). "The legacy of Adolf Meyer's comparative approach: Worcester rats and the strange birth of the animal models." *From Past to Future, 4*(1): 25-38

Morgan, C. L. (1892). "The law of psychogenesis." *Mind, 1* (n.s.): 72-93.

Morgan, C. L. (1894). *An introduction to comparative psychology.* London: Walter Scott.

Morgan, C. L. (1896). "On modification and variation." *Science, 4* (No. 99): 733-740.

Morgan, C. L. (1897). "The realities of experience." *Monist, 8,* 1: 1-18.

Morgan, C. L. (1903). "Preface." In C. L. Morgan, *An introduction to comparative psychology.* 2nd ed. London: Walter Scott.

Morgan, C. L. (1909). "The natural history of experience." *British Journal of Psychology, 3,* 1: 1-20.

Morgan, C. L. (1961). "C. Lloyd Morgan." In C. Murchison, *A history of psychology in autobiography.* Vol. 2. 2nd ed. (pp. 237-264). New York: Russell & Russell [original 1932].

Osborn, H. F. (1896). "Ontogenetic and phylogenetic variation." *Science, 4* (No. 100): 786-789.

Robinson, D. N. (1977). "Preface to Morgan's Introduction to Comparative Psychology and 'Limits of Animal Intelligence.'" In D. N. Robonson (Ed), *Significant contributions to the history of psychology, 1750-1920.* Series D. *Comparative psychology.* Vol. 2 (pp xxi-xxxvii). Washington, D.C.: University Publications of America.

Staudinger, U., & Werner, I. (2002). "Wisdom: its social nature and life-span development." In J. Valsiner & K. J. Connolly (Eds), *Handbook of Developmental Psychology.* London: Sage.

Valsiner, J. (2000). "Thinking through consequences: the perils of pragmatism." *Revista de Historia de la Psicologia, 21,* 4: 145-175.

Valsiner, J. (2001). *Comparative study of human cultural development.* Madrid: Fundacion Infancia y Aprendizaje.

Valsiner, J., & van der Veer, R. (1993). "The encoding of distance: The concept of the zone of proximal development and its interpretations." In R. R. Cocking & K. A. Renninger (Eds.), *The development and meaning of psychological distance* (pp. 35-62). Hillsdale, N.J.: Lawrence Erlbaum Associates.

Valsiner, J., & van der Veer, R. (2000). *The social mind: Construction of the idea.* New York: Cambridge University Press.

van der Veer, R. & Valsiner, J. (1991). *Understanding Vygotsky: A quest for synthesis.* Oxford: Basil Blackwell.

Wozniak, R. H. (1993). "Conwy Lloyd Morgan, mental evolution, and the Introduction to Comparative Psychology." In C. L. Morgan, *An introduction to comparative psychology* (pp. vii-xix). London: Routledge/Thoemmes [reprint of 2nd edition of 1903].

10

Other Minds Than Ours[1]

Conwy Lloyd Morgan

A distinguishing feature of modern psychology is the employment of the comparative method. So long as the psychologist restricts himself to the introspective study of the workings of his own consciousness, his conclusions rest on a basis which, however sure it may appear to himself, must be limited by the inevitable restrictions of his own individuality. When he compares and correlates his own results with those of other introspective observers, he becomes so far a comparative psychologist, and by widening his basis renders his conclusions more comprehensive. A further stage of the comparative method is reached, when he endeavors to correlate the results of introspective psychology with the conclusions reached by the physiological study of those nervous processes which are the concomitants of psychical states. On the hypothesis of monism, he is thus comparing two wholly different aspects of the same natural occurrences; on the hypothesis of dualism, two wholly different occurrences, which are nevertheless invariably associated. In any case, by proceeding to this comparison, he links his subject with the science of biology in such a way that has proved eminently helpful to his own branch of study. Now, the keynote of modern biology is evolution; and on the hypothesis of scientific monism here adopted, though not necessarily on that of empirical dualism, we are not only logically justified in extending our comparative psychology so as to include within its scope the field of zoological psychology, but we are logically bound to regard psychological evolution as strictly co-ordinate with biological evolution.

I propose to consider in this chapter what we can know of other minds than ours, and how we may gain this knowledge. It follows from what has just been said, that since biological evolution has given rise to individuals of divergent types of organic structure, there may be—nay, there must be—in these divergent biological individuals divergent types of mind, using the word "mind" in the widest and most comprehensive sense as embracing all modes of psychical activity. The question arises, however, how we are to gain acquaintance with these divergent types of mind. And here we are met by the fundamental difficulty which comparative psychology, both human and zoological, encounters when it leaves the broad field of general considerations, to enter upon the more particular study of individual and concrete cases with divergent possibilities of interpretation. For we have direct and immediate acquaintance with no other psychical process than those which we can study by the introspective method in ourselves. Hence, introspective study must inevitably be the basis and foundation of all comparative psychology.

I will endeavor to illustrate the fundamental difficulty of comparative psychology by means of an analogy. Suppose that a chronometer were gifted with intelligence and reason, and were to enter upon the study of other timepieces, all access to their works being inexorably denied it. It would be able to observe the motions of the hands over the dial-plate, and perhaps gain some information by attentively listening to internal sounds. But when it came to the interpretation of these observed phenomena, and when it attempted to explain their inner causes, the chronometer would be forced to frame all such interpretation and such explanation in terms of its own works. With no other works would it have any acquaintance. It would infer, and justly infer under the circumstances, that the works of other timepieces were, on the whole, of like nature with those which actuated the movements of its own hands over the dial-face. There can be no question, moreover, that the more thorough and accurate the acquaintance of the chronometer with its own works, the more valid would be its inferences with regard to the hidden works of other timepieces. For example, it might learn by introspection that it possessed a mechanism of compensation for changes of temperature; and noticing that in other timepieces the rate of movement of the hands varied with the rise or fall of the thermometer, it might infer that in them such mechanism was absent. It is probable, however, that the chronometer would interpret all the phenomena as due to the action of a mainspring, since it would necessarily be unacquainted with the impelling motive power derived from the descent of heavy weights; and the outflow of energy from the spring would, in its interpretation, be regulated by some sort of balance-wheel, since the principle of the pendulum would nowhere be found through introspection of its works. Thus there would be for the chronometer inevitable possibilities of error. And although it could do little more than speculate concerning these possibilities, it would certainly be wise in refraining from anything like dogmatism concerning the insides of other timepieces which it must interpret, if it interpret at all, in terms of its own chronometer works, but which might not impossibly, could it only get at them, exhibit the application of other mechanical principles.

Now this analogy must certainly not be pressed too far. It is here adduced to illustrate the fact that just as the supposed chronometer would be forced to interpret the mechanism of other timepieces in terms of its own mechanism, so man is forced to interpret the psychology of animals in terms of human psychology, since with this alone he has first-hand acquaintance through the study of the nature and sequence of his own mental processes. But it will perhaps be said that the analogy is invalidated on the principles I have myself adopted, by the fact that in animals a knowledge of the organic mechanism, the functional activity of which is the objective aspect or correlate of psychical processes, is not beyond our reach, but is attainable through psychological research. Access to the works of other timepieces, at any rate from the objective side, is, it may be said, *not* inexorably denied to man the investigating chronometer. So far from this being the case, it is the comparative study of other "works," taken in connection with the comparative study of the life-activities effected through their means, that affords the justification of *inferential* conclusions concerning the psychical processes of animals. This view of the matter in which I concur, does not seem to me wholly to invalidate the chronometer analogy; but it does suggest a modification, and further development of the analogy.

The chronometer, we will suppose, is acquainted through introspection with its own psychology, and is able to take to pieces the works of other timepieces. It finds a number of chronometers whose works are all practically identical, and as it believes, but cannot demonstrate without taking itself to pieces, just like its own; and it is led to the inference that their psychology is similar to its own. It finds also a number of other timepieces whose works are constructed on similar principles, and differ chiefly in their being less highly finished and somewhat less complex; and it is led to the inference that their psychology, though less developed and less complex than its own, has probably been evolved on similar lines. But when it comes to the kitchen clock, it finds certain general similarities, cog-wheels and chains and so forth. But it also discovers principles of construction so different, the weights and the pendulum being so unlike its own balance-wheel and escapement, that it hesitates to draw any positive and definite conclusions. It sees that though the psychology of the kitchen clock may be closely analogous to its own, it may be quite different. It refuses to express a definite opinion on the psychology of the kitchen clock.

To apply the analogy in this modified form. Man, by anatomical and physiological research, has found in other men cerebral hemispheres with sensory-centers, control-centers, and so forth, similar to those which he believes that he individually possesses; and he infers that their psychology is of like nature to his own. He also finds in other vertebrates cerebral hemispheres, with sensory-centers and so forth, differing from man's chiefly in mass and complexity; and he infers that their psychology, though less developed and less complex than his own, has probably been evolved on similar lines. But when he comes to the insect, the crustacean, the mollusc, not to mention the worms, the sea-anemone, or the amoeba, he finds nervous systems so different in types of structure from his own, that he hesitates to draw any definite and positive conclusions concerning the psychical states of these animals. It is true that there are nerve-fibers and nerve-cells; but the manner of their arrangement is so different from that of the vertebrates to which he belongs, that the careful student of zoological psychology is forced to conclude, that though the psychical states of insects and crustacea may be similar to those of man, they may be markedly dissimilar.

It may indeed be contended that community of environment—the joint-tenancy of the same world—must necessarily beget community of psychical faculty to meet the requirements of that environment. But while admitting the soundness of this argument so far as it goes, I venture to submit that it does not go far. For why should the community of psychical nature be greater than that of physical nature? The anatomy or the physiology of insects, for example, differs tolerably widely from that of man; why then should he suppose that their *psychical* endowments are more closely similar? Both physical nature and psychical nature are so to speak molded in accordance with the environment. To both the argument of a joint-tenancy of the world applies. The physical nature being widely divergent from that of man, is it not reasonable to suppose that the psychical nature is, or at least may be, also widely divergent?

No one can study with any attention and care the habits and activities of such insects as ants and bees, without feeling convinced that they profit by experience and that their actions are under control. It is true that at present we know little about the physiology of this control, and of the relation of control centers to automatic centers. But this may sooner or later be remedied by an extension of our knowledge of the nerve-physiology of insects. I am the last to think of counseling any abatement of zeal in the fascinating study of the activities, and of the minute anatomy and physiology of the higher invertebrate forms of life. But I am of opinion that students in this department of investigation may do well to lay to heart the lesson conveyed by the analogy of the chronometer and the kitchen clock. In any case, in an introduction to comparative psychology, I feel bound to lay stress on the necessity for the greatest caution in the psychical interpretation of insect activities and I feel justified in restricting myself, in this work, to a consideration of the psychical states which we may infer to be associated with the functional activity of the cerebral hemispheres in the higher vertebrates.

Now it is clear that the validity of our inferences concerning the mental processes which underlie the actions of our human neighbor, is primarily dependent on the similarity of his mind to our mind. If he is an Englishman, of the same social grade as ourselves, of like tastes and habits of thought, educated under the same school system, the similarity will be fairly close, though even here there must be slight individual differences. But if he be a foreigner, of a different social grade from ours, differing from us in tastes and habits of thought, educated on other school systems than ours, there will be a wide margin of dissimilarity. We shall find no little difficulty in putting ourselves in his place, in understanding how with such and such facts staring him in the face he can hold the views he says he holds, and in conceiving how he can derive any pleasure from that which would bore us to death, or would set our aesthetic teeth on edge, or would painfully shock our moral sensibility. In dealing with

North Australians, or Maori or South Sea Islanders or Red Indians, our difficulties are proportionally increased. These are peoples who have been living,
generation after generation, under circumstances widely different from those
in which our own race has been nurtured. How difficult it is justly to interpret
their thoughts and feelings, and to reach the mental processes which are the
psychical accompaniments of their actions, to us so strange and meaningless!
And the difficulty is due to the fact, that the only mind with which we can claim
any first-hand acquaintance is the civilized mind, that of which we are conscious
within ourselves. In terms of this mind, that of the aboriginal Australian or Red
Indian has to be interpreted. We must remember that among civilized men careful
introspection and comparative study have led to the formation and adoption of
tolerably clear-cut and self-consistent views of the world, and of our relations
as individuals to that which we regard as universal. But among primitive folk,
of less introspective and reflective power, we must not expect such definiteness
and self-consistency. And I confess that I read with some skepticism much that
is written on the animistic or fetishistic or other interpretations which are read
by philosophers into the vague and often contradictory beliefs of uncivilized
peoples. It is difficult for us to realize with what content such peoples can hold
a number of beliefs which *to us* appear self-contradictory, and how readily
they are satisfied with isolated fragments of explanation, having little or no
desire to combine them into a consistent whole. Again, in our very midst there
are beings, so like us, and yet so different, the understanding of whose mental
processes is difficult and yet most important. I refer to our own children. How
unexpected are often the actions of children! How strange their whims and
moods and fancies! How charmingly illogical and irrational they sometimes are,
and yet often how surprisingly sharp and clever! Notwithstanding the excellent
work that has been done in this branch of study, the psychology of the child is
a field in which much careful observation and much cautious inference is still
needed. And why are the difficulties of interpretation so great? Because we
have to interpret in terms of the adult-mind the child-mind, in which the relative development of the faculties, like the relative development of the bodily
organs, is so different from that of men and women. It is true that we ourselves
have once been children. But what most of us remember of our child-days is
not the nature of our mental processes, but certain salient products. A greater
or less number of striking external incidents, a few occasions of keen joy or
bitter sorrow, constitute for most of us the sum-total of our memories of childhood. To reach mental processes needs introspection, and few children have the
power of introspection, or the knowledge by which such introspection must be
guided. We have no recollection of the mental processes of childhood, because
those mental processes could not then for most of us be objects of thought and
contemplation.

Even in human psychology, therefore, if we include not only the psychology of sages, but of ordinary folk, of savages, and of children, there are serious

difficulties of interpretation. Since the validity of our inferences concerning the mental processes which underlie the actions of our neighbor is primarily dependent on the similarity of his mind to our mind, it is clear that, if through divergence of development, or imperfection of development, his mind has come to differ from ours, the validity of our inferences will be so far impaired. For we cannot get at his mind directly; our inferences must always be, for better for worse, in terms of our own mental processes.

It will thus be seen that in studying other minds through their objective manifestations, it is primarily essential that we should have, so far as is possible, a thorough and accurate acquaintance with the only mind we can study at first-hand and directly, namely our own. Without this, anything like scientific interpretation is manifestly impossible. All rational human beings have, however, some acquaintance with the workings of their own consciousness. And many of those who are not professed psychologists have, through unusual powers of introspection and keen insight, reached conclusions which are just and true, though they are apt to be somewhat lacking in balance. Psychologists make, or should make, no claim to any monopoly of knowledge in the subject they study; their province is mainly to systematize that knowledge. They bear to the acute and accurate observer the relation of the trained biologist to the amateur naturalist. And just as the amateur naturalist is apt to regard the scientific biologist with some suspicion, as one who is over-subtle, and relies too much on the delicate methods of the laboratory and the dissecting table; so is the plain man of shrewd insight apt to regard the psychologist also with some suspicion, as one who is over-subtle in his distinctions, too introspective, and not sufficiently objective in his study of mind. And the psychologist should accept the criticism, not with impatience and the assumption of an air of superior knowledge and wisdom, but with a quiet determination to justify his procedure by the results which, through its means, he is enabled to reach. From the position that the first duty of a psychologist is to attain accurate and systematic acquaintance with the workings of his own mind, as the cipher in terms of which all other minds must be read, he cannot recede without abandoning the only basis of scientific method possible under the circumstances of the case.

With this as a basis, he may proceed to the so-called objective study of mind—that is to say, to the study of the objective manifestations in other beings of a consciousness more or less similar to that of which he has, through introspection, some first-hand knowledge his aim being, by such study, to reach an inferential or second-hand knowledge of the nature of the consciousness which actuates the conduct of these beings. And here the student of human psychology is in a position of great advantage, as compared with that which the student of zoological psychology must rest content with. For, by means of specialized objective manifestation, especially of language, self-conscious human beings can signify to each other the nature of their individual conscious experiences. Objective manifestations of some kind are the only index we have of the inner psychical experience. But by means of a common language, human beings can purposely set the index, so as to suggest the particular nature of this psychical experience.

Let us revert once more for a moment to the analogy of the chronometer. In two similar chronometers the position of the index-hands at any moment indicates the exact configuration of the wheels of the internal mechanism. Either of these two, then, which knew from introspection the psychical aspect of its own inner processes, would be able to infer with accuracy the exact configuration of the wheels of its neighbor's works from the position of the index-hands. If it had also a pair of subsidiary hands which it could shift at will, it would be able to indicate at any moment to its neighbor the particular configuration of some previous moment. Thus each could gain inferentially and indirectly through the objective study of the index-hands and accurate knowledge of its neighbor's inner mechanism. Everything, however, would depend upon the similarity of the internal mechanism, in the two chronometers. If they were slightly different, they would have very great difficulty in conveying to each other the nature of this difference. So too with human beings. In so far as men are similar in psychical endowments, they can convey to each other through the index of language the nature of their psychical experience. They have great difficulty in making each other acquainted with their individual differences. And the difficulty is the greater the more these individual differences are qualitative, and not merely quantitative. Among civilized men, of like social grade, and somewhat similarly educated, the individual differences are mainly quantitative—that is to say, differences in the relative development of similar faculties. Careful objective study enables us to gauge and assign a value to the ratio of the faculties in our friends and neighbors. But in the study of uncivilized men, not only of different social grade, but living under a different social system, men whose education and upbringing has been far other than those under which our own character has been molded, we find differences which are not merely quantitative but qualitative. There is not merely a difference in the ration of similar faculties, but a greater or less divergence in the nature of the faculties themselves. In such cases our inferences are much more difficult and less trustworthy.

The realization of the difficulties inseparable from the subject, and of his liability to error in the interpretation of the facts, does not, however, deter the student of human psychology from a careful investigation of the objective manifestations of mind. He takes every opportunity of studying these manifestations, not only in normal men and women of all grades and of all races, not only in normal children and infants, but in pathological cases in hospitals and asylums, and under those abnormal conditions which are presented by patients in the somnambulistic or hypnotic state. Throughout the whole of these objective investigations, the wide and cautious student never forgets that the interpretation of the facts in psychical terms is based upon the inductions he has reached through introspection. The facts are objective phenomena; the interpretation is in terms of subjective experience; and no one has or can have any subjective experience other than that afforded by his own consciousness.

We are now in a position to see clearly what is the distinctive peculiarity of the study of mind in beings other than our own individual selves. Its conclusions are reached not by a singly inductive process, as in Chemistry or Physics, in Astronomy, Geology, Biology, or other purely objective science, but by a doubly inductive process. Inductions reached through the objective study of certain physical manifestations have to be interpreted in terms of inductions reached through the introspective study of mental processes. By induction I mean the observation of facts, the framing of hypotheses to comprise the facts, and the verification of the hypotheses by constant reversion to the touchstone of fact. Our conclusions concerning the mental processes of beings other than our own individual selves are, I repeat, based on a two-fold induction. First the psychologist has to reach, through induction, the laws of mind as revealed to him in his own conscious experience. Here the facts to be studied are facts of consciousness, known at first-hand to him alone among mortals; the hypotheses may logically suggest themselves, in which case they are original so far as the observer himself is concerned, or they may be derived—that is to say, suggested to the observer by other observers; the verification of the hypotheses is again purely subjective, original or derived theories being submitted to the touchstone of individual experience. This is the one inductive process. The other is more objective. The facts to be observed are external phenomena, physical occurrences in the objective world; the hypotheses again may be either original or derived; the verification is objective, original or derived theories being submitted to the touchstone of observable phenomena.

Both inductions, subjective and objective, are necessary. Neither can be omitted without renouncing the scientific method. And then finally the objective manifestations in conduct and activity have to be interpreted in terms of subjective experience. The inductions reached by the one method have to be explained in the light of inductions reached by the other method.

I am anxious to make this matter quite clear, and I will therefore endeavor to illustrate it diagrammatically. In the first diagram (Figure 10.1) the line *a b* represents the conduct, activities, and other objective phenomena exhibited by other beings or organisms than the individual psychologist, while *c d* represents the states of consciousness of which he alone has direct knowledge.

Then the diagram is intended to show how the psychologist must combine both objective induction and subjective induction, that he may reach a subjective interpretation of *a b* in terms of *c d*.

In the second diagram (Fig. 10.28) the curve represents the living beings under investigation comprising the psychologist himself and other organisms. The upper line represents the physical objective aspect, the lower line the psychical subjective aspect. The whole of the upper line is open to the inductive investigation of the psychologist. But of the lower line only the firm part,

Figure 10.1

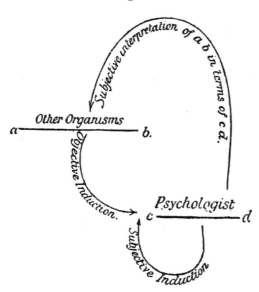

that representing his own inner consciousness, is open to his inductive study. The dotted part, that representing the mental side of other organisms, has to be interpreted by the inferential prolongation of the known part of the curve, or in other words, has to be interpreted in terms of the subjective inductions reached through the introspection.

Now it is idle to assert that one set of inductions is more important than the other, since both are essential. But there can be no question that the subjective inductions are in some respect more subtle and difficult and delicate than the inductions concerning objective phenomena. There can be no question that false assumptions and vague generalizations more commonly pass muster with regard to mental processes than with regard to their physical manifestations. And there can be no question that in the systematic training of the comparative psychologist the subjective aspect is not *less* important than the objective aspect.

The question now arises whether in passing from human to animal psychology any other method of interpretation is possible than that which holds good for the former. Can the zoological psychologist afford to dispense with that systemic training in introspective or subjective analysis and induction which is absolutely essential for the student of human psychology? I venture to contend that he cannot. The scheme of interpretation exhibited diagrammatically in Figure. 10.2 holds good I maintain as well for animal psychology as for the psychology of man. There are, I am well aware, many people who fancy that by the objective

Figure 10.2

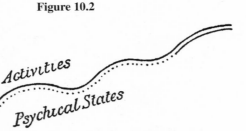

study of animal life they can pass by direct induction to conclusions concerning the psychical faculties of animals. But this is, I think, through ignorance of the methods of psychology; or perhaps one may say, without injustice, through ignorance of the method that they themselves unconsciously adopt. All that is necessary, these people will tell you, is to observe carefully, and to explain the actions you observe in the most natural manner. "In the most natural manner," here means and is equivalent to, in just the same way as you explain the actions of your human neighbors and acquaintances. And these human actions are explained on the assumption that your neighbor is actuated by motives and impulses similar to your own. Thus these observers who think that their explanations are reached by direct induction are really proceeding unconsciously on the method they affect to disregard. Reduced to its logical basis their contention is that the thorough and systematic study of that mind in terms of which they unconsciously interpret all other minds is unnecessary if not misleading.

Now it appears to me that the foundation of this erroneous view, for as such I must regard it, is the tacit assumption that what suffices for practical purposes suffices also for scientific purposes. All fairly successful men and women acquire, and must acquire, a knowledge of human nature sufficient for the practical needs of everyday life under social conditions. Over-subtlety and refinement of analysis, too great nicety of interpretation, are rather disadvantageous than otherwise in the practical conduct of affairs. Hence practical men are wont to look with some suspicion at the psychologist as one who is prone to be a mere theorist. In the same way practical politicians not uncommonly look with suspicion on sociologists and political economists, practical engineers regard with similar eyes the subtler theories of the physicist, practical metallurgists look askance on the more delicate methods and more advanced hypotheses of the chemist, and in general the practical man is inclined to utilize the results of the man of science but to regard his more refined interpretations of natural phenomena as mere theory.

There can be no question that the interpretation of the actions of animals as the outcome of mental processes essentially similar to those of man amply suffices for practical needs. The farmer, the keeper of a kennel, the cattle-breeder, the gamekeeper, the breaker-in of horses, all the practical men who are employed in the breeding, rearing, and training of animals, and the great number of people who keep animals as pets or in domestic service find a somewhat rough and ready interpretation amply sufficient for their purposes in hand. And not unnaturally they are surprised that the explanation which suffices for them with their wide practical experience is found by the man of science to need serious revision and correction. Often unacquainted with the method and aims of science in its intellectual aspect as endeavoring to interpret the phenomena of nature, often regarding science as the generally unpaid servant of practical utility, they smile if they do not sneer, at the arrogance of the man of science who tells them that the explanation which is good enough for the practical purposes of daily life is not sufficient for the more subtle and refined purposes of scientific interpretation. Be this as it may, I venture to affirm that whereas the man who has to deal with animals for practical purposes can afford to be ignorant of psychological methods and results, the man who would deal scientifically with the psychical faculties of animals cannot afford to be thus ignorant. For the practical man accuracy of observation and careful induction there from are of primary importance, validity of psychological interpretation being for him altogether subsidiary. But for the scientific investigator thorough and accurate knowledge of and training in psychology is of at least co-ordinate importance with accuracy of objective observation.

Unfortunately many able men who are eminently fitted to make and record exact observations on the habits and activities of animals have not undergone the training necessary to enable them to deal with the psychological aspect of the question. The skilled naturalist or biologist is seldom also skilled in psychological analysis. Notwithstanding therefore the admirable and invaluable observations of our great naturalists, we cannot help feeling that their psychological conclusions are hardly on the same level as that reached by their conclusions in the purely biological field.

For in the study of animal psychology as a branch of scientific inquiry, it is necessary that accurate observation, and a sound knowledge of the biological relationships of animals, should go hand in hand with a thorough appreciation of the methods and results of modern psychology. The only fruitful method of procedure is the interpretation of facts observed with due care in the light of sound psychological principles.

What some of these principles are we have considered, or shall consider, in this work. There is one basal principle, however, the brief exposition of which may fitly bring to close this chapter. It may be thus stated – *In no case may we interpret an action as the outcome of the exercise of a higher psychical faculty, if it can be interpreted as the outcome of the exercise of one which stands lower in the psychological scale.*

To this principle several objections, none of them however of any real weight, may be raised. First there is the sentimental objection that is ungenerous to the animal. In dealing with one's fellow-man it is ungenerous to impute to him lower motives for his actions when they may have been dictated by higher motive. Why should we adopt a different course with the poor dumb animal from that which we should adopt with our human neighbor? In the first place, it may be replied, this objection starts by assuming the very point to be proved. The scientific problem is to ascertain the limits of animal psychology. To assume that a given action may be the outcome of the exercise of either a higher or a lower faculty, and that it is more generous to adopt the former alternative, is to assume the existence of the higher faculty, which has to be proved. In the case of our neighbors we have good grounds for knowing that such and such a deed may have been dictated by either a higher or a lower motive. If we had equally good grounds for knowing that the animal was possessed of both higher and lower faculties, the scientific problem would have been solved; and the attribution of the one or the other, in any particular case, would be a purely individual matter of comparatively little general moment. In the second place, this generosity, though eminently desirable in the relations of a practical social life, is not precisely the attitude which a critical scientific inquiry demands. Moreover, an ungenerous interpretation of one's neighbor's actions may lead one to express an unjust estimate of his moral character and thus to do him grave social wrong; but an ungenerous interpretation of the faculties of animals can hardly be said to be open to like practical consequences.

A second objection is, that by adopting the principle in question we may be shutting our eyes to the simplest explanation of the phenomena. Is it not simpler to explain the higher activities of animals as the direct outcome of reason or intellectual thought, than to explain them as the complex results of mere intelligence or practical sense-experience? Undoubtedly it may in many cases seem simpler. It is the apparent simplicity of the explanation that leads many people naively to adopt it. But surely the simplicity of an explanation is no necessary criterion of its truth. The explanation of the genesis of the organic world by direct creative fiat, is far simpler than the explanation of its genesis through the indirect method of evolution. The explanation of instinct and early phases of intelligence as due to inherited habit, individually acquired, is undoubtedly simpler than the explanation which Dr Weismann would substitute for it. The formation of the cañon of the Colorado by a sudden rift in the earth's crust, similar to those which opened during the Calabrian earthquakes, is simpler than its formation by the fretting of the stream during long ages under varying meteorological conditions. In these cases and in many others the simplest explanation is not the one accepted by science. Moreover, the simplicity of the explanation of the phenomena of animal activity as the result of intellectual processes, can only be adopted on the assumption of a correlative complexity in the mental nature of the animal as agent. And to assume this complexity of mental nature on grounds other than those of sound induction, is to depart from the methods of scientific procedure.

But what, it may be asked, is the logical basis upon which this principle is founded? If it be true that the animal mind can only be interpreted in the light of our knowledge of human mind, why should we not use this method of interpretation freely, frankly, and fully? Is there not some contradiction in refusing to do so? For, first, it is contended that we must use the human mind as a key by which to read the brute mind, and then it is contended that this key must be applied with a difference. If we apply the key at all, should we not apply it without reservation?

This criticism might be valid if we were considering the question apart from evolution. Here evolution is postulated. The problem is this: (1) Given a number of divergently ascending grades of organisms, with divergently increasing complexity of organic structure and correlated activities: (2) granted that associated with the increasing organic complexity there is increasing mental or psychical complexity: (3) granted that in man the organic complexity, the complexity of correlated activities, and the associated mental or psychical complexity, has reached the maximum as not yet attained: (4) to gauge the psychical level to which any organism has been evolved. As we have already seen, we are forced, as men, to gauge the psychical level of the animal in terms of the only mind of which we have first-hand knowledge, namely the human mind. But how are we to apply the gauge?

There would appear to be three possible methods, which are exemplified in Figure 10.3. 9. Let a represent the psychical stature of man, and 1,2,3, ascending faculties or stadia in mental development. Let b c represent two animals the psychical stature of each of which is to be gauged. It may be gauged first by the "method of levels," according to which the faculties or stadia are of constant value. In the diagram, b has not quite reached the level of the beginning of the third or highest faculty, while c has only just entered upon the second stadium. Secondly, it may be gauged by the "method of uniform reduction." In both b and c we have all three faculties represented in the same ratio as in a, but all uniformly reduced. And thirdly, it may be gauged by the "method of variation," according to which any one of the faculties 1,2 or 3, may in b and c be either increased or reduced relatively to its development in a. Let us suppose, for example, that b represents the psychical stature of the dog. Then, according to the interpretation on the method of levels, he possesses the lowest faculty (1) in the same degree as man; in the faculty (2) he somewhat falls short of man; while in the highest faculty (3) he is altogether wanting. According to the interpretation on the method of uniform reduction he possesses all the faculties of man but in a reduced degree. And according to the interpretation of the method of variation he excels man in the lowest faculty, while the other two faculties are both reduced but in different degrees. The three "faculties" 1,2,3 are not here intended to serve any other purpose than merely to illustrate the three methods of interpretation.

On the principles of evolution we should unquestionably expect that those mental faculties which could give decisive advantage in the struggle for existence would be developed in strict accordance with the divergent conditions of

Figure 10.3

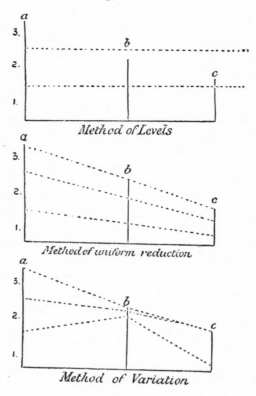

Method of Levels

Method of uniform reduction

Method of Variation

life. Hence it is the third method, which I have termed the method of variation, which we should expect *a priori* to accord most nearly with observed facts. And so far as we can judge from objective observation (the only observation open to us) this would appear to be the case. Presumably there are few observers of animal habit and intelligence who would hesitate in adopting the method of variation as the most probable mode of interpretation. But note that while it is the most probable it is also the most difficult mode of interpretation. According to the method of levels the dog is just like me, without any higher faculties. According to the method of uniform reduction he is just like me, only nowise so highly developed. But according to the method of variation there are many possibilities of error in estimating the amount of such variation. Of the three methods that of variation is the least anthropomorphic, and therefore the most difficult.

In the diagram by which the method of variation is illustrated, the highest faculty 3 is in *c* reduced to zero—in other words, is absent. It may, however, be objected that this is contrary to the principles of evolution, since the presence of any faculty in higher types involves the germ of this faculty in lower types. This criticism only holds good, however, on the assumption that the evolution of higher faculties out of lower faculties is impossible. Those evolutionists who accept this assumption as valid are logically bound to believe either (1) that all forms of animal life from the amoeba upwards have all the faculties of man, only reduced in degree and range, and to interpret all animal psychology on a method of reduction (though not necessarily uniform reduction), or (2) that in the higher forms of life the introduction of the higher faculties has been effected by some means other than that of natural evolution. I am not prepared to accept the assumption as valid; and it will be part of my task in future chapters to consider how the transition from certain lower to certain higher phases of mental development may have been effected.

If this be so it is clear that any animal may be at a stage where certain higher faculties have not yet been evolved from their lower precursors; and hence we are logically bound not to assume the existence of these higher faculties until good reasons shall have been shown for such existence. In other words, we are bound to accept the principle above enunciated: that in no case is an animal activity to be interpreted as the outcome of the exercise of a higher psychical faculty, if it can be fairly interpreted as the outcome of the exercise of one which stands lower in the psychological scale.

Note

1.   Reprinted from Morgan, C.L. (1894). *An introduction to comparative psychology.* L.: Walter Scott Ltd. Chapter 3, pp. 36-59.

11

A Holistic Perspective in Natural Sciences

Camilo E. Khatchikian
Clark University

In any approach taken to the natural world, it ought to be easy to perceive that living systems are extremely complex. Thus, any scientific approach used in its interpretation should take into account this complexity and the evident presence of hierarchical levels of organization. Each one of those hierarchical levels shows, concordantly, increasing levels of complexity in their quantity and quality of their novel, emergent properties (Teller, 1992; Kauffman, 1993; Richardson, 1997). For example, molecules are combined into one organizational level; cells present a new set of characteristics and properties which are not equal to the sum of the characteristics and properties in the lower level, resulting in an entirely new entity. This sequence can be followed to higher levels to reach other entities, as could be considered tissues, organs, systems, organisms, populations, species, communities, ecosystems, and landscapes. The exact identification of those levels does not appear to be critical in this context (several biologists may consider including or excluding different levels), but clearly it is the notion that the organizational properties in each level are not the result of simply adding the characteristics of its components. Emergent properties are those that appear in specific hierarchical levels and can neither be predicted nor resolved based on the analysis of lower level properties (see Healey, 1991, for a dialectic criticism). Evidently, some properties that are present in any given level would be present in the following level as well, nevertheless, not all of them are (an extensive emergence framework is presented by Paul Humphreys, 1997). Biology, as the science that studies living organisms and their processes, is confronted on a regular and consistent basis with the phenomena of emergence, and, thus, has adopted a holistic and integrative approach as a core part of its heuristic program. The path toward the recognition of a holistic attitude was concurrent with its own development as a modern science in recent times.

In this chapter, I will present how the philosophical and epistemological context prevalent during the scientific revolution, predominantly mechanisms associated with a methodology of reductionism, profoundly influenced the initial attitude of biology towards the natural world.

It is only after centuries of compiling discoveries, advances, and concomitant changes in biology conceptual frameworks (as well as other disciplinary frameworks) that the initial influence of the scientific revolution has progressively been ameliorated and finally reverted. Contributions from biologists to initially perceived dissimilar fields such as genetics, development, physiology, ecology, and evolution were critical in the progressive realization of a natural integration between disciplines. It is my intention to present how the study of the biological phenomena, where wholes and parts are intangibles changing according to the level of study, has converged in a coherent holistic point of view.

Early Biology

It seems clear that early human communities had intense contact with the natural world; these communities subsisted by a combination of various forms of hunting, gathering, and throve by a developing plant and animal domestication (see Lewin, 1998). Their perceptions regarding the properties of the natural world, if any, remain unclear for us, though we know that several pre-Grecian civilizations had a considerable amount of biological or medical knowledge that could be sporadically discerned from sculptures, utensils, papyri, and a few scattered fragments of manuscripts (Sirks & Zirkle, 1964). The first recorded attempts, in the Occidental world, to explain life and its properties should be accredited to the Greeks. Considering the extension and complexity of the Hellenic period, it is difficult to summarize the different philosophers' concepts regarding this issue—as each one was a distinct personality, with highly individualistic views. The philosophers most prevalent in their legacy, as a general rule, were essentialists (i.e., they were willing to find the true essence of things), often related with invoking forces or materials to explain the natural world, rejecting supernatural explanations.

Several philosophers of the Hellenic period, such as Thales of Miletus, Anaximander, and Anaximenes maintained the existence of one or more essential or primary elements as constituents of the world. In a similar manner, Heraclitus or Empedocles argued that the presence of properties or basic laws rule natural phenomena, such as ether (or "fire"). The inherent conclusion of these positions is that given a total knowledge of the essential elements and a complete understanding of the laws that govern them, a consummate understanding of the natural world is possible. Special consideration should be taken with Aristotle (384-322 BC), as his points of view prevailed in all sciences for almost twenty centuries. Aristotle saw the body as composed of four primary substances (fire, earth, air, and water), each with different organization. A strong essentialist concept of the world can be found in Aristotle's philosophy, as he looked for the first principles and the essential attributes of existence (see Gardner, 1965). Aristotle's natural philosophy can be characterized by its dynamism, the importance of the principle of movement (but no mechanical implication), and a universal vitalism where the existence of the soul is strongly recognized (Sirks & Zirkle, 1964)—this soul being the principle of movement itself. Interestingly, different interpretations of Aristotle's arguments would be taken either by mechanist or vitalist positions later on.

The Scientific Revolution

During the fifteenth and sixteenth centuries, when the Renaissance began, drastic changes took place in Europe establishing the end of the middle ages and the beginning of modernity. Classical works were recovered in this period, mainly from the Arabic world, which acted as a foundation for the developing science, technology, and scholarship. Despite the increasing critical attitude of Renaissance scholars toward Greek traditions, classical works played a relevant role in the development of sciences, especially Aristotle's works, which often were taken as starting positions. This period was characterized by a mechanistic standpoint of the world, mainly due to the significant impact of Descartes, Galileo, Kepler, Boyle, and Newton in the conceptualization and interpretation of Nature. During this period, Aristotle's fundamental principle of dynamism evolved into a mechanistic view of the natural world. Mechanism was the common vision that all science would eventually be reduced to mechanics, a purely physical component.

The early versions of mechanism were characterized by the belief that all of science could be derived from the science of mechanics and the resulting conclusion was that living creatures could be treated as machines, pure and simple. In this way, to reach a full understanding of the biological processes, these machines should be dissected and reduced to their smallest components. The mechanism movement had the enormous merit in refuting much of the magical thinking that had characterized the preceding centuries. Mechanism's greatest achievement was to provide natural explanations of physical phenomena and, thus, eliminate much of the reliance on supernatural entities as was previously accepted (Mayr, 1998). The mechanism made a hierarchical interpretation of the Nature, where the explanations for any phenomenon should be sought by carefully analyzing its elemental components, dividing the whole into the smallest parts. This position can be easily observed in contemporary writings. Descartes (1958/1701) wrote in his *Rules for the guidance of our native powers,* Part II, Rule XIII:

> For the perfect understanding of a question we must abstract it from all that is superfluous, rending it as simple as possible, and, resorting to enumeration, divide it into its minimal parts. (p. 71)

. . . we seek the whole by way of the parts, as when, having several numbers, we seek their sum by adding one to another; or when, having two numbers, we seek their product by multiplying the one by the other. (p. 75)

This was the context within which modern biology was established, providing ways of explaining and investigating biological processes and phenomena without the need of divine intervention (Agutter et al., 2000; see also Mandelbaum, 1974). This new scientific competence over life itself was a radical and revolutionary position long sought by thinkers and opponents of church and state throughout Western Europe. In those early days of the scientific revolution, analyses of the nature of the organic compounds were performed showing that living organisms were not composed of special matters or substances, but rather regular compounds also commonly found throughout the Earth (Haldane, 1914). In a similar way, advances in anatomy and physiology of organisms allowed anatomists to attribute specific functions to particular parts of the body, such as organs or systems. As a result of those theoretical frameworks, modern biology was stigmatized with a strong mechanical approach, in similar way as physics and chemistry. It was clear, thus, that if an organism is constituted of a large number of small parts that together form the whole, the only viable analytic approach in biological processes should be to analyze each part independently in its minimal expression to reach the whole as an additive result of these parts.

After the initial mechanism homogeny, biologists in different fields started finding that natural phenomena; especially those related with growth, reproduction, embryology development, and reaction to the environment; were completely incompatible with the pure concept of organism as machines (Agutter et al., 2000). Slowly but steadily different perceptions of the biological world started to appear among biologists. Those new positions, which are broadly included under the term vitalism, were extreme variables with each other, but they shared two main characteristics; they were opposed to the organism-machine concept and, as pointed out by Driesch (1914), considered to some extent a declaration of independence of organisms from the inanimate world.

Vitalism

The origins of vitalism philosophy in modern biology can be found during the seventeenth century as a reaction to the prevailing mechanistic view of the Scientific Revolution. It is relevant to mention, at this point, that several naturalists and biologists at that time belonged to the clergy, and thus, were willing to believe in some kind of divine intervention. Some early versions of vitalism argued that life was connected with a special substance (protoplasm) or a special state of matter (such as colloidal state) that could not be found in inanimate matter and thus, were outside the scope and incumbency of physicochemical sciences. These early vitalism positions were promptly criticized and revised, not only by mechanists but also by the following generation of vitalists as no evidence of such substances or states had ever been found. Later vitalist authors, such as G. E. Stahl, J. Müller, G. L. Buffon, or J. F. Blumenbach, argued that there was a special vital force (called either *Lebenskraft, Entelechie, élan vital,* or *nisus formativus*) which, again, physical sciences were unable to explain or deal with. Several authors, such as G. E. Stahl and H. Driesch himself, argued as well that life should have some ultimate purpose (for an extended revision of early vitalism see Driesch, 1914).

A variety of different vitalism schools flourished during the eighteenth and nineteenth centuries, obtaining support from some observations of natural phenomena, but never reaching a unified, coherent program. Bray (1958) pointed out that most positions of vitalism share the concept that life was made of different substances, or that there was an additional vital substance, a natural extra-sensory element or force that governs and rules the natural world and its behavior. In general terms, any vitalism position from any period shares the belief in the existence of some operating principle which is not found in the inorganic world and that it is particular to living organisms (Lipman, 1967). Vitalism positions ruled undisputed among biologist until the first part of the nineteenth century, as almost all biologists recognized the action of some "vital property" or "vital force" peculiar to living substance, which rules over the mechanical elements (for example, see Myers, 1900; Agutter et al., 2000). Thus, the vitalism marked a brief but nontrivial change in biology's ruling paradigm as it began taking into account living systems as wholes, not only as parts or elements.

Mechanistic Materialism

During the nineteenth century, biology was becoming an experimental discipline, especially in the physiological field. The physiological schools were introducing methods commonly used in other distinct disciplines, such as physics and chemistry, in an experimental context. In conjunction with new methodology, new batches of scientists were incorporated into the biological sciences that had formal training in physics or chemistry, sciences still under a tight mechanical vision. Biologists were able to rigorously test their conclusions through experimentation, and they gradually expanded experimentation to the study of most kinds of biological phenomena promoting biology as a new, independent, and accepted natural science paired with physics and chemistry (see Gardner, 1965).

In 1839, M. Schleiden and T. Schwann announced the cell theory, establishing cells as the unit of structure, growth, and minimal organizational expression of life and, thus, supporting an elemental and reductionist explanation of the vital phenomena. In correspondence, studies on organic compounds showed that the chemistry of life was similar to inorganic chemistry, as exemplified by Liebig's and Wöhler study on benzoyl radicals, among others, where chemists were able to identify, produce, describe, analyze, and duplicate organic compounds and processes (see Lipman, 1967; Rosenfeld, 2003). These studies and advances contributed to generate the belief that the difficulty with understanding organic chemistry came from ignorance, not from a mysterious vital force (see Lipman, 1967). At the same time, medicine started using "chemical remedies," being able not only to clearly explain why but also how those compounds worked. The newly acquired competence of biology caused a major decline in vitalism, which was already having problems stating a testable hypothesis, and as a result, was progressively considered a mystical belief by the scientific community (Haldane, 1913; Mayr, 1998). These new schools of thought brought again a strong mechanistic philosophy to the forefront. A new revitalized version of mechanistic materialism arose fundamentally in physiological schools of Germany, which held that all phenomena of animal and plant physiology could be explained in terms of physics (Agutter et al., 2000), as illustrated by von Nägeli invoking, in 1884, the "movement" of the smallest parts to explain the mechanics of organic life. Huxley (1877) noted that biology is a physical science, and thus, the methods of study must be analogous to those followed in other scientific disciplines. Once again, in biology the whole was the sum of its parts, and nothing more.

Formally, this scientific philosophy is known as mechanistic materialism, which holds that the ultimate understanding of phenomena comes from studying the individual parts that interact; the parts are studied in isolation, and the whole is reconstructed as a sum (and nothing more) of those parts. Mechanistic theory is a special form of a the general principle of determinism, deriving its specific characteristics from the introduction of a temporal factor, and from the use of geometrical, kinematical, mechanical, and physico-chemical terms (Hoernle, 1918). Mechanistic materialism has often been associated with the methodology of reductionism, which implies that the most thorough understanding of any phenomenon occurs when that phenomenon can be broken down, or reduced, to its lowest accessible level of organization (Allen, 1978). Not surprisingly, most mechanist positions usually imply reductionist methodologies. Hull (1974) pointed out that one of the contentions of mechanistic reductionism is that, in the course of time, scientists will produce theories that can be synthesized into a single unified theory (see also Lotka, 1925). Many scientists, especially biologists and social scientists, argue against both the possibility and desirability of such a program, recognizing the inherent qualities, components, and autonomies of the diverse sciences (e.g., Kincaid, 1986; Rosenberg, 1994; Mayr, 1996). Mechanism, even that which was predominant in the second part of the nineteenth century, was unable to completely rule out vitalism—as mechanism was incapable of accounting for the whole in any other way but as the sum of its component parts. The major failure of mechanism was that it did not provide consistent research programs to deal with the hierarchical levels and emergent properties present in biological systems.

Hans Driesch's Contribution

Hans Driesch (1867-1941) was a notable embryologist who made several observations and experiments in relation with the early stages of development of embryos that refuted the previous developmental theory proposed by August Weismann in 1883. Weismann's theory proposed that there was an early determination of the fate of each cell after each division, even after the very first division (in the two-cell stage). Later, Wilhelm Roux performed a series of experiments and found that destroying one cell of a two cell frog embryo results in the development of a half, non-viable embryo. Roux concluded that the frog embryo was a mosaic of self-differentiating parts (see Gilbert, 2000). Driesch found a quite different picture studying the development of sea urchin's larvae. He performed slightly different experiments by pulling apart individual cells from the embryos resulting, each one, in a smaller, fully viable larva. Based on his results, Driesch concluded that the development of organisms does not proceed in a mechanical, isolated way but in an integrative holistic fashion. The production of a normal organism despite disturbance in the embryo is, in its very nature, a violation of a mechanical process, as pointed out by Elkus (1911). Mechanism involves the principle that similar effects must be produced by similar causes, nevertheless, in Driesch's experiments, quite different causes are observed to produce similar results. An unaltered embryo produces a normal organism, but an altered embryo produces a normal organism as well. Driesch (1934) stated that, in that way, the machine theory of development has been completely refuted; the mechanistic theory cannot be applied, at the very least, in the field of embryology.

According to Driesch, the shaping of highly differentiated organisms from a single-cell embryo (composed of undifferentiated material) could only be attributed to the action of the *entelechy* or vital force, as physicochemical agents were unable to account for it by themselves. Later in his life, Driesch stopped working in embryology and focused on the philosophical aspects of the nature of life. He emphasized the action of a vital force acting shaping and regulating the development of embryos (see Driesch, 1934). Driesch realized that there were additional considerations that can not been taken into account by the mechanistic theory of life. He assumed that the *entelechy* was outside the physical world, and thus, science was never going to be able to experiment, manipulate, or measure this non-physical factor. Considering our incapacity to know the completed whole of life, biological knowledge would always be hypothetical.

Later biologists, such as T. Boveri, found that certain structures are present in unfertilized eggs of the sea urchin and others organisms—circumstance unknown during Driesch's experiments. Three zones can be identified inside an unfertilized egg demarking a rough pre-formation of the main axis of the embryo (Figure 11.1a). The first two divisions are parallels to this axis,

Figure 11.1
Early Stages of Development of Sea Urchin

Figure 11.1 a

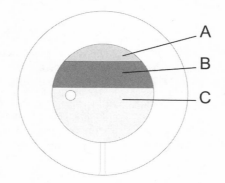

Figure 11.1 b

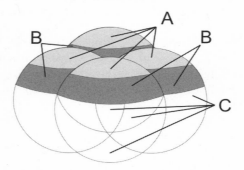

Representation of early stages of development of sea urchin embryo depicting the areas that can be recognized: a small clear cap (A), a pigmented ring (B), and the rest unpigmented (C). Figure 11.1a represents a single-cell stage, and Figure 11.1b represents a four-cell stage, after two parallel to the axis cell divisions, where each cell contains one-fourth of the original regions (modified from Loeb, 1916).

producing four equal cells; that is, with equal distribution of egg regions (Figure 11.1b). In this stage, if these cells are pulled apart, the product would be four complete larvae. The following sets of division are perpendicular to the axis, and thus, produce unequal cells. From this point, pulling apart cells will not produce fully developed larvae. Nevertheless, embryos would still be able to compensate for the loss of a few cells in later stages of development (see Loeb, 1916; Przibram, 1926). Even though Driesch's and his followers produced interpretations of the natural world that were found to be partially inaccurate, they certainly made two major contributions to the biological sciences. First, vitalists proposed an alternative view of the nature of biological systems, using an experimental approach. Second, they showed that mechanism approaches provided several trivial and superficial explanations to biological phenomena and, in that way, showed that central questions and problems still remained unsolved. Driesch's himself found a major flaw in the previously accepted mechanical explanation for embryo development, which could not account at all for the biological process under study.

Twentieth-century Biology

In the beginning of the twentieth century, a new generation of physiologist such as F. Magendie, C. Bernard and J. S. Haldane arrived rejecting the mechanistic view of organisms and started to study the larger problems of animal physiology—involving the integration of functions of many organs and systems together. Once again, physiology played a major role in the change of the biological sciences, as it soon became clear that any animal physiological process was such a complex system that an oversimplified mechanistic approach was unable to provide a comprehensible solution (Allen, 1978). Haldane (1931) pointed out that by the early days of the twentieth century, biologists had abandoned vitalism as an acknowledged belief but at the same time argued that a pure mechanistic interpretation could not satisfactorily account for life phenomenon. Based on the observation that all biological processes tend towards being highly coordinated, and this coordination is critical in biological systems, Haldane concluded that biology should find a different theoretical base. In this regard, Haldane stated that:

> . . . not merely the difficulty, but the impossibility, of interpreting life as a physico-chemical process on the general conception of physics and chemistry as formulated on the lines of Galileo and Newton . . . the attempt to eke out the physico-chemical interpretation by assuming the interference in vital process of an agency which, since it is neither visible nor tangible, we can properly call a supernatural agency, is equally unsatisfactory in enabling us to comprehend life. (Haldane, 1929: 73)

Organicism: A New Paradigm

During the end of the nineteenth and the beginning of the twentieth century, paired with the rejection of mechanism in biology, similar changes occurred in physical and chemical sciences leading to a new view of the physical world. Allen (1978) underscores the discovery of X-rays and the rise of quantum and relativity theories as breaking points in the physical concepts of the natural phenomena. Atoms were no longer regarded as mechanical bodies but were centers of electrical force with magnetic properties and subatomic particles; electrons could not be located in space but had to be described in terms of areas of probability. In a similar way, it became clear in chemistry that knowing all the subatomic structures and properties of an element provided no way to predict the properties of any compound in which the element took part; similar aware-ness occurred in related disciplines as well (such as medicine, see Lawrence & Weisz, 1998). The question of what was the nature of matter could no longer be answered in a simplistic way; in fact, to some, nothing seemed real, and science came to be regarded more and more only as a conceptual framework that man imposed on the universe. The biological sciences were prepared to develop and enunciate their own heuristic program and philosophy of science.

W. E. Ritter called this philosophy "organicism" in 1919, under the premise that parts, as can be known as independent entities, are not wholly explanatory of their wholes. This new philosophy was based on the premise that the exclu-sive characteristics of biological systems are not due to their composition but to their organization, including their hierarchies and the properties associated with them. Thus, he writes:

> . . . wholes are so related to their parts that not only does the existence of the whole depend on the orderly cooperation and interdependence of its parts, but the whole exercises a measure of determinative control over its parts . . . The whole is not merely something that is intact, something not torn, or cut to pieces, or smashed into fragments. Rather a whole is something the original and necessary parts of which are so located and so functioning in relation to each other as to contribute their proper share to the structure and the functioning of the whole. A natural whole stands in such relation to its parts as to make it and its parts mutually constitutive of each other. Structurally, functionally, and generatively, they are reciprocals of one other. (Ritter & Bailey, 1928: 308)

Since the 1920's, the terms holism and organicism have been used inter-changeably, but in current biology the more restricted term organicism is used more frequently (Mayr, 1998), probably as a biology reassertion of its own identity. It should be noted, however, that different terminologies could be used, even nowadays, by different authors implying slightly different concepts but quite similar ideas (Hull, 1974). At this point, biologists began to explain in detail why there was a need for a holistic approach to the study of living organisms. In the second half of the twentieth century, an increasing body of references to this issue can be found in the biological literature; for example, Novikoff (1949) states:

> In the continual evolution of matter, new levels of complexity are superimposed on the individual units into a single system. What are wholes on one level become parts on a higher one. Each level of organization possesses unique properties of structure and behavior which, though dependent on the properties of the constituent elements, appear only when these elements are combined in the new system . . . No matter how complete our knowledge of the chemistry and physics of living systems becomes in the future, living substance must still be recognized as matter on a higher level, with new, unique properties which have emerged in combination of the lower-level units. (p. 209-210)

According to this new strain of thought, biological systems are composed of various hierarchical levels acting as wholes or parts according to the specific object of study. The characteristics of each whole cannot be deduced, even in theory, from the most complete knowledge of the components taken separately or in any other combination (after Mayr, 1982). Simpson (1969) believed that these distinctions serve to distinguish biology from physics or others exact sciences, but Mayr affirmed that the holistic approach apply in other scientific disciplines as well. Mayr (1998) mentioned an interesting anecdote, that it is relevant for this topic:

> At first I thought that this phenomenon of emergence, as it is now called, was restricted to the living world; and indeed, in a lecture I gave in the early 1950's in Copenhagen, I made the claim that emergence was one of the diagnostic features of the organic world. The whole concept of emergence was at that time considered to be rather metaphysical. When the physicist Niels Bohr, who was in the audience, stood up to speak during the discussion period, I was fully prepared for an annihilating refutation. However, much to my surprise, he did not at all object to the concept of emergence but only to my notion that it provides a demarcation between the physical and the biological sciences. Citing the case of water, whose "aquosity" could not be predicted from the characteristics of its two components, hydrogen and oxygen, Bohr stated that emergence is rampant in the inanimate world. (Mayr, 1998: xvi)

In this way, it is easy to see that a holistic approach is critical for all sciences where even a complete knowledge of the parts and their interaction in any given physical system is insufficient to provide meaningful insights into the properties of that system as a whole. As Mayr (1996) mentioned, it is the organization of these parts what determine the properties of the entire system.

Final Thoughts

The recognition of the natural complexity and uniqueness of biological systems was crucial in the development of a holistic approach in the biological sciences. An integrative holistic point of view that considers hierarchical levels and wholes, and the interrelations and interactions among them, remains the only proper heuristic approach for biology. As Mayr (1998) pointed out, every system loses some of its characteristics when taken apart, and many important interactions only occur at higher levels and remain undetected at lower levels of integration. It is clear that the nature of biology's heuristic program plays a relevant role in its abilities to provide results and developments but, even more critical, is its effective capacity to formulate proper questions, interact with other scientific disciplines, and promote a plentiful critical view of its own philosophy as an autonomous science. In this way, biology is able to establish its own competences and limitations.

Acknowledgments

This publication was only made possible by the help and contribution of different people. R. Diriwächter was invaluable in the conceptualization of this work and providing valuable suggestions and helpful discussions that significantly improved this work. J. Valsiner provided meaningful insights to an early version of this manuscript. J. Willis provided her support in all stages of the manuscript and suggested multiple critical improvements to the manuscript readability and internal coherency. T. Livdahl provided help and support in the development and exploration of ideas and concepts. I am grateful to my former advisors and mentors M. Martinez, G. Denegri, M. Favero, and A. Vassallo for their encouragement and support that developed my interest and passion for biology.

References

Agutter, P.S., Malone, P.C. & Wheatley, D.N. (2000). "Diffusion theory in biology: A relic of mechanistic materialism." *Journal of the history of biology, 33*: 71-111.

Allen, G.E. (1978). *Life science in the twentieth century.* West Hanover: Cambridge University Press.

Bray, J.R. (1958). "Notes toward an ecological theory." *Ecology, 39*: 770-776.

Descartes, R. (1958/1701). "Regulae ad directionem ingenii." In *Descartes philosophical writings*, translated by NK Smith. New York: The Modern Library.

Driesch, H. (1914). *The history and theory of Vitalism.* London: MacMillan and Co., Limited.

Driesch, H. (1934). "The breakdown of materialism." In Mason, F. (Ed.). *The great design, order and progress and nature.* New York: The MacMillian Company.

Elkus, S.A. (1911). :Mechanism and Vitalism." *The journal of philosophy, Psychology and Scientific Methods, 8 (13)*: 355-358.

Gardner, E.J. (1965). *History of Biology.* Minneapolis: Burgess Publishing Company.

Gilbert, S.C. (2000). *Developmental biology.* Sunderland: Sinauer Associates, Inc.

Haldane, J.S. (1914). *Mechanism, life and personality. An examination of the mechanistic theory of life and mind.* London: John Murray.

Haldane, J.S. (1929). *The sciences and philosophy.* Garden City: Doubleday, Doran, and Company, Inc.

Haldane, J.S. (1931). *The Philosophical basis of biology.* London: Hodder and Stoughton.

Healey, R.A. (1991). Holism and Nonseparability. *The Journal of Philosophy, LXXXVIII (8)*: 303-421.

Hoernle, R.F. (1918). "Mechanism and Vitalism." *The Philosophical Review, 27 (6)*: 628-645.

Hull, D.L. (1974). *Philosophy of biological science.* New Jersey: Prentice-Hall, Inc.

Humphreys, P. (1997). "How Properties Emerge." *Philosophy of Science, 64*: 1-17.

Huxley, T.H. (1877). "A lecture on the study of biology, in connection with the loan collection of scientific apparatus." In *America addresses, with a lecture on the study of biology.* New York: D. Appleton and company.

Kauffman, S.A. (1993). *The origins of order: Self organization and selection in evolution.* New York: Oxford University Press.

Kincaid, H. (1986). "Reduction, explanation, and individualism." *Philosophy of Science, 53*: 492-513.

Lawrence, C. & Weisz, G. (Eds.). (1998). *Greater that the parts: Holism in biomedicine, 1920-1950.* London: Oxford University Press.

Lewin, R. (1998). *Principles of Human Evolution.* Malden: Blackwell Science, Ltd.

Lipman, T.O. (1967). "Vitalism and Reductionism in Liebig's Physiological Thought." *Isis, 58(2)*: 167-185.

Loeb, J. (1916). *The organism as a whole.* New York: The Knickerbocker Press.

Lotka, A.J. (1925). *Elements of physical biology.* Baltimore: Williams & Wilkins Company.

Mayr, E. (1982). *The growth of biological thought. Diversity, evolution and inheritance.* Cambridge: Harvard University Press.

Mayr, E. (1996). "The autonomy of biology: The position of biology among the sciences." *The quarterly review of biology, 71*: 97-106.

Mayr, E. (1998). *This is biology.* Cambridge: Harvard University Press.

Mondelbaum, M. (1974). *History, man, & reason: a study in nineteenth century thought.* Baltimore: John Hopkins Press.

Myers, C.S. (1900). Vitalism: A Brief Historical and Critical Review. *Mind: New Series, 9(34)*: 218-233.

Nägeli, C.V. (1884). *Mechanisch-physiologische theorie der abstammungslehre.* München und Leipzig: R. Aldenbourg.

Novikoff, A. (1949). "The concept of integrative levels and biology." *Science, 101*: 209-215.

Przibram, H. (1926). "Transplantation and Regeneration: Their Bearing on Developmental Mechanics." *Journal of Experimental Biology, 3*: 313-330.

Richardson, R.C. (1997). "Natural and Artificial Complexity." *Philosophy of Science, 64*: 255-267.

Ritter, W.E. (1919). *The unity of the organism.* Boston: The Gorham Press.

Ritter. W.E. & Bailey, T. (1928). "The organismal conception." *University of California publications in zoology, 31*: 307-358.

Rosenberg, A. (1994). *Instrumental biology, or the disunity of science.* Chicago: University of Chicago Press.

Rosenfeld, L. (2003). "William Prout: Early 19th Century Physician-Chemist." *Clinical Chemistry, 46(4)*: 699-705.

Simpson, G.G. (1969). *Biology and man.* New York: Hardcourt, Brace and World.

Sirks, M.J. & Zirkle, C. (1964). *The evolution of biology.* New York: The Ronald Press Company.

Teller, P. (1992). "Supervenience, Emergence, and Reduction." In Berkermann, A., Flohr, H. & Kim, J. (Eds.), *Emergence or reduction?: Essays on the prospects of nonreductive physicalism.* (Pp. 94-118). New York: Library Ed.

12

Dynamic Adaptive Psychology: Viewing the Individual through the Lens of Evolution and Development

Rosemarie I. Sokol
University of San Francisco

Philip J. Rosenbaum
Yeshiva University

Evolutionary Psychology (EP) has found itself on the forefront of modern psychological research as a result of its unique inclusive approach. Based on Darwin's theory of evolution by natural selection, this comprehensive field draws also from fields such as anthropology, sociology, biology, genetics, and psychology. While this inclusiveness allows EP to act as a popular interface of study, the mainstream research on evolutionary processes does not incorporate or emphasize the developmental and holistic nature of these processes. Accordingly, the explanatory statements offered by EP are themselves not as insightful as they otherwise could be. Thus, the goal of this chapter is to provide a theoretical model of EP that is both developmental and holistic by introducing a new method of study called Dynamic Adaptive Psychology.

In attempting to accomplish this goal, we begin by with a backdrop of our argument by developing our claims about EP by contrasting it with Developmental Systems Theory (DST) and *Ganzheitspsychologie*. Following this, an historical overview of both EP and DST is offered in an attempt to show how the developmental history of both fields shaped how they approached research. This in turn leads to the central goal of this paper, where we draw from both DST and *Ganzheitspsychologie* in order to address the weaknesses exposed earlier, by explaining the new Dynamic Adaptive Psychology (DAP). Lastly, we conclude with an example of how this new DAP can be applied to the study of human behavior.

Limitations of Evolutionary Psychology

EP is limited in its focus because it fails to incorporate development in explanations of human behavior. Although it avoids genetic determinism, EP theories tend to emphasize the role of past environments to the exclusion of the current context. Part of this context is the influence of individual development on species-typical behavior. Accordingly, EP views the behavior of the individual not as being a product of their current environment, but rather as a result of their previous environments. The current environment is only important if it differs dramatically from that in which humans evolved. This view does not take into account the role that the individuals' previous experiences, current social situations, and changing cultural values has upon them, and this as a result limits the explanatory power of EP.

Though EP takes an epigenetic approach, examining interactions between adapted traits and the environment, the view appears to be that of predetermined epigenesis. From this perspective, species-specific behaviors are viewed as invariant—given trait x and experience y, the behavior will emerge. Instead, a probabilistic epigenetic approach (Gottlieb, 1999), much like that of developmental systems theory (DST), emphasizes the role of development in the expression of evolved traits.

Therefore, one way of introducing development into EP comes from adopting the developmental perspective taken by DST. This field is, in part, in direct influence of probabilistic epigenesis, which supposes that "behavioral development of individuals within a given species does not follow an invariant or inevitable course, and, more specifically, that the sequence and outcome of individual behavioral development is probable (with respect to norms) rather than certain" (Gottlieb, 2001: 43). Structure and function influence each other as bidirectional relationships between genetic activity, the environment, neural activity, and behavior.

Another way of enhancing the developmental perspective in EP comes from *Ganzheitspsychologie*. In particular, the holistic focus of *Ganzheitspsychologie* would ensure developmental inclusion by attending to the complete and constantly changing organism. Much like probabilistic epigenesis and DST, *Ganzheitspsychologie* emphasizes the whole organism as it exists in the environment.

History of Evolutionary Psychology

Darwin predicted that natural selection would influence all areas of scientific study, particularly psychology (Darwin, 1859/1936). Darwin's influence spread to the natural world via Ethology; to emergent group properties with Sociobiology; and, more recently, to EP, which attempts to explain specific human behaviors and psychology based upon the principles of Darwinian natural selection. (For an extensive review of evolutionary psychology, see Barkow,

Cosmides, & Tooby, 1992; and Cosmides & Tooby, 1997).

In the early twentieth century, the ethological movement formed after the influential Konrad Lorenz (1903-1989) and later Nikolaas Tinbergen (1907-1988) began observing and explaining animal behavior as patterns that occur even in the absence of conditioning, as a result of natural selection (Gould, 1982). To explain animal behavior, Ethologists employed comparisons between closely related species, observed the relevance of particular behaviors to the survival of the individual, and inferred the social and ecological consequences of behavior.

The ethological movement, and in particular Lorenz (and in opposition, Lehrman, and Kuo), is most notable for its generation of the Instinct Wars of the mid-twentieth century (see Thompson, 2000). These wars split those who believed that all behaviors are learned and those who believed certain behavioral traits are instinctual. Instincts are stereotypical behaviors present at birth, and therefore are genetic in nature. From such a view, genetic activity leads directly to species-specific behavior. For example, geese have an imprinting instinct, in which newly hatched goslings are predisposed to follow the first thing they see moving within the first two days of their life, which is in most cases the mother (Lorenz, 1970). From this perspective, goslings do not learn to follow their mothers but do so out of an inborn behavior. Further, if a human is inserted in the place of the mother, the human-adopted goslings would grow into geese that then tried to court humans rather than other geese.

Though many instincts were described for other animals, (i.e., the pecking of chicks and aggression in many social species), William James (1842-1910) believed humans were characterized as having more instincts than other animals (James, 1918), referring to instincts as "native reactions." According to James, "every acquired reaction is, as a rule, either a complication grafted on a native reaction, or a substitute for a native reaction, which the same object originally tended to provoke" (James, 1899/2005: 38). Even the childhood tendency to snatch for toys was described as a native "snatching" reaction, or an instinct. William McDougall (1871-1938) believed that all of human behavior is instinctive (Johnston, 2001). Luther Lee Bernard (1881-1951) tracked a list of 850 instincts proposed in the psychological literature between 1900 and 1920, referring to the overuse of instincts as a "peculiarly and psychologically almost meaningless use of the term" (Bernard, 1924: 122). The list included "instinct with contempt" and "instinct with the breath of heaven."

Instinct theory was influential to modern Evolutionary Psychology since the theory was an attempt to explore the role of natural selection on behavior. In a systematic way, the Ethologists (though not necessarily psychologists) espousing instinct theory laid out ways in which behaviors are adaptive, and thus come to characterize a species. However, more recently, instinct theory has been noted for its limitations. Labeling a trait instinctive does not offer an explanation for the trait. Further, instinct theory was never intended to account for individual differences; rather the theory broached only the realm of species-specific behaviors. With a modern understanding of psychology, and Darwin's emphasis on variation among individuals, evolutionary psychology must necessarily go beyond behaviors that characterize a species. Despite the current opinions of instinct theory, it has proved generative of future theories—from psychotherapist John Bowlby (1969/1982) and his theory of attachment to Wilson's (1975) Sociobiology.

Towards the last quarter of the twentieth century, E.O. Wilson set forth an extensive theory to explain the evolution of human behavior: Sociobiology (Wilson, 1975). With this theory, Wilson posited that all behavior can be explained by seeking out the evolutionary advantage of each behavior. It is an inclusive theory in that behavior is considered from multiple perspectives including biology, anthropology, sociology, and population genetics. Further, this theory draws from the principles of holism, stating that individual behavior is determined by emergent group properties. Thus, the properties of any given social group cannot be studied by breaking the group into pairs or individuals but must be examined during the interactions of the group as a whole. This theory compliments instinct theory in that both require an examination of the individual within its group, yet Wilson goes one step further by studying behavior unique to the individual while in the group. Wilson used this holistic view to explain the behavior of many creatures, including the particularly relevant primates living in social groups. That humans are adapted for group living means that their behavior cannot be isolated from the group and still remain the same.

Wilson (1975) viewed the relationship between structure, behavior, and genes essential and considered social organization furthest removed from genes. He explained this in terms of the multiplier effect seen often in nature when a small evolutionary change in the behavior of individuals produces major social effects. Examples of this effect are strongest among colonizing insects, such as termites. Between species of termites, though morphological differences may be few, behavioral differences may be vast. A trained eye can often identify varying species based on the structure of nests alone. From the observance of the multiplier effect, and following Darwin's lead, Wilson considered behavior to be the evolutionary pacemaker. Therefore, behavior is most likely to be the first change in response to long-term changes in the environment, followed by structure. This idea holds important implications when studying the evolution of human psychology, namely, that the evolution of specific behaviors should not take as long as the evolution of physical traits.

Sociobiology appeared to be the necessary compliment to early theories of instinct. Like modern Evolutionary Psychology, it is inclusive and requires an examination of the environment as well as genetics in behavior. However, Wilson's reliance on insect and non-human animals for support of the evolved social structure of humans left the theory of Sociobiology open to many critiques from those longing for a more human-supported theory. These critiques would lead to the more modern approach of the evolution of human behavior, as seen in Barkow's, Cosmides', and Tooby's (1992) version of Evolutionary Psychology.

A separate movement came to light in the middle of the twentieth century comparing the mind to a computer. The cognitive revolution set forth with the assumption that the brain is made up of separate and independent modules contributing to various behaviors and cognitions (Fodor, 1983). A module is a structure in the mind with an evolutionarily defined function that is distinct from the function of other brain structures. Further, each module was designed based on different problems in the environment at a given time—for example, when posed with the problem of retaining a mate, a module for jealousy might have evolved. These modules are present at birth and account for all of human psychology. As a computer, the mind is composed of modules that are connected to each other to produce an end product in the form of a behavior.

Drawing heavily upon cognitive psychology, Barkow, Cosmides, and Tooby (1992) were able to construct an elaborate field of human psychology drawing from the principles of natural selection. These principles are that individuals vary in the traits that they possess, traits are passed down through inheritance, more individuals are produced than can survive to reproductive age, and those with favorable variations will reproduce more often (Darwin, 1859/1936). Barkow et al. (1992) apply these principles in their approach, focusing specifically on how evolution shaped the modules comprising the mind. These modules have been fashioned by natural selection during relatively important times of early species development. Modules, as specific mental adaptations, evolved in response to recurring problems in the environment. For example, the language module evolved sometime after the human brain expansion (around 2 million years ago). However, the specific problems to which language provided a response is the cause of speculation. Some believe that language is like grooming and serves to solidify social relationships (Dunbar, 1998); while others see language as a response to the need to regulate an infant's behavior that has been placed down while the mother gathers food (Falk, 2004). From a standard EP perspective, the underlying commonality is that language evolved in isolation from other evolved modules as a solution to a recurring problem.

From this view, one would argue that human behavior results from the development of these inherited modules that evolved independently, thus behavior is reducible down to specific neural networks. These modules interact with the environment in the sense that they either remain adaptive if the environmental conditions mimic those in which we evolved, or appear maladaptive if the current environment is drastically different from that in which we evolved. A popular example of an evolved module that is no longer matched with our current environment is our tendency to crave sweets. Our sweet tooth used to be adaptive when high-energy foods (i.e., sweets) were limited, but now our sweet tooth is maladaptive (Fox, 2006). In the current context, craving sweets in a time when they are prevalent often leads to health problems. This view excludes development by characterizing behaviors as resulting first as a result of genetic activity, which then leads to a particular development path, and given the appropriate environment, the particular species-specific behavior.

History of Developmental Systems Theory

Developmental Systems Theory (DST) has recently emerged in biology as a popular approach to the study of developing organisms. By viewing development as a dynamic interaction between the organism and its environment, systems theorists are able to propose complex and holistic accounts of how behavior can influence development and vice versa. DST "views both development and evolution as processes of *construction* and *reconstruction* in which heterogeneous resources are contingently but more or less reliably reassembled for each life cycle" (Oyama, Griffiths, & Gray, 2001: 1; italics in original).

While seen as progressive—and currently considered a popular alternative to the "gene-for" talk—DST is not a new field. DST has early roots in the work of (among others) Daniel Schneirla, Gilbert Gottlieb, and Daniel Lehrman, whose critique of Konrad Lorenz's theory of instinct is considered a landmark paper (Lehrman, 1953/2001). Lorenz's well developed theory of instinct led others to believe that specific stereotyped behaviors present at birth have to be endowed in the individual by virtue of belonging to a species. Accordingly, the importance of the concept of instinct was in relation to the role it played in behavior. At the time considered to be an innate, heritable, and unchangeable core, instinct was seen as a way to group and organize behaviors but did not explain from where such behaviors emerged. Teleological in nature, one can see how the argument about the importance and makeup of instinct was a precursor to the modern form of the nature/nurture debate. Instinct theory ignores the role of development *and* environment in species-specific behavior.

Lehrman (1953/2001) criticizes Lorenz's theory on a number of grounds—but most importantly for DST, on the use of instinct to explain behavior. The radical behaviorist, Zing-Yang Kuo (1898-1970) performed many studies on the embryonic conditions of chicks in the mid-twentieth century (Kuo, 1932). This line of research emerged from the claim that chicks, upon hatching, pecked for food out of an instinct for such a behavior (Lehrman, 1953/2001). Kuo pointed out that what was considered to be very instinctual (that of pecking) was instead a result of learning in the embryo. In the confined conditions of the egg, when the chick's heart beats, its head moves forward in a movement not unlike the pecking observed upon hatching. Kuo concluded from this study that chicks in fact learn to peck for food by the natural movement occurring in the embryonic stage.

Similarly, Gottlieb (1999) performed experiments challenging the instinct for Mallard ducklings to follow the species-specific maternal call. At birth, ducklings can distinguish between the maternal calls from their own species and those from even closely related species (for example, mallard and wood duck calls). Gottlieb first speculated that rather than being instinctual, the differential responses were likely based on exposure to the mother's call while still in the egg. However, even after being isolated from their mothers in incubators, hatched ducklings still had the ability to respond differentially to maternal calls. From this Gottlieb later showed experimentally that the embryonic ducklings were primed to respond to the maternal calls based upon the vocalizations that they themselves made while in the eggs. In other words, the ducklings made their own species-specific vocalizations in the eggs and in essence trained themselves to respond to such vocalizations once hatched. That ducklings do not need to hear their mothers in order to identify them is an example of how the genetic activity (in this case the duckling's vocalization) interacts with developmental maturation (the ability of the duckling's to differentiate maternal calls) in a bidirectional nature.

These experiments led to Gottlieb's (1999) theory of probabilistic epigenesis, which stresses the multitude of different pathways an organism can take towards an end point. The organism is seen as developing through a series of continuous interactions with the environment, genetics, and behavior that shape the developmental pathways being taken. That organisms develop in a predictable and reliable fashion is probable, but not obligatory—thus Gottlieb has labeled his theory *probabilistic* epigenesis. This view then puts an emphasis on the emergence of developmental features which cannot be understood as isolated but rather part of a dynamic system. This theory can be exemplified as:

Genetic activity ↔ neural maturation/development ↔ experience ↔ species-specific behavior

DST, both historically and in present day studies, is seen as holistic in two ways. The first is in its approach towards the study of development. DST's eclectic makeup is meant to incorporate all fields of scientific study interested in the role of development in organisms, including psychology, sociobiology, ethology, biology, and chemistry. Pointing to scientific advances as specifically a product of DST is more difficult. Indeed, by attempting to study the whole of the process rather than the parts, papers would seem often times more complex and as a result not as attractive to a lay audience, especially one enraptured by the apparently easy possibility of gene-for language. This complexity is seen easily in the example of the "learning" of pecking behavior in contrast with the simple claim of a "pecking instinct," or in more modern terms, a "gene-for" pecking in chicks.

The second way one sees holism in DST is in how it approaches the study of development. Systems theorists are interested in the interaction of the organism and its environment. Believing that behaviors are not isolated events, as in one behavior occurring independent of another behavior—and that they did not occur in the isolation of the lab is in line with the holistic approach as described by Diriwächter (this volume). The rest of this chapter will show how this approach can be appropriated by EP.

A New Approach: Dynamic Adaptive Psychology

Recently, EP has begun to incorporate a developmental aspect. This new branch, appropriately termed Evolutionary Developmental Psychology (EDP) has begun to apply the principles of natural selection toward understanding how organisms develop. This point of view is not without potential problems. Researchers often propose studying development in the traditional bottom-up modular approach that focuses upon stages and isolated processes. Traditionally, aspects of childhood development have been presumed to be necessary for future reproductive success; EDP presumes that the same aspects are necessary for survival in the moment, in addition to reproductive success. However, we do not feel this altered view goes far enough.

EDP is more akin to one of two common views toward integrating evolution and development in the world of biology. Like EDP, one approach examines traits that have been produced via evolution for a specific period of development only. For example, a recent examination of the horned beetle species *Onthophagus* shows that the sexual dimorphism of thoracic horns only occurs in the adult form (Moczek, 2006). The thoracic horn is present in males and females in the larval form, and appears to serve the vital function of assisting in the molting process. Those without the thoracic horn do not properly molt and die prior to reaching the pupal form. However, the females in the *O. nigriventris* species go through a resorption period, leaving them hornless as adults, as do the males of the *O. Sagittarius* species. Thus the thoracic horn has been selected for a specific period of development for either the males or females, depending on the species. Like the EDP espoused by Blasi and Bjorklund (2003; see below), the emphasis is on the role of evolution in shaping particular aspects of development.

In their recent chapter Blasi and Bjorklund (2003) lobby for EDP, pointing out that such an approach would explicate the why's of human development. They draw upon DST as a non-deterministic model of gene-environment interaction in an attempt to broaden the scope of EP. However, at the same time they cannot avoid what seem to be the pitfalls of contemporary EP. Their research focus is "to elaborate a catalogue of different types of behaviors and cognitions characteristic of humans from birth to adult in different cultures and to classify them according to their adaptive status" (Blasi & Bjorlklund, 2003: 267). Such a catalogue feels reminiscent of both Bernard's instinct catalogue and of deterministic contemporary evolutionary psychology models. Equally problematic is their advocacy that "researchers may take a bottom-up approach and begin with interesting or important phenomena and search for an evolutionary explanation of them" (Blasi & Bjorlklund, 2003: 268). This approach is at odds with what we consider to be the necessary holistic approach towards development and evolution.

A different biological approach views the bi-directionality of evolution and development. For example, changes in the environment can cause heritable changes in offspring independent of genetic changes, such as seen in the Mongolian gerbil (Jablonka & Lamb, 2005). Mongolian gerbils are sensitive to the uterine environment, so that if a female embryo develops in a uterus in which most embryos are male, she will be exposed to high levels of testosterone. This exposure affects her development, making her more likely to display male-typical behaviors such as aggressive territorial markings. Moreover, she is likely to have a more male-dominant litter of her own, repeating the cycle of female offspring that display male-typical behaviors. This example provides evidence for the perspective that espouses the bidirectional influences that development and evolution have on each other.

We feel that evolution and development can no longer be examined in a unidirectional manner. Both biological views above need to be incorporated to fully understand human psychology. We find the recently revived *Ganzheitspsychologie*, and Developmental Systems Theory both pave the way for a powerful alternative to the bottom-up approach inherent in the Evolutionary Developmental model. To emphasize the holistic and bidirectional nature of evolution and development, we prefer the term Dynamic Adaptive Psychology (DAP), which connotes the active change that an individual undergoes psychologically both within the lifespan and across generations.

Ganzheitspsychologie and its Contributions to DAP

Ganzheitspsychologie operates from the basic principle that the "whole is more (or different) than the sum of its parts" (see Chapter 3 of this volume). This approach is based on four interconnected theses: holism, development, structure, and feelings—each of which is necessary to understand behavior. The holistic approach is a way of viewing the non-reducibility of the whole. Accordingly, to gain holistic insight requires attending to the organism's development—viewing how life changes are integrated within the whole. The totality of an organism is not just additive, rather can only be understood by examining the dynamic components in union with one another (see Chapter 3 of this volume). Thus, an individual's behavior must be accounted for by rigorous examination of the developmental pathway leading up to the behavior. This understanding of holism also provides insight into how *Ganzheitspsychologie* approaches development. By viewing development as continuous and based upon the organism's previous developmental experiences, *Ganzheitspsychologie* is interested in the dynamic unfolding processes of development. This view of development is both similar and compatible to that endorsed by systems theorists.

We are interested in focusing upon the holistic integration of development into Evolutionary Psychology. In keeping with the perspective of *Ganzheitspsychologie,* the four theses (holism, developmental, structure, and feelings) are not to be viewed separately, but rather, as interwoven together. Within *Ganzheit-spsychologie* holism is more than just a thesis, it also provides the overarching link. We feel this link necessary to evolutionary theories of behavior.

DST and its Contributions to DAP

By holistically studying the organism's previous developmental history, a better understanding of how the organism arrived at their present state in the world and how they might behave in the future is understood (Valsiner, 2003). From the DST perspective, behaviors develop as a result of a series of unfolding interactions between the organism and distinct objects (stimuli) within its environment. While the organisms are always integrated with their environment, their interactions with distinct objects within their environment are constantly guided by their previous interactions. These interactions are bidirectional—any level leading to a behavior can influence another (see Gottlieb, 1999 model previously mentioned). An example of the bi-directional, holistic approach towards development taken by systems theorists can be found within contemporary genetic research. Far from reductionist "gene-for" talk, genetic research has moved towards trying to understand the complex interactions of genetic networks. From this lens, the expression of genes as phenotypes results from a series of interactions. As Evelyn Fox Keller notes:

> . . . the gene has lost a good deal of its specificity and its agency. Which protein should a gene make, and under what circumstances? And how does it choose? In fact it doesn't. Responsibility for this decision lies elsewhere, in the complex regulatory dynamics of the cell as a whole. It is from these regulatory dynamics, and not from the gene itself that the signal (or signals) determining the specific pattern in which the final transcript is to be formed actually comes. (Keller, 2000: 63)

The notion of genes controlling the entirety of development has been replaced by a more complex one involving various regulatory processes. Here, the developmental nature of the cell is emphasized; the proteins that are made do not arise from a pre-conceived genetic program but rather through a constant flow of interaction with the environment and the organism's developmental position in the moment.

Another example of the bi-directional interaction between an organism and objects in the environment can be seen in the research on other non-genetic inheritance systems. Eva Jablonka and Marion Lamb (2005) have focused upon the holistic and developmental nature of these systems. For example, by studying epigenetic transferences, which are changes in gene functions that are both reversible and heritable, a new non-genetic aspect of development is being understood. Non-genetic inheritance is phenotypic material that is passed from a cell or a multi-cellular organism without being encoded in the DNA. This form of development is more Lamarckian than Darwinian in that it is not blind to function. Along these lines, epigenetic transmission has been used to explain how cells are differentiated into specialized organs by a process of cell-memory. For instance, while an individual's liver cells, skin cells, and kidney cells function and look different, the genetic materials that comprise them are the same. The specific developmental history of these cells at one point influenced how their products acted, leading to the specialized function that we see in organs. This specialization is then transmitted to following generations of daughter cells, which behave in a similar way. For the purpose of development, epigenetic transference of material is important in emphasizing the constant bi-directionality where changes in function can lead to changes in form. This bi-directional nature has importance for evolution as heritable changes in function can very much influence natural selection (Jablonka & Lamb, 2005).

Bringing this view of development into EP emphasizes not just the organisms' past environments, but also their current environment. In this way, EP could explain behavior not as something pre-determined by evolved traits, but rather as a result of the unique interaction between an organism's evolutionary background and their current developmental experiences. At the same time, this approach broadens the evolutionary perspective to include other dimensions of evolution. Thus, we find DST a necessary addition to our Dynamic Adaptive Psychology.

Elements of Ganzheitspsychology Applied to DAP

Within *Ganzheitspsychologie* structure refers to the configured parts of a system that contribute to the whole. These parts can be conceptualized as complexes, for instance, as hierarchical levels of human physiology or the relationship between an organisms biological potential and their developmental history. However, as these parts both derive meaning from the entire organism and provide meaning to it, when studied they have to be related to the whole (Diriwächter, Chapter 3). This type of research focuses upon understanding the partial structure of specific components, for example, we cannot simply study memory in isolation but rather have to study memory in the holistic organism. Thus, one holistic view of memory might include researching how memory is related to development, speech, and acting (Bartlett, 1932/1964).

These parts provide the framework from which the organism's experiences emerge. Recent work on "hidden" genetic material that only emerges in certain situations provides demonstrable evidence of the effects of environment and development on the structure of the organism. The example of polyphenisms shows a phenotypic adaptation of coloration in the larvae of *Manduca Sexta* (Suzuki & Nijhout, 2006). Responding to environmental stimuli (in this case, thermal stress), the larvae's color will change. The ability to change coloration is considered evolutionarily adaptive by providing an alternative phenotype which could be of use when faced with external selective pressure. When studying this "hidden" phenotype we can see structure—the adaptation is seen as useful to the organism and, at the same time, only derives meaning itself in relation to other states of being.

In a similar way, the rapidly changing environmental conditions, in terms of our hominin (human and pre-human) history, combined with our adapted minds produce behaviors that may be likewise adaptive or seemingly maladaptive. Regardless, the changing environment produces variations in human development and behavior that are interactive with our genetics.

The experienced totality of the whole must also be examined. This is known as feelings in *Ganzheitspsychologie*. Since DST has largely been applied in the realm of biology, the experience of the organism has most often been overlooked. However, one can begin to see speculations of experience in examples from Gottlieb's work on Mallard ducks (above). We will also explain the role of feelings in explaining human behavior in the example below.

DAP Applied: Attachment as an Example

As a combination of DST and *Ganzheitspsychologie,* DAP can be applied to the understanding of human attachment. We conceive of attachment as a bidirectional relationship between caregiver and child, in which each seeks the physical closeness, or proximity, of the other (Bowlby, 1969/1982). Attachment has been examined in natural settings and laboratory experiments as well as among humans and non-human animals, such as monkeys (Harlow & Harlow, 1962) and Mallard ducks (Gottlieb, 1999). The proximity seeking nature of attachment has also been broken down into different types of behaviors, including vocalizations (see Fernald, 1992; Sokol, Webster, Thompson & Stevens, 2005; Thompson, Dessureau, & Olson, 1998 for examples), gestures (Tomasello, 2003), and movement towards the partner (Ainsworth & Wittig, 1969; Bowlby, 1969/1982). We will attempt to apply the theoretical assertions of DAP to attachment, separated by the main principles of *Ganzheitspsychologie*.

Development

Bowlby (1969/1982) observed the long-term ill effects on children suffering separation from a primary attachment figure. Children who do not form early attachments have difficulty forming attachments later in life. Whether or not there is a critical period for attachment is a controversial matter; what is worth pursuing are the developmental indicates of how attachment forms. For such speculation, we return to Gottlieb's (1999) research with Mallard ducks.

Attachment is generally assumed to be formed between caregiver and offspring shortly after the offspring is born. However, Gottlieb's (1999) research challenges such assumptions by expanding the development of attachment behavior to the embryonic stage. In the case of Mallard ducks, the attachment, or proximity seeking behaviors, is observed when a newly hatched duckling follows the maternal call from his own species (most likely the mother) rather than from other related species. This behavior is a result of developmental events that occur before the duckling has hatched; however, the vocalizations of the un-hatched duckling prepare him to follow the specific maternal call of a member of his own species.

Extending this prenatal attachment formation to humans would require the examination of the influence of prenatal development on the attachment between caregiver and child. A caregiver's attachment to her prenatal child is associated with her attachment to the infant after the birth (Benoit, Parker, & Zeanah, 1997). Viewing attachment as both evolved and developmental would require an examination of the precursors to attachment related behaviors before birth, such as any vocalizations the infant may make or other aspects of the womb environment that transfer to the environment post-birth, much like the Mallard duckling embryonic vocalizations.

Structure

The structures of an organism both influence and draw influence from the whole. Attachment is one structure that influences the whole organism, but is also influenced by the other experiences of the organism. For example, not forming an attachment to a primary caregiver early in life makes forming permanent friendships and intimate relationships later in life extremely difficult (Bowlby, 1969/1982).

As a structure, attachment is also composed of substructures which build the entire attachment relationship. A partner can attempt to get nearer to the other partner early in life by vocalizing—in the case of humans, crying, and later, whining. These vocalizations encourage the caregiver to close the physical gap, in the case of infant cries, before an infant can close that gap on her own. The caregiver can also vocalize to the child to encourage proximity, often with the specific form of speech known as "motherese." Pre-linguistic children will also gesture to be picked up by a caregiver. Both partners, once the child can walk, can move towards the other as well. Each of these behaviors solidifies the attachment relationship, but is likewise determined by the previous relationship. For instance, if a caregiver has signaled inconsistency in responses, only bridging the physical gap occasionally when requested, the child will form an insecure attachment style and seek proximity less reliably.

Feeling

Feeling is the experienced aspect of holism. Feeling can be seen in attachment relationships from the perspective of the child, who will build his/her understanding of the world based on this early relationship. As Chisholm (1995) has proposed, attachment relationships cue people into the stability of the surrounding environment. If a caregiver consistently responds to the infant, the infant will experience the environment as stable, and act accordingly in future endeavors. These children will form secure attachments. However, if the caregiver either cannot or will not respond consistently, the infant will experience the environment as instable and will have to plan accordingly when navigating the environment. These children will form insecure attachments.

Interestingly, Chisholm (1995) toys with the idea of a developmental toggle, or a sort of genetic predisposition to adopting a certain attachment style early in life. Drawing from the influence of an epigenetic approach, a researcher might question whether this toggle is a matter of genes or other influences. For example, when a mother rat licks her newborn pups, the female pups will then carry this tendency into their own maternal behaviors and lick their future pups (Francis, Diorio, Liu, & Meaney, 1999). Moreover, this will affect the pups' behavioral and endocrine responses to stress. However, those that remain unlicked will not show the same maternal care and stress responses, even when cross-reared. Maternal licking triggers hormones and physiological changes in the pups that are then carried into their own future maternal behavior. Extending this research to the psychological realm would require looking into hormonal and physiological changes that occur during each type of human attachment relationship and charting correlated changes in future attachment relationships. The feelings of attachment likely correspond to physical changes within the caregiver and child.

A caregiver will experience attachment in different ways as well. Caregivers often experience attachment before the infant is born—as is seen with the common Western practices of determining the sex of the prenatal infant, naming the prenatal infant, and reading to the "infant" via the pregnant woman. The attachment experience is solidified with the birth—clearly, this attachment is strong since mothers can even discriminate their own infants by smell (Kaitz, Good, Rokem & Eidelman, 1987). Attachment serves the purpose of the survival and future reproduction of the infant evolutionarily, but experientially is felt as love between caregiver and child.

Holism

In attachment relationships, the whole is clearly not equal to the sum of its parts. The whole organism is shaped by early attachment relationships, as the attachment relationship is shaped by proximity seeking behaviors. Conversely, attachment relationships are shaped by the past experiences of the organism.

Attachment begins as a way of experiencing the world and familial relationships. Cues of investment on the part of the caregiver, such as consistent response to cries, shape how the infant views the world—in this case, as stable and reliable. This early relationship then leads to an understanding of the world at large—if a caregiver reliably responds to the infant, once the infant grows into a child, adolescent, and adult, he or she may be more likely to seek out reliable and stable relationships. Thus, future relationships are shaped by past intimate relationships.

Though attachment behaviors can be broken into parts—vocalizations, gestures, mobilization towards a partner—the whole attachment relationship is not so simplistic. A child cannot merely "walk the walk" by making empty gestures towards a caregiver to mimic cues of attachment. The feeling, or experienced aspect, of attachment must be sincere to be believed. Humans not only have a tendency to become attached to other individuals, but have a tendency to perceive when they are being deceived. The parts of attachment are not sufficient to form a lasting attachment relationship.

Conclusion

We set out in this chapter to posit a method for making EP more developmental and holistic in order to gain a better understanding of complex and dynamically changing behavior. Adopting the perspectives of DST and *Ganzheitspsychologie* to evolutionary explanations of human behavior forces the researcher to go beyond the assertions that we are the product of our stone-aged minds and current environmental conditions. Applying DAP by incorporating both developmental and evolutionary approaches forces one to look at the organism as a whole that interacts dynamically with the environment based on past experiences and development. Rather than building the whole from a bottom-up approach, we feel DST and *Ganzheitspsychologie* both enforce a top-down approach of viewing the organism as more than the sum of its parts. Further, each approach allows for a bi-directional view of evolutionary and developmental influences of behavior. Such approaches are necessary when viewing a complex, dynamic system.

A focus on Dynamic Adaptive Psychology appears a good way to achieve these goals. Such an approach highlights not only evolved mechanisms and common developmental milestones, but also ways in which development across a lifespan can produce changes to evolved mechanisms (for example, the Mongolian gerbils). Another example is the developmental influence of embryonic vocalizations on the recognition of maternal calls in Mallard ducks. One could conceive of an experiment in which the vocal cords of embryonic ducklings were suppressed (as Gottlieb did to show that ducklings prime themselves to respond to maternal calls) repeatedly across a number of generations, which might then produce the inability for the offspring of these ducklings to respond to maternal calls. Behavior in this case becomes less genetically determined and more influenced by developmental and environmental aspects of an organism's world.

Viewing behavior as bidirectional and influenced by many aspects forces a reexamination of how we study human behavior. As with the example of human attachment, behavior is influenced by development, the organism's experience, structures that make up the organism, and the totality of all of these elements.

Neglecting that each behavior is influenced by so many complex aspects causes oversights and incorrect generalizations, such as assuming that Mallard ducklings have an "instinct" to respond to maternal calls and humans have an "instinct" to be attached to caregivers. Admitting that humans have been shaped by evolution on a behavioral level is a good step towards describing behavior. Incorporating aspects of *Ganzheitspsychologie* and DST will provide great steps towards explaining it.

Acknowledgements

We would like to acknowledge the many conversations with and feedback from Nicholas S. Thompson in each stage of this text. We are also grateful for Rainer Diriwächter's constant patience and editorial comments.

References

Ainsworth, M.D.S., and Wittig, D.S. (1969). "Attachment and exploratory behavior of one-year-olds in a strange situation." In B.M. Foss (Ed.), *Determinants of infant behavior*, (v. 4, pp. 113-136). London: Methuen.

Barkow, J.H., Cosmides, L., and Tooby, J. (1992). *The adapted mind: Evolutionary psychology and the generation of culture.* New York: Oxford University Press.

Bartlett, F.C. (1932/1964). *Remembering: A study in experimental and social psychology.* London: Cambridge University Press.

Benoit, D., Parker, K.C. and Zeanah C.H. (1997). "Mothers' representations of their infants assessed prenatally: Stability and association with infants' attachment classifications." *Journal of Child Psychology and Psychiatry, 38* (3): 307-313.

Bernard, L.L. (1924). *Instinct: A study in social psychology.* New York: Henry Holt and Co.

Blasi, C. H. and D. Bjorklund, D (2003). "Evolutionary Developmental Psychology: A new tool for better understanding human ontogeny." *Human Development, 46:* 259-281.

Bowlby, J. (1969). *Attachment and loss*, vol. 1: *Attachment.* New York: Basic Books.

Chisolm, J.S. (1995). *Death, hope and sex: Steps to an evolutionary ecology of mind and morality.* Cambridge: Cambridge University Press.

Cosmides, L. and Tooby, J. (1997). "Evolutionary psychology: A primer." Retrieved January 7, 2008 from http://www.psych.ucsb.edu/research/cep/primer.html.

Darwin, C. (1859/1936). *The origin of species by means of Natural Selection.* New York: The Modern Library.

Diriwächter, R. (2008). "Genetic Ganzheitspsychologie." In R. Diriwächter & J. Valsiner (Eds.) *Striving for the Whole: Creating Theoretical Syntheses.* New Brunswick, NJ: Transaction Publishers.

Dunbar, R. (1998). *Grooming, gossip, and the evolution of language.* Cambridge, MA: Harvard University Press.

Falk, D. (2004). "Prelinguistic evolution in early hominins: Whence motherese?" *Behavioral and Brain Sciences, 27* (4): 491-503.

Fernald, A. (1992). "Meaningful melodies in mother's speech to infants." In U.J. Hanus-Papousek & M. Papousek (Eds.), *Nonverbal Vocal Communications.* New York: Cambridge University Press.

Fodor, J. (1983). *The modularity of the mind.* Cambridge, MA: MIT Press.

Fox, R. (2006). "Food and eating: An anthropological perspective." *Social Issues*

Research Center. Retrieved January 7, 2008 from http://www.sirc.org/publik/food_ and_eating_12.html.

Francis, D., Diorio, J., Liu, D. and Meaney, M.J. (1999). "Nongenomic transmission across gene rat ions of maternal behavior and stress responses in the rat." *Science, 286* (5442): 1155-1158.

Gottlieb, G. (1999). *Probablistic epigenesis and evolution.* 1999 Heinz Werner Lecture Series, vol. 23. Worcester, MA: Clark University Press.

Gottlieb, G. (2001). "A developmental psychobiological systems view: Early formulation and current status." In S. Oyama, P.E. Griffiths, & R.D. Gray (Eds.) *Cycles of Contingency: Developmental Systems and Evolution* (pp. 41-57). Cambridge, MA: MIT Press.

Gould, J.L. (1982). *Ethology: The mechanisms and evolution of behavior.* New York: W.W. Norton & Company, Inc.

Harlow, H., and Harlow, M. (1962). "Social deprivation in monkeys." *Scientific American, 207*: 136-146.

Jablonka, E. and Lamb, M. J. (2005). *Evolution in four dimensions: Genetic, epigenetic, behavioral, and symbolic variation in the history of life.* Cambridge, MA: MIT Press.

James, W. (1899/2005). *Talks to teachers on psychology and to students on some of life's ideals.* Whitefish, MT: Kessinger Publishing.

James, W. (1918). *The principles of psychology.* New York: Henry Holt and Company.

Johnston, T.D. (2001). "Toward a systems view of development: An appraisal of Lehrman's critique of Lorenz." In S. Oyama, P.E. Griffiths, & R.D. Gray (Eds.) *Cycles of Contingency: Developmental Systems and Evolution* (pp. 15-22). Cambridge, MA: MIT Press.

Kaitz, M., Good, A., Rokem, A.M., and Eidelman, A.I. (1987). "Mothers' recognition of their newborns by olfactory cues." *Developmental Psychobiology, 20*: 587-591.

Keller, E. F. (2000). *The Century of the Gene.* Cambridge, MA, Harvard University Press.

Kuo, Z.Y. (1932). "Ontogeny of embryonic behavior in Aves. III: The structural and environmental factors in embryonic behavior." *Journal of Comparative Psychology,* 13: 245-271.

Lehrman, D.S. (1953/2001). "A critique of Konrad Lorenz's theory of instinctive behavior." In S. Oyama, P.E. Griffiths, and R.D. Gray (Eds.) *Cycles of Contingency: Developmental Systems and Evolution* (pp. 25-39). Cambridge, MA: MIT Press.

Lorenz, K. (1970). *Studies in human and animal behavior,* vol. 1. Cambridge, MA: Harvard University Press.

Moczek, A. P. (2006). "Pupal remodeling and the development and evolution of sexual dimorphism in horned beetles." *The American Naturalist, 168* (6): 711-729.

Oyama, S., Griffiths, P.E., and Gray, R.D. (2001). "Introduction: What is developmental systems theory?" In S. Oyama, P.E. Griffiths, & R.D. Gray (Eds.) *Cycles of Contingency: Developmental Systems and Evolution* (pp. 69-85). Cambridge, MA: MIT Press.

Sokol, R.I., Webster, K.L., Thompson, N.S., and Stevens, D.A. (2005). "Whining as mother-directed speech." *Infant and Child Development,* vol. *14* (5): 478-490.

Suzuki, Y. and Nijhout, F.H. (2006). "Evolution of a polyphenism by genetic accommodation." *Science, 311* (5761): 650-652.

Thompson, N.S., Dessureau, B., and Olson, C. (1998). "Infant cries as evolutionary melodrama: Extortion of deception?" *Evolution of Communication, 2* (1): 25-43.

Thompson, N.S. (2000). "Z.-Y. Kuo and the historical amnesia of contemporary evolutionary psychology." *From Past to Future*, 2 (2): 53-56.

Valsiner, J. (2003). "Beyond social representations: A theory of enablement." *Papers on Social Representations 12* (7): 1-7, 16.

Wilson, E.O. (1975). *Sociobiology: The new synthesis.* Cambridge, MA: Harvard University Press.

Conclusion:
Returning to the Whole—A New Theoretical Synthesis in the Social Sciences

Jaan Valsiner
Clark University

Rainer Diriwächter
California Lutheran University

The theme this present volume has brought to its readers focus on theory construction that preserves the integrity of the wholes while abstracting relevant features from them. This book continues the focus of its predecessor (Valsiner, 2007a) on how psychologists think about complex phenomena. We are convinced that a re-analysis of selected ideas from the past of the social sciences helps us in the present. Learning from both successful and failing (or just from the forgotten) avenues of theoretical thinking widens our horizon of possibilities for new approaches. Our aim was to highlight these ideas of the whole (and our various views on them) and make them a fruitful basis for the further advancement of our science.

Constructive learning from the history of science was the focus of the series of issues of *From Past To Future: Clark Working Papers on the History of Psychology* that were published at Clark in 1998-2004. The majority of contributions to this volume originated in that series of investigations. However, in this book we went beyond merely bringing the bibliographically rare work from that local technical reports series to the wide public access domain. The empirically over-flooded social sciences of today are in a deep crisis. Their objects of investigation are increasingly complex, yet the methods that are used for making sense of complexity are reducing the crucial aspect of the phenomena—their holistic qualities—to elementary constituents. While paying lip service to the catchphrase "the whole is bigger than the sum of its parts"—occasionally remembered from some history of psychology course—psychologists in good conscience continue to use linear models and elementaristic coding schemes for phenomena that are most likely of some non-linear and holistic kind. This is "normal science" at its utmost—to use the Kuhnian term. It is unlikely to give us new knowledge—but it surely creates massive databases. Yet, much of the busy-work of such "normal science" entails repetition of what we already know.

Consider the example of axiomatic acceptance of additivity of parts in a complex phenomenon. The complexity of the mysterious term technically called "the variance" becomes reduced to components (and their "interactions") through analysis of variance type additive models. All factors work for the ha-bitual acceptance of the way of thinking in terms of analyzing "the variance" into its parts and treating the latter as if these are additive. This can be done out of habit and because of the convenience of statistical data analyses packages. Furthermore, such work is supported by the social norms for how not to perish in the academic evaluation systems. Myriads of empirical papers all show how they "account for variance" in their object domains and how causal functions are easily projected into the separated parts of "the variance" (through the notion of "effects"). Yet the assumption of the additivity of parts of variance remains intact—guaranteeing the "conceptual blindness" of the researcher to the nature of the whole as not reducible into its parts. Furthermore, the assumption of ad-ditivity guarantees psychology a similar "blindness" to the development of the whole—and emergence of new parts within it.

Variance is a vague technical term. From the perspective of *Ganzheits*-think-ing—that axiom of additivity of variance is untenable. First, the complex we call "variance" cannot be divided into additive parts (as there are holistic qualities that stand above the elements and unite them into complex con-figurations—see Chapter 3 of this volume). This of course has been the historically old Gestalt argument present since the 1890s—the question of a special "Gestalt quality." Secondly—following the notion of dynamic nature of *Ganzheit*—the distinctive parts of the "variance" are not given, they may differentiate from the whole under some circumstances. In other terms, the "variance" is never finitely given. Hence, it cannot be analyzed into its components for any other reason than momentary description (at moment t, the "variance" of X could be "accounted for" by X factors[1]). The notion of "accounting for" part of "variance" is purely descriptive—yet the explanatory power is projected into it through the use of quasi-causal terminology ("effects," "interactions").

Complexity is Real—and Needs to be Studied as Such

It is time to overcome the trivialization of complexity of psychological and other social phenomena and bring the importance of modeling complex-ity—wholeness (*Ganzheit*) of the phenomena—to our methodological focus. This book is a starting point from a historical perspective, while other work towards the same objective occurs through theoretical elaboration (Abbey & Diriwächter, 2008; Valsiner, 2007b) and through reuniting the social sciences with advanced forms of mathematics (Rudolph & Valsiner, 2009).

By bringing together the contributions to this book, we have aimed at a new synthesis of ideas of the holistic perspectives of the past with the needs of our post-postmodernist science of today. All biological, behavioral, social, and cultural sciences have reached, by the beginning of the twenty-first century, the point where they were a hundred years before—the holistic and dynamic complexity of the phenomena under study cannot be reduced to their elementary components. The theoretical efforts of the holistic theoretical constructs in the past—forgotten for most of the past century—are a fertile place to restart our movement to new understanding.

Ganzheitspsychologie gets a new start in our time. Complexity of phenomena does not disappear when our models deny their holistic nature—as much of the late twentieth century psychology has done. Now, a century later, the ideas of *Ganzheit* come back to us as we are informed by the complexities of the phenomena in the genomes of sea urchins (Davidson, 2006) and gene regulation mechanisms (Carthew, 2006), the discovery of "mirror neurons," cognitive and social complexities of primate behavior (Matsuzawa, 2001; Matsuzawa, Tomonaga, & Tanaka, 2006; Segerdahl, Fields, & Savage-Rumbaugh, 2005), the focus on generalized meaning of the environment (von Uexküll, 1982/1940), and embodiment of affective processes (Laird, 2007). They all lead to the need to create a scientific language for the social sciences that maintains the holistic nature of the complex phenomena. At the same time, the new language needs to preserve the theoretically relevant aspects of the phenomena in their generalized abstract form.

This movement within the social sciences signals a major turn. The time of self-proliferating empiricism is over, and it is time to overcome that theoretical iconoclasm that post-modernism has done for the social sciences. Publishing ever more large-samples based survey results or using "standardized methods" in psychology can only multiply the kind of knowledge we already have. However, it seems to fail in creating new knowledge. Statistical methods—which are currently taken to the status of quasi-religious orthodoxy in psychology—need to be subordinated to the greater scheme of knowledge construction that unites theoretical, phenomenological, empirical, and philosophical sides of methodology (Branco & Valsiner, 1997). Tools should not be treated as theories (see Gigerenzer, 1993; Gigerenzer et. al, 1989) any longer. The primacy of inductive inference in psychology, in relation to its deductive and abductive counterparts, needs to be questioned. In this, our contemporary science has much to learn from C. Lloyd Morgan's "two inductions" (Chapter 9 & 10 in this book).

How does science develop? It is through the processes of *abstracting generalization* (as emphasized by Karl Bühler, 1934/1990) that sciences produce new knowledge. Starting from the phenomena, and inductively derived first knowledge, science proceeds beyond the common sense (and common language) to arrive at axiomatic general views, from which (deductively) a theoretical framework is created. The latter becomes tested through empirical work—in crucial loci that make critical distinctions for the abstract nature of the theory. But how can this happen?

Uniting Levels of Analysis

The social sciences need theoretical perspectives that simultaneously focus on the whole and its constituent parts. This need is not new in science. A look into the history of chemistry shows how abstraction paid off. Chemistry moved from direct (common-sense) description of its substances—and their transformations into other substances—to the abstract depiction of relevant properties of the substances through chemical formulae (around 1800-1860—see Klein, 2004). For instance, the formula for water—H_2O, introduced by Jacob Berzelius in 1813—has no sensorial connections to any form of the substance (liquid, steam, or ice) yet it fully and abstractly characterizes both the whole molecule and its constituents. Through such abstractions (i.e., chemical formulae) chemists could concentrate on the kinds of chemical reactions of their choice, rather than be lost in the high complexity of the real-life manifestations of substances (cf. Roberts, 1991). Furthermore, all molecules of water are one in their holistic organization; the formula H_2O fits a water-drop in our basin as well as the whole of an ocean, or an iceberg, or in our own body cells. The abstracting (formulaic) language that chemistry adopted in the nineteenth century allowed it to preserve the connection of general knowledge with very concrete practical applications.

Are such abstractions confusing? No chemist would claim that planning an experiment on the basis of deductive prediction from abstract formulae is an obstacle to the reality of chemical processes as those might occur in their "situated reaction contexts." This is in dire contrast with our contemporary social sciences' efforts to "go native"—situate their empirical observations within "situated activity contexts" on the grounds of general axiom that all social phenomena are "context-bound." The phenomena may be context bound—but it does not follow from that property of the phenomena that there are no general laws that set up both the phenomena and their context-boundedness. In our "situated activity contexts" we may experience and produce water in its different forms (ice, steam, liquid)—yet all these situated forms remain those of the same general chemical formulae. The experiences would change drastically if that abstract formula were to be changed (e.g., instead of H_2O we encounter H_2O_2).

General knowledge is constructed in its abstract form, tested through concrete acts in selected real setting, and generalized further towards further abstract knowledge. Abstraction and generalization—often through formal-mathematical means—expands the horizon of knowledge by exploring those of its domains that have not happened to become objects for empirical investigation or to which direct access may be impossible.

Psychology's Conceptual Enterprise—Higher Complexity

Psychology and other social sciences start from the phenomena that are experienced by their form—be that behavioral action or internal ruminations of "the soul." If we were to draw parallels with other ("hard") sciences, it is chemistry—more than physics—that may be a fitting comparative counterpart for us. Both deal with complex structured phenomena that are characterized by transformations. Furthermore, both encounter their phenomena in a variety of forms in a variety of locations. Yet they differ in the kind of complexity of their phenomena. The complexity of the phenomena in the social sciences is by *three qualitative levels* more complex than that of chemistry.

First, beyond the complexity of chemical substances remains the qualitative *synthesis of chemical components into living systems*. The first qualitative difference we need to bear in mind is that between the non-living and living systems. The latter are open systems; they depend, for their emergence and maintenance, upon exchange relations with the environment. Thus, the irreversible nature of time is to be included in any holistic account of biological systems while such inclusion is not obligatory for the chemical systems. The question of emergence of life is that of the making of a new qualitatively different organizational order.

Second, the psychological and social systems include a novelty not present in biological systems[2]—that of *self-reflexivity*. Through the use of signs, human beings can account for their own ways of behaving and orient themselves towards the uncertainties of the future (Rosa, 2007). The *Ganzheits* perspective of this book, of course, captures the dynamic indeterminacy of such self-reflexivity very well (e.g., see Chapter 8 of this volume for a detailed analysis through culture). What is to happen, but has not happened yet (but see Buller, 2006 for an effort), is formal modeling of such self-reflexivity dynamics.

Finally, at the highest level of complexity, human beings and social systems *can generate intentional and persistent ways of striving towards some future* goal orientations. Systems of self-reflexivity can move to project their expected states into the not-yet-known domain—the future—and differentially evaluate such projected states. Hence, we get the distinctions of "AS-IS" (self-reflection of the present) and "AS-IF" —exemplified in the history of philosophy by Hans Vaihinger (1911). From the "AS-IS" <> "AS-IF" contrast, a number of scenarios can follow: "AS-COULD-BE," "AS-SHOULD-BE," (and its counterpart) "AS-SHOULD-*NOT*-BE." The emergence of the "moral reflection" upon the world is an effort of the systems to reduce the uncertainties of their current "AS-IS" experience of the world. Such "moral reflection" is an emergent feature of human psyche and functions as a tool for facing the ever-unknowable future.

What emerges from the expositions in this book is the understanding that the general *Ganzheits* perspective is well fitted to look at the unity of the present fears of uncertainty leading to moral feelings of the (seemingly) determinate decisions of "right" and "wrong." The whole guides the differentiation of its parts towards local (and usually temporary) moments of clarity. Human construction of what SHOULD-BE and SHOULD-*NOT*-BE are outgrowths of the AS-IS <> AS-IF contrast. Morality has no explanatory power for science but it is a most important object for investigation precisely as it has no such power.

All this complexity leads to the need we faced in our Introduction: any truly holistic approach needs to be developmental in its nature. A holistic theoretical system has to include both the presently existing *whole<>parts* relations and their potential for transformation into new forms. It is here where productive relationships with contemporary qualitative mathematics are expected to lead to new perspectives (Rudolph, 2006a, 2006b, 2006c; Rudolph & Valsiner, 2009). Instead of un-reflexive efforts to "measure" invented essences "in the mind" (see Michell, 1999; Molenaar, 2004; Molenaar, Huizenga, & Nesselroade, 2003) psychology should move towards modeling dynamic patterns of complexity similar to other sciences. Psychological traditions of "measurement" have created a huge family of illusory causal entities that are conveniently usable in psychology's interaction with the laypersons. Who could doubt that a "high level" of "intelligence" is perceived to be "good" (and desirable) by laypersons (who may be worried about their "level of intelligence"). Or who could doubt the social usefulness of "measures of risk" or of "well-being"—all these presumably existing entities are as good an explanatory tool for contemporary laypersons as attributions to "evil eye" or "ancestors' spirits" were not too long ago. They have only one problem—their common sense (and language) based ease of explanation for complexity misses the opportunity to explore that complexity as it exists. Psychology's constructions of explanatory principles have proceeded along the lines similar to those of alchemy—and not those of chemistry.

Science is One—and Philosophical Questions Set its Stage

At the heart of psychology lies philosophy. While it was by no means exhaustive, we have tried to highlight some of the philosophical underpinnings (i.e., through Leibniz and Ehrenfels—see Chapters 1-3 of this volume). After all, what psychology ultimately seeks to understand is human nature, both objectively and subjectively seen. The traditional "textbook" definition of psychology; namely, *the study of human behavior and mental processes* (Myers, 2007); does not go far enough in its emphasis.

Textbooks never make science—they trail far behind its cutting edge. Aspiring young scientists are strongly advised to ruminate while visiting some art museum rather than preparing for a multiple-choice test based on textbook knowledge. It takes a philosophical orientation to make sense of what is meant by "behaviors" and "mental processes" in order to articulate the reality in which humans find themselves. And it is here where psychology has hardly progressed since William James (1842-1910) recognized the holistic flow of human mental processes in his description of "*the stream of consciousness*" (Bailey, 1999; James, 1890). In the beginning of the twenty-first century, the processes of consciousness are only starting to be studied anew (Petitot, Varela, Roy, & Pachoud, 1999). It is a collective and interdisciplinary effort. Psychology has much to learn from other sciences about how to think of its own subject matter.

International and Interdisciplinary Effort

The quest for understanding human nature has transcended national boundaries and disciplines. What ultimately emerges—be it in Germany, Japan, South Africa, or the United States—is a drive to synthesize past approaches into a novel form. The multi-linearity by which different people (from different nations and disciplines) attempt to reach equifinal solutions to problems of basic understanding of nature and humanity has gone underappreciated. In our case, such equifinality would be a coherent holistic theory of psychology that can explain the complexity of experience and the reality of phenomena. That effort was started in the 1890-1930 time period—led by scientists in continental Europe (Toomela, 2007) and extended widely through the rest of the world. *Ganzheitspsychologie* was in the air—the entire world was a whole, in peace and in war.

In this book, we got glimpses of such unity. We can see how pervasive the *Ganzheitspsychologie* kind of thinking has been in different disciplines. The reality of complex phenomena leads thinkers in psychology, sociology, and biology to the need to reflect upon the world in holistic terms. Yet, it has also been evasive; after some talk about the basic relevance of the whole (that is more than the sum of its parts), little has followed in terms of constructive leads into methodology.

What are the premises for creating adequate methodology? Consistency between the phenomena, basic assumptions, theory, and methods is the basis for all science. How can such consistency be obtained in case of studying dynamic, vague, generalized, and little differentiated wholes—like the ones to which the *Ganzheits*-perspective alerts us? The central question we need to address is the general issue—*how does one depict the whole?* An answer comes from a renewed look at field-theoretical constructions in different sciences.

Approaches to Fields

Obviously, the basic idea of *Ganzheit* pertains to the use of field terminology of some kind. Such use is our axiomatic prerogative, as Figure C.1 demonstrates.

Figure C.1a includes a dot (a point) on a non-discriminate background. In terms of our usual (exclusively separating) mindset, this point stands independently "on its own." However, from the axiomatic stand of inclusive separation, that is not the case. The point is a point only in relation to its (non-discriminate) background. This is in line with the co-genetic logic (Herbst, 1995) where any figure is given as a triplet (figure, boundary, and ground). The triplet comes into being as a whole (i.e., you cannot draw a circle without drawing a boundary between the figure, its "inside;" and the ground, its "outside").

Figure C.1
Where is the Field Here? All Around the Point.

a.   b.

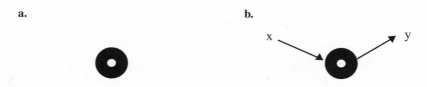

Thus, from the axiomatics of genetic logic, the point in Figure C.1a is not a point—but a field with minimal boundary (that of the point itself) and *infinite extension of the field* (which includes all the space, extended to infinity, *around* the point). That extension is a holistic phenomenon—infinitely so—without any structure. It could also gain structure, for instance, that of the whole—"the world." That latter whole, from any individual's perspective, entails the whole geological, social, and other structural formations on the surface of the Earth, starting from my personal standpoint here-and-now (i.e., the position of "the point" as the boundary of the "whole" around it—"the world"). This rather abstract quasi-geometrical story may gain greater reality if we look at our contemporary discourses about "global warming." Somebody—"we" (a person or a group located in place X on Earth's surface) are worried about something that happens "in the World"—perhaps in the atmosphere above Antarctica from the vantage point of what such holistic cataclysms may bring as consequences to us in our concrete "here-and-now" location.

In the latter example, we may blame ourselves (or our industrious or industrialized profit-making conspecifics) for bringing about the "effects" which the transformed world has on us. Hence, the field, including the "minimal field" kind of depiction, allows for the study of the *relationships at the boundary of the field* (Figure C.1b). The point—seen as a discrete point (Figure C.1a)—has no "relations" with the ground that are worth investigating. The point—seen as minimal boundary of an infinite field (Figure C.1b)—allows us to think of specifiable relations (vectors x and y). This fits the open-systemic nature of all living beings—they exist thanks to exchange relations between the "system" and "its environment." These exchange relations are processes of boundary transitions (in the formal sense)—hence the holistic axiomatics of co-genetic logic is the imperative starting point for all biological, social, behavioral, and cultural sciences.

The feature most relevant to stress about the field is that it is a totality where structural form may emerge. However, this is not obligatory. This makes *Ganzheits*-thinking theoretically more potent for innovation (see Chapter 3 of this volume) than its subordinate (structured) counterparts, such as the Berlin Gestalt tradition. The entire set of *Ganzheit* includes all forms of the wholes—from non-form to rigid classificatory forms. The "wide open field" is as much a whole as a strictly structured pattern of connections on a microchip.

Furthermore, the wholes are dynamic (Abbey, 2006). The structure of the field, and of the boundary between the ground and the figure, changes in its course of existence. Reaching the phenomenological "state of nothingness" in a Buddhist life course is a higher order structural form (of hyper-generalized field kind, see Valsiner, 2005a). Since Johann Wolfgang von Goethe (1749-1832) we can observe *differentiation<>de-differentiation* models proliferating in developmental biology and psychology (e.g., Heinz Werner's "orthogenetic principle," see Valsiner, 2005b). These are examples of dynamic fields of the theoretical kind. It is true that the fields implied, nor their dynamics, were never formally elaborated—which may be yet another lead for us in the twenty-first century to pick up a trajectory of development of our science and carry it further.

Duality of Wholes

It is time to stop the intellectually useless witch-hunt on "dualisms" that has been a habit in post-modernist social sciences and recognize the inevitable duality of all open systems. That duality relates the system and its environment (rather than separates them). According to an Igbo proverb, "A boundary is not the point at which something stops . . . A boundary is the point from where something begins to be present" (Beneduce & Taliani, 2006: 442).

The issue of transitions *through* boundaries is the core for our understanding of complexities. The boundary processes become the core of scientific investigation—be it those of translation of genetic backgrounds into actual proteins, permeability of biological membranes, or passport control points on borders, persons' feeling happy or sad at a given cocktail party, or social institutions attempting to make peace (or war). These are all holistic phenomena of boundary transitions—obviously operating at vastly different levels of biological, psychological, and social organization of living.

Possible Forms of Boundary Transitions

We can ask the question, "If boundary is the place where holistic processes operate, what kinds of boundary processes can exist?" Basically, we can see two kinds: (1) boundary processes that *maintain themselves* and (2) boundary processes that *innovate themselves* (with transformation of the fields).

The former are of obvious kind—an established boundary remains in its given form until broken or changed. The traditional borders of well-defined, real objects are of such kind. The German word for object, *Gegenstand*, entails the notion of position (*Stand*) against (*Gegen*) something.[3] In order for some part of the field to "be an object" there needs to exist a boundary process that leads to the objectification of something and, thus, maintains that something. Objectification entails discontinuity of the object and non-object. That may be organized into a form of clear boundary—a contour, a membrane, or the like. On the other extreme, this maintenance can take the form of fluid *fusion* of the sides relating through the boundary (see Figure C.3 below). From the angle of *Ganzheits* thinking, even a "seamless" boundary between an object and its environment is still a boundary. Objects cannot exist without the contrast with some opposite (non-object).

The self-innovating boundaries are of course the priority of our new approach. These boundaries have rarely been conceptualized in psychological theories where qualitative parts are usually treated as ill-defined essences only to be turned into specific forms through quantification. Thus, the common sense term "self-esteem" —vague and variable from person to person—becomes a concrete "variable" if turned into a quantified form through some "self-esteem measure."

In contrast, the historical parallels of science and developmental psychology—that of embryology—has had to deal with the core transformation of the boundaries of growing biological organisms in their most visible geometric forms (see also Chapter 11 of this volume). While the "growth of intellect" has no visible geometry to it; the "growth of an embryo" very much does! Hence the new synthesis that returns to the *Ganzheits* framework promises that we can learn from contemporary embryology (e.g., the *morphodynamic* field theory, see Cherdantsev, 2006) in ways parallel to the nineteenth century connections of the disciplines (e.g., William Preyer, whose contributions to developmental psychology were based on his embryological work).

What Kinds of Field Accounts have been Used in Psychology?

Psychology's history entails the borrowing of the field notion from physics—albeit in ways that mixed the deductive-theoretical power of the latter with the enchanting possibilities of describing human life experience in all of its fullness. Yet the fullness can be captured in two ways: through an all-encompassing phenomena-level term (e.g., "all the life") or through an abstraction. The latter is the way of science—the notion of the field in physics was an abstract, distanced from phenomena and generalized, construct. Likewise, any positing of a "N-dimensional space" where N>4 or the notion of infinity leaves the common sense experiences far behind and brings the thinker to the domain of pure abstraction. In contrast, the history of adoption of field theory in psychology can be viewed as that of finding a phenomenologically fitting analogy, rather than a generalized abstraction that innovates theory.

Thinking in terms of common sense attributes, psychology can be seen as an envious discipline. It has been caught in between its "physics envy[4]" (leading to importation of key ideas) and the ambivalence about the fullness of psychological phenomena. The latter entails the repetitive dance between the need to analyze the phenomena to their elements—while understanding that such analysis gets rid of precisely the phenomena because of the holistic nature of the latter.

Hence, the efforts to use field-kind terminology in psychology have been located in the phenomenological side of psychology and have fused the richness of common sense notions of the field with those of the generalized abstract possibilities of the field as a theoretical concept.

The "field at the given time"—Kurt Lewin

Lewin's application of field-theoretic notions was closely coordinated with insights into everyday life experience and its phenomenological structure. In a relatively late retrospect upon his efforts, Lewin himself confessed the limited nature of his efforts to build a psychological field theory:

> I am afraid, those psychologists who, like myself, have been in favor of field theory for many years have not been very successful in making the essence of this theory clear. The only excuse I know of is that this matter is not very simple. Physics and philosophy do not seem to have done much analytical work about the meaning of field theory that could be helpful to the psychologist. In addition, *methods like field theory can really be understood and mastered only in the same way as methods in a handcraft, namely, by learning them through practice.* (Lewin, 1943: 292, added emphasis)

Given that the field-phenomenological orientation was present in Lewin's own work since World War I and culminated in his formalization of his version of the field theory in the late 1930s (Lewin, 1936, 1938), this retrospect corroborates the claims of commentators (e.g., Deutsch, 1954: 189) that his uses of topology in psychology have been closer to phenomenology than to generalizing science.

In that regard, Lewin's field theory emphasized the subjective phenomena of relating to the present field that included reflections upon the past, and upon the future (see Figure 2). In Lewin's own words:

> . . . the psychological past and the psychological future are simultaneous parts of the psychological field existing at a given time t. The time perspective is continually changing. According to field theory, any type of behavior depends upon the total field, *including the time perspective at that time, but not, in addition, upon any past or future field and its time perspectives.* (Lewin, 1943: 303, added emphasis)

What Lewin theoretically accomplished was the translation of past and future into the present—through including the present reflection upon both into the same immediate person<>environment relation. The relationship of person and environment becomes a closed system—a "monad" of $B= f \{P, E\}$ that transforms *in* time—but *not through* time (cf. Lewin, 1936: 34-35). The uncertainty of facing the future, for example, was viewed by Lewin as a *fully certain* feeling of "uncertainty":

> Indeterminateness leads to special difficulties in representing the life space. *How shall one represent something that in itself is indefinite?* How, for instance, can one speak of the direction toward an indefinite goal? . . . I see the solution of this difficulty in that the indeterminateness of mental events is the indeterminateness of the

Figure C.2
Lewin's Topography of the Past-Present-Future Relations in Ontogeny
(a= younger child, b= older child) from Lewin, 1951: 246

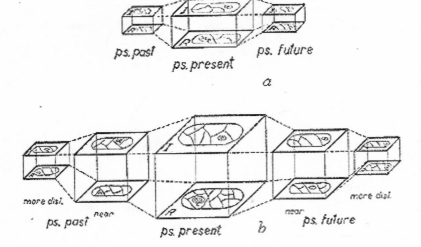

content and not of the psychological fact itself. *Fear in the face of an uncertainty that dominates a man at a certain moment is in itself a perfectly definite psychological fact whose properties it is possible to describe. One of these uniquely determined properties is the specific degree of indeterminateness of what the man fears.* (Lewin, 1936: 40, added emphases)

It is possible to observe the opening up of the phenomenological richness of the life-world (person-in-environment as a field) while closing down the analytic alley to very traditional point like notions (of a fixed quality, "fear," and its fixed measurable extent, "the *specific degree of* indeterminateness"). Here, Lewin solved the problem in the way all psychology had done before him—by separating the quality (and considering it determinate) from its quantity and considering the latter indeterminate. The difference between Lewin and the psychometric traditions in psychology are only in how the indeterminate (quantity) aspect of the determinate (quality) should be dealt with. For Lewin that took the form of looking at dynamic variability in the person and the field-whole. For psychometrics, it took the form of eradicating that dynamics through positing the existence of a "true score" and looking for ways that could help the researcher to by-pass the "noise" ("error") that stands on the way of the researcher to the "measuring" of that "true score."

In contrast, the *Ganzheits*-perspective allows for indeterminateness in the qualities of the wholes—with, of course, the corresponding analytical difficulties. The notion of "measurement" of any presumed "static state" is a contradiction in terms for this perspective. However, the observation (extrospective or introspective) of the process of differentiation of the whole is perfectly possible (and preferred).

Static Duality Field—Fusion of Person and the World

The personological system of William Stern (1935, 1938) provides a good example of such focus on the psychological level of lived-through experience. This is a theoretical system that emphasized person<>world relations within the present (see Figure C.2) and did not include the temporal transformation of the present into a new one ("The personal present is spatio-temporally neutral, it is the unseparated 'here-now.'" Stern, 1938: 93).

Stern's account (Figure C.3) that sets up person in one's "here-and-now" state as the center point of experiencing interestingly represents the *boundary structure* in terms of our depiction of the field. In a sense, Stern solved the problem of definiteness of the personal experiencing by locating the person in the "here-now" of the boundary between two fields—those of "outer infinity" and "inner infinity." The notion of *fusion* (of the person and situation) follows from the static fixing of the personal present as "neutral"—rather than "striving towards X" or "moving away from Y" (which would entail the adoption of a non-neutral, agentive position of the person within the flow of experiencing).

In Stern's own words:

> *The inward direction* leads first to the regions of the person that are nearest his present; in so far as these are separate from the world while still confronting it, they constitute the personal *surface*. Further inward the personal *depths* are reached, i.e., those moments of the person that have no immediate reference to the direct external situation, but which represent in a specific way the self-contained being of the person. Further progress in the same direction signifies passage from the explicit and concrete to the implicit, the underlying, the potential. At the fictitious limit of this incursion into the personal depths is the complete indeterminateness and inner infinity of the person. (Stern, 1938: 93)

In the outward direction (Figure C.3) the person's concrete experiencing moves to the field of ever far exteriors of infinity, and "finally lapses fictively into the wholly contentless, into outer infinity" (ibid.: 93).

Stern's person-centered perspective creates the contrast of two open-ended phenomenological fields (inner and outer infinities) as those are defined by the boundary relation (the person in the "here-and-now"). His contrast with the "objective" situation explains his need for creating the static "snapshot" of the field at the given time:

> My seat-mate in the street-car is distant from me while the friend toward whom I am riding is already near to me—in contradiction to the linear distance from both;—all that counts is personal relevance to my present life. (Stern, 1938: 94)

Figure C.3
**William Stern's Field-Theoretic Personalism—The Field of the "Spaceous
Present" at the Border of Two Quasi-infinite Fields**
(from Stern, 1938, p. 94)

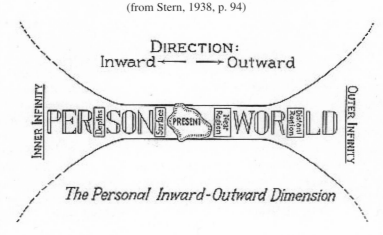

While not denying movement within one's life-world, Stern theoretically
focuses on the static moment within that movement. The dual field system here
is ontological while its content matter is necessarily dynamic. The same person's
"present" is always filled with new material, yet the system of experiencing
in-between two infinities remains unchanged.

Dynamic Duality Field: C. S. Peirce's Abductive Generalization

A contrast between two infinity fields in person's experiencing in the here-
and-now moment was also a focus for Charles S. Peirce. In Peirce's version,
these infinite fields are relating the person's past and future at the indeterminate
boundary moment of the present. The result is a synthesis of the new movement
towards the future through abductive synthesis (see Figure C.4).

As Figure C.4 shows, Peirce attempted to describe the "insistency" of past
ideas for the present, and of the present's relevance for the immediate future.
For our purposes it suffices to emphasize that both the "ideas of the past" and
(especially) of the future are fields of practically infinite boundaries. The only
existing and specifiable boundary is the meaning-making person in the "here-
and-now" moment. That boundary is characterized by tension (depicted by
the never-meeting lines of the two equilateral hyperbolas in Figure C.4). The
boundaries of the hyperbolae indicate the field that is functional in the infinitely
small center point between past and future (shown by the arrows—our addition
to Peirce's scheme) and between positive and negative "insistencies." At that
point semiotic synthesis—the abductive "jump"—is likely to happen.

Figure C.4
C. S. Peirce's Infinite Fields of Future, Past—At the Infinitely
Small Boundary of the Present
(after Peirce, 1935: 104)

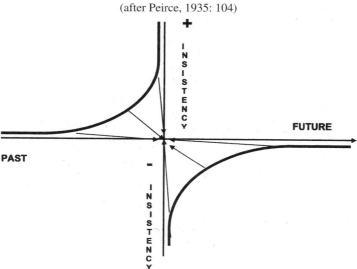

In phenomenological terms, Peirce remarked:

> . . . feeling which has not yet emerged into immediate consciousness is already affectible and already affected. In fact, this is habit, by virtue of which an idea is brought up into present consciousness by a bond that had already been established between it and another idea while it was still <u>in futuro</u>. . . the affected idea is attached as a logical predicate to the affecting idea as subject. So when a feeling emerges into immediate consciousness, it always appears as a modification of a more or less general object already in the mind. The word suggestion is well adapted to expressing this relation. The future is suggested by, or rather is influenced by the suggestions of, the past. (Peirce, 1935: 104-105 [6.141 and 6.142])

The flow of irreversible time guarantees the possibility for active novelty construction through the semiotic processes. The person is constantly moving beyond the "here-and-now" temporal situation through abductive synthesis of one's life experiences.

In contrast to Lewin's and Stern's depiction of the boundary conditions as determinate (the spatially and temporally extended present) "switch stations" between the internal/external or past/future links (in the present), Peirce's model implies the infinitely small moment of the present where the "discharge" of innovative abduction occurs. This happens in-between the two heterogeneously structured fields (past and future) through sign construction that necessarily entails a "jump" to novelty. The time extension, from past through present to future (see also Gurwitsch, 1964), is crucial for emergence. Peirce's view is open to processes of emergence as it specifies the location of that emergence at the ever-moving border between past and future and the mechanism (tension) between the constructive infinities of imagination and memory.

Central Focus on Becoming

As highlighted in Chapter 3 of this volume, the *Ganzheitspsychologie* approach has made development one of its central tenets. The complexity of developmental systems, which are intransitive and open in their nature, makes it particularly difficult for researchers to capture the actual process and subsequently analyze it from a morphological and "unfolding" point of view. But difficulties are there to be overcome, rather than to lament about. If a given area in science finds itself in "difficulty" (or "crisis") because of the inability to understand a particular phenomenon it is probably the axiomatic system used by the given scientists at the given time, rather than the phenomena, that are creating the "difficulty." The phenomena out there in the universe do not care if they are "easy" or "difficult" for scientists to study. They are not "intentionally hiding" from the scientists. It is the latter who may have entered an impassé in their effort to assume an appropriate viewing position or who look for something in the phenomena they most dearly cherish to be there.

Methodology of psychological investigation cannot stop at describing the existing structure of the *Ganzheits* field, but needs to capture the expected and subsequently actual movement of the field as a whole. If our general presentation of the *Ganzheits* assumptions is adequate, there is no such thing as "the field at the given time" as an ontological entity but only as a transitory "snapshot" within which the movement orientations of the parts of the field and of the total field remain hidden. Processes of such field transformations need to be studied precisely as such: transformations of quasi-determinate fields.

It is important to emphasize that *Ganzheitspsychologie* did develop the empirical method along these lines—that of *Aktualgenese*. However, even in this method the process of *genese* seems to have become prioritized over what the actual field (the *Aktual*) is. For example, in usual empirical studies of the *Aktualgenese* kind, the person is moving from a fuzzy to a clear (strictly organized) percept or meaning, rather than to (yet another) uncertain field that floats in further tensions. But what if there is no certainty of "the given?" The *Aktual-genese*-maker is creating this "given" as one moves along within the process of such generation. Our perceptual systems surely provide us with visual scenes (Kanizsa, 1980) that call out construction of reality that is not "given" in the stimulus field. And, last but not least, the whole construction of sound *Ganzheiten* of the kind we call music is a testimony of making of the whole while perceiving it.

The latter moment—making a whole while perceiving it—is crucial for understanding of the evolutionary processes *in action*. Specific results of the *Aktualgenese* in the case of a specific organism cannot be evaluated in terms of their evolutionary function. Yet processes of reality construction that converge across individuals—and are maintained over history of the species may become parts of the whole in the evolutionary story as constructed with a prospect towards the future (see also Chapter 12 of this volume). This is in dire contrast to the comforts of retrospective stories about how "evolutionarily adaptive" one or another outcome (an established clear pattern) is.

Thus, *Ganzheitspsychologie* did set the stage for the study of complex fluid and constantly self-transforming complex phenomena. It provided a preliminary look at how to observe those phenomena, be it in the laboratory or in "real" life. The orientation of investigators' minds towards the study of the processes was the innovative focus that is novel even a century later. But that vague feeling of novelty in the minds of our contemporary scientists is but a historical artifact. It is largely due to the loss of interest in the study of processes in psychology over the last half-century.

From our present vantage point, we reach the conclusion that *Ganzheitspsychologie* did not go far enough. That is, it failed to provide a formal language for dealing with emergence of novel forms (rapidly or slowly) that might (but need not) survive. It did not develop much further from Ehrenfels' idea of development of higher-order *Gestalts* and their role in organizing lower-order *Gestalts* (see Chapter 2 of this volume). Lack of this coverage made it an easy target for constructive critics (like Vygotsky) who could easily refer to its limits when higher psychological functions were the focus of attention. In a way, the intra-psychologically available phenomena made the establishment of the holistic perspective complicated through the prism of the "two inductions" of C. L. Morgan (see Chapters 9 and 10 of this volume).

The Whole in the Biological Field

Any thinker about human personality—be it in the clinic of Pierre Janet (see Chapter 7 of this volume) or in the thought of Jan Smuts (see Chapter 6 of this volume), —or a biologist who takes an organismic view (see chapter 11 of this volume) would end up with the need to conceptualize multi-level structure of fluid processes of the kinds of holistic fields. Yet that structure consists of fields that maintain the relative stability of the whole: the structure is fluid, and fluidity supports the structure. Nowhere is this unity of the solid and the fluid more visible than in embryology where field-theoretic perspectives were introduced around the same time as in psychology (Gurwitsch, 1914, 1922, 1947).

Alexander Gurwitsch's productive life work (for description, see Beloussov, 1997) entailed the introduction of the cellular (embryonal) field concept into embryology (Gurwitsch, 1922). The simple fact that the organism is a whole was no news for biologists; yet Gurwitsch transcended the tendency to view the whole as a static structure and treat it in the process of development. For a histologist, development is the transformation of cell patterns from one macro-level configuration into another. The "whole" (configuration) and its "parts" (cells in various versions of mutual transformation) are inseparable.

In the case of transformation of the embryo, the reality of time (the already developed state of the organism and its next state of potential transformation) is the research question. Embryology is necessarily based on the perception of form and on the transformation of form into new states. That transformation is real: cells realign themselves, new cells grow, and the entire configuration moves into new geometric pattern over ontogenetic time (Figure C.5).

Embryologists detect the transformation of the curvature of the shape of the organ (I→ II → III → IV in Figure C.5). Such mapping of curvature change over time can be seen as a descriptive equivalent of psychologists' accounts of "stages" in development (e.g., Piaget's or Erikson's). Yet the material with which the embryologists work does not allow them to stop at the description of mere "stages"—it is necessary to explain how the cell assemblies from one curve (e.g., I) transform into another (e.g. II).

Figure C.5
Geometry of Development—Four Developmental
Contours of the Nasal Area of *Scyllium*
(Gurwitsch, 1914: 541)

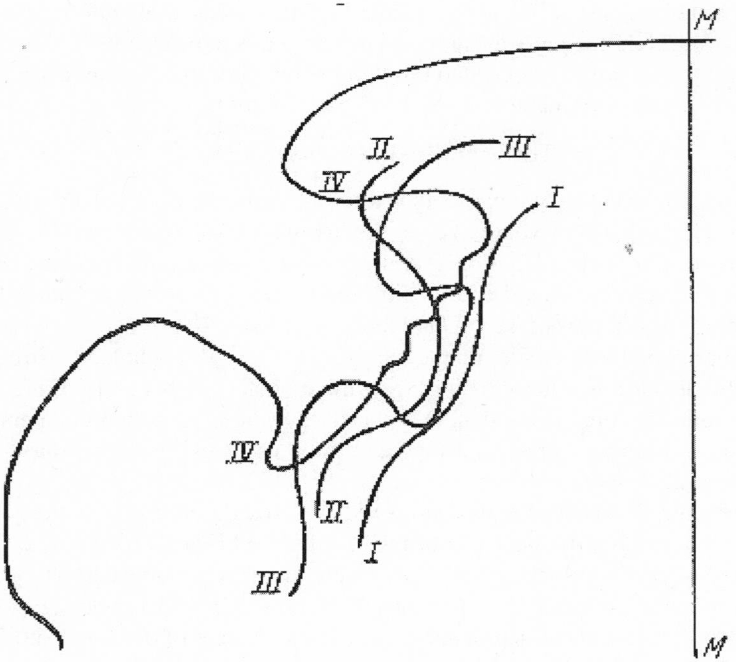

Hence, different from psychologists' readiness to translate time into the structure of the present (Stern, Lewin, see above Figures C.2 and C.3), in embryology the move from the present state of the multi-cellular organized assembly to new form (eventually that of an adult organism) is at stake. What is theoretically at stake is the question of functional ties from the present to the expected (by "blueprint") but not determined (by epigenesis) next future. This locus of the theory construction is analogous to developmental psychology's continuous interest in "zone of proximal development" (Valsiner & van der Veer, 1993).

The basic blueprint of morphodynamics is pre-formist since the range of open alleys for morphological development may be limited (to mostly 1) for the given species. Yet the actual movement to the next state of cellular organization is epigenetic (Gurwitsch, 1947: 97). Both the pre-formed morphological stability and its possible modifications at specific developmental time periods are parts of the same field for embryology.

The Embryonal Field

The starting point for Gurwitsch's introduction was of course empirical, that is, it involved careful depiction of the forms of embryos in their development (Gurwitsch, 1914). Yet the field terminology made it possible to transcend the empirical description towards positing the uniform presence of field forces that operate through "coordination points" located at different distances from each cell. Here the introduction of "field" notion allowed for the look at the expected next step in the transformation of form (Figure C.6). What is modeled through the geometric model is the structured processes (Gurwitsch, 1947: 53) of qualitative transformation of the cell based on the impacts from neighboring cells.

The two "vector initiation points" (K and its counterpart on the right) create a field of "pulls" for each cell in the given contour that is about to move in the direction of the resultant vector of the two "pulls." Each cell is initially located in a different position in the structure. Hence, the transition of the structure occurs in a collective—yet new form creating—ways. Thus, the form can move from concave to convex (or back) as a result of collective transition within the cellular field (Cherdantsev, 2006; Cherdantseva and Cherdantsev, 2006).

In the case of multi-cellular organisms, it is the external boundary of the organism (the outer contour) underneath which the cellular "collectives" move so as to lead to qualitative transformation of the form. Such movement processes are non-linear[5] (as the example in Figure C.7 demonstrates).

In the contemporary, non-linear, morphogenetic field theoretic mindset, it is the circular set of forces (F1, F2, F3) which—relating to one another cyclically—bring about the movement of cells bounded by the external contour of the body. That movement leads to the qualitative transition of the contour itself. The biological constraint becomes remade in the cellular actuality genesis as the

Figure C.6
Gurwitsch's Ccheme of the Embryonal Field
(from Gurwitsch, 1922: 412)

Figure C.7
Field-Theoretic Depiction of the Change in a Hypothetical Cell Assembly
Around the Contour
(after Cherdantseva and Cherdantsev, 2006: 162)

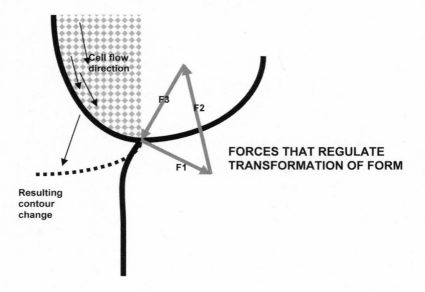

embryo moves on in its individual development. The cyclical causal system can be located in the specific location where the "breakthrough" can occur, or it can situate it randomly at some boundary point. In terms of contemporary dynamical systems theory, that situated cyclical vector system (F1→F2→F3→F1) might be viewed as an "attractor" (Valsiner, 2005c). In any case, the causal system is a non-linear (cyclical) system that can locate itself in different parts of the field—anatomically specifiable—and "pull" for transformation.

This glimpse into the history of field theory in embryology is instructive in two ways. First, the empirical basis for theoretical efforts is very clear: cell assemblies that form describable structures transform into new structures (Figure C.5). Here a parallel with thorough ethological description of behavior (or of an introspective flow of feelings or ideas in a psychological study) would be obvious. However, while embryologists carefully preserve the information about transformation of one cell assembly into another, tracing the changing location of individual cells and the emergence of new ones, psychologists move quickly to eliminate such information of structural transformations and "accumulate data" taking them out of their spatio-temporal *loci*. Hence, psychologists tend to lose the whole at the first step of data generation.

Secondly, the embryonal field theory was an act of abstraction beyond the description of cell assemblies in their movement. The vectors (and their linear or non-linear configurations) are generalized abstractions that are in their epistemological status close to formulae in chemistry. In contrast, both Lewin's and Stern's field accounts in psychology (Figure C.2 and C.3) were descriptive translations of the potentially productive (if generalized) notions of topology into an alternative (indeed richer than elementary accounts) presentation of the phenomena. Psychology's empirical orientation has reduced its theoretical creativity and created a situation where ever-new "collection of data" is not in a position to innovate the core theoretical state of the science.

Theoretical Challenges and New Directions

It is clear that psychologists today are currently ill prepared to tackle the basic problem of theory construction that preserves the holistic nature of their phenomena. As all science is a semiotic enterprise of creating new (and generalizing) theoretical languages, we can look at the kinds of signs that are "ruled in" in construction of psychological accounts. Thus, the use of real numbers in the quantification efforts is positively privileged in contemporary psychology, despite arguments to the principal irreducibility of psychological phenomena to real numbers (Rudolph, 2006c: 68). Similarly, the treatment of non-ergodic phenomena as if these fit ergodic data construction is socially accepted in psychology (Molenaar, 2004).

In terms of types of signs, psychology's theory construction is fossilized by using point-like signs to denote the data: categories, prototypes, averages, or any other "measures" of something (Diriwächter & Valsiner, 2005; Michell, 1999). The adoption of premises of statistics as if it was *the* objectivity-granting miracle for data analysis has served as the blinder over the past century. It has excluded from scientific consideration the complex, fluid phenomena that *Ganzheitspsychologie* brought to the focus of scientists and that, of course, continue to be lived through in real life and in art. What we capture through our investigation into the history of *Ganzheitspsychologie* is interestingly very contemporary—for mathematicians, rather than for psychologists! The irony of history of sciences is in their episodic "spurts" interspersed with long periods of stagnation in the cycles of "normal science." Here, of course, is another reason to study history of sciences as an innovation tool for potential futures.

Overcoming the Ghosts of the Socio-political Context

Of course, the history of *Ganzheitspsychologie* has another reason for being forgotten; it has been caught in the middle of the major ideological wars of the twentieth century. The historical mixing of *Ganzheits* terminologies of science and in political discourses that has happened in Germany and in Japan (see Chapter 4 of this volume)—with stigmatizing results—can also be seen from the other side. *Ganzheits* thinking captured some very basic aspects of the psychological and social realities. These aspects were subsequently exploited for political purposes. Such exploitation included terminologies—as the Japanese use of the notion of *Ganzheit* or similar issues in the rhetoric in Germany in the 1930s are documented. The political institutions which attempted to establish total control over the given societies and the minds in people in these societies surely moved to operate at the level of ideologically important wholes rather than elements.

We might want to see our present in terms of what happened in the past. We are not different in our contemporary social sciences where there are parallels between the ideologies of "identity" from that of research on identity in psychology. The ideology of "European identity"—to be developed into the European Union of twenty-seven countries under the conditions of historical unification of the economic and political systems is monological. It overlooks the opposite claims for separation of Basque or Catalan regions from their current homelands—the other side of the dialogical opposition UNITY <> DISUNITY. There is a holistic presumed (vague and general) phenomenon like "European identity" that supposedly exists "in" the citizens of the EU and the "quantity" of which could be "measured." Following from the focus in our current book, fulfilling such contemporary social demand would not give us any more new knowledge than the "diagnostics of Aryan personality" research did in the 1930s. "Identity" may be a socially desirable topic for psychology to be ordered to study. Yet how scientists actually study identity processes cannot be reduced to any socio-political agenda, nor can it benefit from yet another "standardized measure" that replaces the complexity of the "Being-Whole" to a quantitative sum of answers to obscurely formulated items. The phenomenon of "European unity" can be studied through the analysis of continuous dialogues within persons' minds of two opposite processes (UNITY ← striving towards → DISUNITY). Under different, specifiable conditions, one of the opposites may establish its temporary domination over the other—leaving the researcher with the impression of the existence of unitary "characteristic" (essence) that underlies the phenomenon.

Redundantly Organized and Hyper-excessive Reality

Biological, psychological, and social wholes are not "economical" in any sense. Just the contrary, they are abundant, they are generated with much "waste" (or "useless" material) that actually functions as a buffer against adaptation pressures. Redundancy of control mechanisms is the name of the game in all complex systems, which lead to their openness to multi-linear ways of adaptation. The result is high inter-systemic variability based on intra-systemic abundance.

The same is the case in cultural worlds. Edmund Leach has phrased it succinctly, "the jumble is the message" (Leach, 2000: 126). Our cultural worlds are redundantly filled with social suggestions of similar directions—encoded into high varieties of forms of signs. This over-abundance makes the *Ganzheits* nature of the human *psyche* functional in its reality. Our psychological systems are set up to handle very complex field-like experiences with relative ease—interspersed with enormous difficulties in decision making as the interaction of Hamlet with the skull amply reminds us. As the environment of human beings is redundantly hyper-prolific in its stimulus wholes, so would its personal counterpart be rich in its creativity yet focused when it is needed.

We claim that science needs to remain at a comfortable, ideologically distanced position in relation to any society at any given time. The *Ganzheitspsychologie* tradition has suffered historically from the elimination of such science/society distance. For the restoration of the scientific focus on the phenomena of holistic kind, biological and social scientists need to borrow new ideas from contemporary qualitative branches of mathematics (Rudolph & Valsiner, 2009). Statistics is but one (and very narrow) area of applied mathematics—not *the* mathematics that could do miracles for psychology. Science involves sensual construction (Sibum, 2004) and integration of intuitive and explorative curiosities; just as C. Lloyd Morgan had long ago understood (see Chapter 9 and 10 of this volume).

There are no miracles in science. There is a need for a laborious process of making sense of complex phenomena. A constructive return to *Ganzheitspsychologie* in order to move beyond the knowledge it reached during the first peak in its history is, therefore, a feasible goal for our contemporary science.

Acknowledgments

The authors are grateful to the "Kitchen Seminar" at Clark University for feedback on a previous version of this manuscript. The discussions of field theory by the first author with Aaro Toomela under the influence of *pel'meny* in *Troika* in February of 2007 has also opened new alleys of contemplation that are partly represented in this chapter.

Notes

1. Furthermore, as a rule, the "total amount" of "variance" usually "accounted for" is small—yet consensually accepted as informative. Through such consensual valida-

tion of research practices social sciences become hyper-productive in the quantity of research results produced and communicated through their publication. At the same time, conceptual understandings are in a stalemate.

2. However, see Hoffmeyer, 2003, for a claim that self-reflexivity—in terms of C. S. Peirce's function of interpretant—is present at all levels of biological systems.

3. This is well expressed by Aron Gurwitsch (1964: 381): "Considering that every object appears within a thematic field and that the pointing references are to the nearer as well as to the most remote zones of the thematic field, we come to assert that whatever description of the object with which we are dealing, it presents itself within a certain order of existence and as a member of that order. To experience an object amounts to being confronted with a certain order of existence." Also J. W. Goethe was deeply interested in this etymological background of the German term (Stephenson, 2005: 565) as it unites the poet and the scientist—in making sense of their (usually resisting) objects.

4. In addition to "physics envy," we can trace many other similar slavish attitudes in psychology—surrendering the complexity of the psyche to the seemingly simple notion of "behavior does it all"; or believing in computer metaphors in cognitive science, or looking for ways of physiological (MRI based) or genetic ("gene for intelligence") simple solutions elsewhere.

5. Where Gurwitsch's innovation ended was precisely here:
    . . . the roots of this true scientific tragedy [of Gurwitsch's field theory] lie in attempting to solve essentially non-linear problems of biological organization with the use of quasi-classical linear fields. Gurwitsch was correct and very much ahead of his time in stressing non-equilibrium orderliness and vectorization of molecular processes essential in living organisms. But he certainly could not foresee that in a modern, largely non-linear self-organization theory . . such vectorization does not require at all the existence of some kind of repulsive field with a definite source. (Beloussov, 1997: 777)

References

Abbey, E. (2006). "Triadic frames for ambivalent experience." *Estudios de Psicologia, 27*, 1: 33-40.

Abbey, E. & Diriwächter, R. (Eds.) (2008). *Innovating Genesis: Microgenesis and the Constructive Mind in Action.* Charlotte, NC: Information Age Publishing.

Bailey, A. R. (1999). "Beyond the fringe: William James on the transitional parts of the stream of consciousness." *Journal of Consciousness Studies, 6*, 2-3: 141-153.

Belousov, L. V. (1997). "Life of Alexander G. Gurwitsch and his relevant contribution to the theory of morphogenetic fields." *International Journal of Developmental Biology, 41*: 771-779.

Beneduce, R., & Taliani, S. (2006). "Embodied powers. Deconstructed bodies: spirit possession, sickness, and the search for wealth of Nigerian immigrant women. *Anthropos, 101*: 429-449

Branco, A. U., & Valsiner, J. (1997). "Changing methodologies: A co-constructivist study of goal orientations in social interactions. *Psychology and Developing Societies, 9*, 1: 35-64.

Bühler, K. (1934/1965). *Sprachtheorie.* Jena-Stuttgart: Gustav Fischer.

Bühler, K. (1990). *Theory of language: The representational function of language.* Amsterdam: John Benjamins.

Buller, A. (2006). "Mechanisms underlying ambivalence: A psychodynamic model." *Estudios de Psicologia, 27*, 1: 49-66.

Carthew, R. W. (2006). "A new RNA dimension to genome control." *Science, 313*; 305-306.

Cherdantsev, V. G. (2006). "The dynamic geometry of mass cell movements in animal morphogenesis." *International Journal of Developmental Biology, 50*: 169-182.

Cherdantseva, E.M. and Cherdantsev, V. G. (2006). "Geometry and mechanics of teleost gastrulation and the formation of primary embryonic axes." *International Journal of Developmental Biology, 50*: 157-168.

Davidson, E. H. (2006). "The sea urchin's genome: where will it lead us?" *Science, 314:* 939-940.

Deutsch, M. (1954). "Field theory in social psychology." In G. Lindzey (Ed.), *Handbook of social psychology* (pp. 181-222). Cambridge, MA: Addison-Wesley.

Diriwächter, R. & Valsiner, J. (2005, December). "Qualitative Developmental Research Methods in their Historical and Epistemological Contexts [53 paragraphs]." *Forum Qualitative Sozialforschung / Forum: Qualitative Social Research* [On-line Journal], 7(1), Art 8. Available at: http://www.qualitative-research.net/fqs-texte/1-06/06-1-8-e.htm. Date of Access: December 30, 2005.

Gigerenzer, G. (1993). "The Superego, the Ego, and the Id in statistical reasoning." In G. Keren & C. Lewis (Eds.), *A handbook for data analysis in the behavioral sciences: Methodological issues* (pp. 311-339). Hillsdale, NJ: Erlbaum.

Gigerenzer, G., Swijtink, Z., Porter, T., Daston, L., Beatty, J. & Krüger, L. (1989*). The empire of chance.* Cambridge: Cambridge University Press.

Gurwitsch, Alexander (1914). "Der Vererbungsmechanismus der Form." *Archiv für Entwicklungsmechanik der Organismen, 39*: 516-577.

Gurwitsch, Alexander (1922). "Über den Begriff des embryonalen Feldes." *Archiv für Entwicklungsmechanik der Organismen, 51*: 383-415.

Gurwitsch, Alexander. (1947). *Une théorie du champ biologique cellulaire.* Leiden: E. J. Brill.

Gurwitsch, Aron. (1964). *The field of consciousness.* Pittsburgh, PA: Duquesne University Press.

Herbst, D. P. (1995). "What happens when we make a distinction: An elementary introduction to co-genetic logic." In T. Kindermann & J. Valsiner (Eds.), *Development of person-context relations* (pp. 67-79). Hillsdale, NJ: Erlbaum.

Hoffmeyer, J. (2003). "Semiotic aspects of biology: biosemiotics." In R. Posner, K. Robering and T. A. Sebeok (Eds.), *Semiotik.* Vol. 3 (p. 2643-2666). Berlin: Walter de Gruyter.

James, W. (1890). *Principles of psychology.* New York: Holt.

Kanizsa, G. (1980*). Gramatica del vedere.* Bologna: Il Mulino.

Klein, U. (2004). "Not a pure science: chemistry in the 18th and 19th centuries." *Science, 306*: 981-982.

Laird, J. D. (2007). *Feelings: the perception of self.* New York: Oxford University Press.

Leach, E. (2000/1983). "The gatekeepers of heaven." In S. Hugh-Jones & J. Laidlaw (Eds.), *The essential Edmund Leach.* Vol. 2. *Culture and human nature* (pp. 119-140). New Haven, CT: Yale University Press.

Lewin, K. (1936). *Principles of topological psychology.* New York: McGraw-Hill.

Lewin, K. (1938). *The conceptual representation and measurement in psychology.* Durham, NC: Duke University Press.

Lewin, K. (1943). "Defining the 'field at a given time.'" *Psychological Review, 50*: 292-310.

Lewin, K. (1951). "Behavior and development as a function of the total situation." In K. Lewin, *Field theory in social science* (p. 238-303). New York: Harper & Brothers.

Matsuzawa, T. (Ed.). (2001). *Primate origins of human cognition and behavior*. Tokyo: Springer.

Matsuzawa, T, Tomonaga, M., and Tanaka, M. (Eds.). (2006). *Cognitive development in chimpanzees*. Tokyo: Springer.

▪ Michell, J. (1997). "Quantitative science and the definition of measurement in psychology." *British Journal of Psychology, 88*: 355-383.

✦ Michell, J. (1999). *Measurement in psychology*. Cambridge: Cambridge University Press.

Molenaar, P.C.M. (2004). "A manifesto on psychology as idiographic science: bringing the person back into scientific psychology, this time forever." *Measurement, 2*, 4: 201-218.

Molenaar, P.C.M., Huizenga, H.M., & Nesselroade, J.R. (2003). "The relationship between the structure of interindividual and intraindividual variability: A theoretical and empirical vindication of Developmental Systems Theory." In U.M. Staudinger & U. Lindenberger (Eds.), *Understanding human development: Dialoques with lifespan psychology* (pp. 339-360). Dordrecht: Kluwer Academic Publishers.

Myers, D. (2007). *Psychology*, 8th Edition in Modules. New York, NY: Worth Publishers.

Peirce, C. S. (1935). *Collected papers of Charles Sanders Peirce*. Vol. 6. Cambridge, MA: Harvard University Press.

Petitiot, J., Varela, F. J., Roy, J.-M., and Pachoud, B. (Eds.). (1999). *Naturalizing phenomenology: Issues in contemporary phenomenology and cognitive science*. Stanford: Stanford University Press.

Roberts, L. (1991). "Setting the table: the disciplinary development of eighteenth-century chemistry as read through the changing structure of its tables." In P. Dear (Ed.), *The literary structure of scientific argument: historical studies* (p.99-132). Philadelphia, PA: University of Pennsylvania Press

Rosa, A. (2007). "Acts of psyche: Actuations as synthesis of semiosis and action." In J. Valsiner & A. Rosa (Eds.), *Cambridge Handbook of Socio-cultural psychology*. New York: Cambridge University Press.

Rudolph, L., (2006a). "The fullness of time." *Culture & Psychology, 12*, 2: 169-204

✍ Rudolph, L. (2006b). "Mathematics, models and metaphors." *Culture & Psychology, 12*, 2: 245-259.

Rudolph, L. (2006c). "Spaces of ambivalence: qualitative mathematics in the modeling of complex fluid phenomena." *Estudios de Psicologia, 27*, 1: 67-84.

Rudolph, L., & Valsiner, J. (Eds.). (2009). *Qualitative Mathematics for the Social Sciences*. London: Routledge.

Segerdahl, P., Fields, W., & Savage-Rumbaugh, S. (2005). *Kanzi's primal language: the cultural initiation of primates into language*. New York: Palgrave.

Sibum, H. O. (2004). "What kind of science is experimental physics?" *Science, 306*: 60-63.

Stephenson, R. H. (2005). "'Binary synthesis': Goethe's aesthetic intuition in literature and science." *Science in Context, 18*, 4: 53-581.

Stern, W. (1935). *Allgemeine Psychologie auf personalistischer Grundlage*. Haag: Martinus Nijhoff.

Stern, W. (1938). *General Psychology From the Personalist Standpoint*. New York: Macmillan.

Toomela, A. (2007). "Culture of science: strange history of the methodological thinking in psychology." *Integrative Psychological & Behavioral Science, 41*, 1: 6-20.

Vaihinger, H. (1911). *Philosophie Als Ob*. Leipzig: J.A. Barth.

Valsiner, J. (2005a). "Affektive Entwicklung im kulturellen Kontext." In J. B. Asendorpf (Ed.), *Enzyklopädie der Psychologie*. Vol. 3. *Soziale, emotionale und Persönlichkeitsentwicklung* (pp. 677-728). Göttingen: Hogrefe.

Valsiner, J. (Ed.). (2005b). *Heinz Werner and developmental science*. New York: Kluwer Scientific/Plenum Publishers.

Valsiner, J. (2005c). "Attractors, repulsors, and directors: making Dynamic Systems Theory developmental." *Annual Report 2003-2004* of Research and Clinical Center for Child Development, Graduate School of Education, Hokkaido University. Sapporo, No. 27: 13-25.

Valsiner, J. (2006b). "From double stars to Dialogical Self: Constructing new theoretical explanatory systems." Paper presented at the Conference *Interaction et pensée: perspectives dialogiques* Lausanne, October 13.

Valsiner, J. (Ed.) (2007a). *Thinking in psychological science: ideas and their makers*. New Brunswick, N.J.: Transaction Publishers.

Valsiner, J. (2007b). *Culture in minds and societies*. New Delhi: Sage.

Valsiner, J., & Van der Veer, R. (1993). "The encoding of distance: The concept of the zone of proximal development and its interpretations." In R. R. Cocking & K. A. Renninger (Eds.), *The development and meaning of psychological distance* (pp. 35-62). Hillsdale, N.J.: Lawrence Erlbaum Associates.

von Uexküll, J. J. (1982). "The theory of meaning." *Semiotica 42,* 1: 25-82. (Original *Bedeutungslehre* from 1940).

Zittoun, T. (2006). *Transitions: Symbolic resources in development*. Greenwich, CT: Information Age Publishing, Inc.

About the Contributors

Rainer Diriwächter is an assistant professor of psychology at the Department of Psychology, California Lutheran University. His current interests lie with the history of psychology and Ganzheitspsychologie in particular. He has published previously on the topics of Ganzheitspsychologie and Völkerpsychologie and is co-editor—with Emily Abbey—of the forthcoming book *Innovating Genesis: Microgenesis and the Constructive Mind in Action.*

Contact Information: Rainer Diriwächter, Ph.D., California Lutheran University, Department of Psychology, 60 West Olsen Rd. #3800, Thousand Oaks, CA 91360, USA. Tel: 805-493-3442, Email: rdiriwae@clunet.edu

Walter H. Ehrenstein is a neuroscientist at the Leibniz Research Center for Working Environment and Human Factors at Dortmund University, Germany. He held additional appointments as adjunct professor at the universities of Bielefeld, Düsseldorf, and Wuppertal since 1985, and positions in psychophysics and neuropsychology at the universities of Freiburg and Constance after a post-doc year at the Neuroscience Department of the University of California at San Diego and receiving his Ph.D. from Göttingen University in 1977. Ehrenstein is an advisory board member of *Gestalt Theory;* his publications concern neuroscience (audition, proprioception, vision), its ergonomic applications (endoscopic systems, perception-action compatibility, virtual depth), and theoretical (Gestalt) accounts.

Contact Information: Walter H. Ehrenstein, Ph.D., Leibniz Research Center for Working Environment and Human Factors, Dortmund University, Ardeystr. 67, D-44139 Dortmund, Germany. Tel: +49 (0)231 1084-274, Email: ehrenstein@ifado.de

Dietmar Görlitz is a (retired) professor of psychology at the Technische Universität Berlin and member of the Zentrum Technik und Gesellschaft, as well as instructor at the Freie Universität Berlin. His research first centered on the social psychology of Fritz Heider, attribution theory in particular, and its application to Developmental Psychology (*Perspectives on attribution theory and research—The Bielefeld symposium, 1980*). Later on, his work included—together with Joachim Wohlwill—concepts of an environmental developmental psychology (*Curiosity, imagination, and play. On the development of spontaneous cognitive and motivational processes, 1987*). Together with Jaan Valsiner, he began to develop an interdisciplinary research program for city life (*Children cities, and psychological theories—Developing relationships, 1998*). Currently, Görlitz is working on the development of a research group that examines the exchange of experiences between generations of craftsmen.

Contact Information: Prof.Dr.habil.Dietmar Görlitz, Universitätsprofessor i.R., (Technische Universität Berlin/Freie Universität Berlin), Enzianstraße 2, D-12203 Berlin, Germany. Email: dietgoerlitz@web.de

Camilo E. Khatchikian is a Ph.D. candidate in Ecology and Evolution at Clark University. His current research interest focuses on evolutionary ecology, adaptation, and phylogeography. Current research includes analysis of life history adaptations, gene flow, population structure, and spatial relationships among populations and genes.

Contact Information: Camilo E. Khatchikian, Clark University, Department of Biology, 950 Main Street, Worcester, MA 01610, USA. Email:ckhatchikian@clarku.edu

Steven C. Kissinger is a professor of psychology in the Department of Psychology at California Lutheran University. Trained in the area of learning and memory, he worked with animal models of hypothermic induced amnesia and the recoverability of memories rendered amnesic. In addition, he is published in the area of the contextual control of tolerance to hypothermia using a compensatory response interpretation.

Contact Information: Steven C. Kissinger, Ph.D., California Lutheran University, Department of Psychology, 60 W. Olsen Road #3800, Thousand Oaks, CA 91360, USA. Tel: (805) 493-3446, Email: kissinge@clunet.edu

Conwy Lloyd Morgan (born 1852, died 1936) was a British natural philosopher and psychologist. He was one of the co-creators - with Henry Osborn and James Mark Baldwin—of the *organic selection theory*, and a pioneer in comparative psychology. He is best known—and most mis-quoted—for the reformulation of the principle of parsimony ("the Morgan's Canon").

Philip J. Rosenbaum is a graduate student in clinical psychology at Yeshiva University: Ferkauf School of Graduate Psychology. He received his MPhil in social and developmental psychology in 2005. His dissertation topic was "Stable Ambiguities: Navigating the Field of Hooking-up."

Contact Information: Philip J. Rosenbaum, M.Phil, Yeshiva University: Ferkauf School of Graduate Psychology, Rousso Building, Albert Einstein College of Medicine, 1165 Morris Park Avenue, Bronx, NY 10461, USA. Tel: 973-886-2237, Email: Aram1836@gmail.com

Tatsuya Sato is professor of psychology at the Department of Psychology, Ritsumeikan University, Kyoto Japan. His general interests are in the history, theory and methodology of psychology. He is a founding editorial board (2000) of the Japanese Journal of Qualitative Psychology (in Japanese) and he actively involved in JAQP *Japanese Association of Qualitative Psychology*. He is also an editorial board of *Japanese Association of Qualitative Psychology* (in Japanese), *History of Psychology and Psychology Studies* (in Japanese), *Japanese Journal of Law and Psychology* (in Japanese) and *The International Journal of Idiographic Science*. In 1999 he was awarded the "Best Article Prize" of Japanese Association of Developmental Psychology.

Contact Information: Tatsuya Sato, Ph.D., Ritsumeikan University, 56-1 Toji-in Kitamachi, Kita-ku, Kyoto 603-8577, Japan. Tel: +81-75-466-3311, Email: satot@lt.ritsumei.ac.jp

Christopher Shelley is clinical director of the Adler Centre for the Adlerian Psychology Association of British Columbia (Vancouver) and is a lecturer in the program in Women's and Gender Studies at the University of British Columbia. A certified Adlerian analyst, he is also co-editor of the British *Adlerian Yearbook*, co-author (with Paul Brinich) of *The Self and Personality Structure* (Open University Press, 2002), and editor of *Contemporary Perspectives on Psychotherapy and Homosexualities* (Free Association Books, 1998).

Contact Information: Chris A. Shelley, Ph.D., M.Phil., Lecturer in Gender Relations, Program in Women's and Gender Studies, The University of British Columbia, 1896 East Mall, Vancouver, BC, Canada, V6T 1Z1. Tel: 604-822-0432, Fax 604-822-9169, cshelley@telus.net

Lívia Mathias Simão received her MA and her Ph.D. at the Institute of Psychology of the University of São Paulo, Brazil, where she has been assistant professor since 1987 and coordinates the Laboratory of Verbal Interaction and Knowledge Construction. She is also a sponsored researcher of the National Council for Scientific and Technologic Development of Brazil. She is author of books and articles concerned with issues embracing the ontological construction of human subjectivity in I–world, I–other and I–self relationships from the perspective of the semiotic-cultural constructivism in psychology and from the broader perspective of the philosophy of psychology.

Contact Information: Prof. Dr. Lívia Mathias Simão, Instituto de Psicologia Universidade de São Paulo, Av. Prof. Mello Moraes, 1721, Cidade Universitária Armando de Salles Oliveira, 05508-900 São Paulo, SP, Brasil. Tel: (55) (11) 3091-4444, E-mail: limsimao@usp.br

Rosemarie I. Sokol is a freelance scholar located outside of San Francisco. She is the editor of a forthcoming book titled *Relating to Environments: A New Look at Umwelt* (for publication as part of the Advances in Cultural Psychology book series) and a founding co-editor of the online, peer-reviewed *Journal of Social, Evolutionary, and Cultural Psychology*. Her research focuses on the role of vocalizations, particularly whining, in attachment relationships. She is interested in the application of evolutionary and developmental theories on human psychology.

Contact Information: Rosemarie I. Sokol, Ph.D., Department of Psychology, University of San Francisco, 2130 Fulton Street, San Francisco, CA 94117, USA. Email: rsokol@jsecjournal.com

Miki Takasuna is professor of psychology at the School of Human and Social Sciences, Tokyo International University in Japan. She is an active member of the International Society for the History of Behavioral and Social Sciences (a.k.a. Cheiron), and co-editor of *Integrative Psychological and Behavioral Science* (2007). She is the co-author of Japanese books on psychology, including *Reading the History of Psychology: In Japan and the World* (2003) and *The History of Psychology* (2005).

Contact Information: Miki Takasuna, Tokyo International University, Waseda Satellite, Nishi-Waseda 2-6-1, Shinjuku, Tokyo 169-0051, Japan. Tel: (+81)33205-7727, Email: takasuna@tiu.ac.jp

Jaan Valsiner is professor of psychology at the Department of Psychology, Clark University. He is the founding editor (Sage, 1995) of the journal *Culture & Psychology*, and of Integrative Psychological and Behavioral Science (Springer, 2007). He is also the author of numerous books, including *The Guided Mind* (1998), *Culture and Human Development* (2000), and *Comparative Study of Human Cultural Development* (2001), *Culture in Minds and Societies* (2007) and the coeditor, with Kevin Connolly, of the *Handbook of Developmental Psychology* (2003) and of *Cambridge Handbook of Socio-cultural Psychology* (2007). In 1995 he was awarded the Alexander von Humboldt Prize in Germany for his interdisciplinary work on human development.

Contact Information: Jaan Valsiner, Ph.D., Clark University, Frances L. Hiatt School of Psychology, 950 Main Street, Worcester, MA 01610, USA. Tel: 508-793-8862, Email: jvalsiner@clarku.edu

Tania Zittoun is professor of Education at the University of Neuchâtel, Switzerland. She is the author of the books *Transitions: Development Through Symbolic Resources* (2006a), *Insertions: A Quinze Ans, Entre Echec et Apprentissage* (2006b) [Being fifteen, between failure and apprenticeship], *Donner La Vie, Choisir un Nom. Engendrements Symboliques* (2005) [Giving life, choosing a name. Symbolic begetting], and co-editor of *Joining Society: Social Interaction and Learning in Adolescence and Youth* (2004) with A.-N. Perret-Clermont, C. Pontecorvo, L. Resnick and B. Burge.

Contact Information: Tania Zittoun, Institut de psychologie et education, Faculté des Lettres et Sciences Humaines, Université de Neuchâtel, Espace Louis Agassiz 1, CH-2000 Neuchâtel, Switzerland. Tel. ++41 (0)32 718 19 89, Fax. ++41 (0)32 718 18 51, Email: Tania.zittoun@unine.ch

Index